I0088592

SUNDAY CONFESSIONS

A FICTIONALIZED CONVERSATION ABOUT SEXUAL VICTIMIZATION, A THEOLOGY PROFESSOR, AND RECOVERY INSPIRED BY ACTUAL PEOPLE AND EVENTS

REBECCA P. FALCO

Copyright © 2014 by Rebecca P. Falco

All rights reserved. No part of this book may be reproduced in any form or by any means, electronic or mechanical, including photocopying, recording, or by any information storage and retrieval system, without permission in writing from the author. Exception is given in the case of brief quotations embodied in critical articles and reviews..

For information: rpfalco@mac.com

ISBN: 978-0692359181

Cover by Barbara Gottlieb
www.gottgraphix.com

Published in Partnership with
Purple Distinctions Self Publishing
www.purpledistinctions.com
Venture, CA 93007

Printed in the United States of America

SUNDAY CONFESSIONS

A FICTIONALIZED CONVERSATION ABOUT SEXUAL VICTIMIZATION, A THEOLOGY PROFESSOR, AND RECOVERY INSPIRED BY ACTUAL PEOPLE AND EVENTS

REBECCA P. FALCO

Also by Rebecca P. Falco

Everything In Its Own Time:
A Mother's Memoir about Adopting Five Children and the
Ones that got Away

Some days are fairy tales
Some days belie
Four and twenty black birds baked in a pie
Could open up their sweet throats
To serenade a king
That's a lot of heat to take
and still be able to sing…
To sing… to sing

-Emily Saliers

DEDICATION

To three marvelous women,
Karen Steinour, Martha Simmons, and
Amelia Stinson-Wesley,
Who aided my recovery from sexual victimization
And worked to spare others from this kind of harm

CONTENTS

Sunday, November 2, 2014

Sunday, November 9, 2014

Sunday, November 16, 2014

ACKNOWLEDGMENTS

I want to thank my diverse group of friends and acquaintances who read an earlier version of this story and prompted me to make many of the changes that have led to this book: Bob Russell, Jill Tolbert, Ann Watson, Joni Laney, Leslie Foge, Linda Bryant, Katherine Russell, Jill Ruhlman, and Emily Washburn. I also want to thank Jack Riggs, author of two published novels, who consulted with me about the fictional aspects of story writing. There have been others in the past who read different presentations of this story, which was a long time coming into the light. Their support helped me stay on the path to publishing. In particular, I want to thank my husband, John Falco, my sister, Joanna Breazeale, and my parents, John and Helen Patton.

Of particular note is friend and fellow writer, Judith Kolberg, who also read my previous manuscript and left little yellow sticky notes throughout the document. Her notes contained questions about issues I had left unanswered or comments regarding the impression my words made on the reader. This was invaluable to me. As I read Judith's notes, I imagined my response and the story began to unfold as a 'conversation' between 'Rachel,' my main character, and someone else. In time, the conversation partner became 'Jennifer,' Rachel's daughter. I had worried about sharing this story with my children. Once I discovered 'Jennifer,' the story became a conversation I *could* imagine having with my own teenage and young adult children.

I owe a special thanks to my wonderful editor, who is also my exceptional mother, Helen Patton. Her support and critique, as well as her copyediting, enabled me to finalize the manuscript before turning it over to Ronni Sanlo of Purple Distinctions Self Publishing who converted my words into this book. I am grateful for the encouragement and expertise that Ronni provided.

Finally, I want to thank the unnamed women and men who shared their stories of sexual violence with me. Your courage, thoughtfulness, and inspiration made this story possible.

INTRODUCTION

*B*efore I became a wife and mother to five children, before I practiced law or ran an adoption agency, I was a daughter, a feminist, a student, a newspaper carrier, and a victim of rape who survived. Of the various "hats" I wore prior to becoming a wife and mother, the one that impacted my life in the most dramatic ways was *rape survivor*. My rape by a stranger in the middle of the night on June 24, 1982 is a matter of public record. There was a trial, a conviction, and an unsuccessful appeal. But surviving rape did more than expose me to the criminal legal process. It changed the way I felt about myself and others. It opened my eyes to sexual victimization everywhere.

Over time, as I worked as a volunteer in rape crisis centers, as a Minister to Youth, as a teacher in psychiatric hospitals, as a legal intern in a District Attorney's office, and as Coordinator of Sexual Assault Support Services at a university, I heard stories of other victims of sexual violence. I was astounded by the complexity of the problem and by the vast numbers of women, men, and children who had been harmed.

Sexual violence is not a new issue. Indeed, in the past few years, rape statistics have become familiar to the current generation of young women and men entering college. They learn that one in four women will experience sexual assault or attempted sexual assault before they graduate, presumably from a male peer. As a society, we have made some progress in addressing sexual violence that takes place in certain environments because of media exposure and open discussion by policy-makers. Date rape on college campuses, military sexual misconduct, and workplace sexual harassment come to mind.

Yet, even when channels for achieving justice are secured for these types of sexual violence, there are often impediments to an individual survivor's recovery that achieving *justice* cannot overcome. Without the proper support of family and friends or professional counselors who understand sexual violence and the individual's personal history, in hostile school or work environments, and absent attention to the way sexual violence affects a person's sexual behavior and thoughts, a survivor can continue to struggle.

In addition to the publicly discussed contexts in which sexual victimization is known to occur, there are other circumstances that allow victimizers to abuse the vulnerable. Survivors, in these cases, often shoulder the burden of their stories privately and with great shame. In my experience as a university's Coordinator of Sexual Assault Support Services, I was shocked to learn about the vast number of instances of sexual violence experienced by women and men *before* they entered college, often perpetrated by older, trusted adults. Here are a few real examples:

- a girl raped in 4th grade by her brother's friend

- 14 and 15-year-old boys raped by their church youth group leader

- a 15-year-old virgin who was raped, became pregnant, miscarried, and then tried to take her own life

- girls raped by an uncle... grandfather... stepfather... cousin

- boys raped by a coach... a minister

- a 14-year-old girl who placed her baby for adoption after being impregnated by a rapist

- a brother and two sisters all raped by their father

- a babysitter raped by the father of her charge while the mother was in the next room

- a young women raped three times: (1) as a "lesson" by five guys for having a black boyfriend; (2) on a counter with a knife against her throat by a potential employer; (3) by a date who got her drunk and held her down on his bed.

For years, I have wanted to expose these stories and others, but fear of bringing pain to the survivors and their loved ones prevented me.

Time passed, and as my teenage and young adult children started to venture into the world without my protective care, I began to realize that shielding them from these horrific stories might be doing them more harm than good. Indeed, telling the stories without revealing actual identities might be a gift I had the power to give them – a gift that might aid them in choosing who to trust and under what circumstances, a gift that might show them how to get help if they did fall victim to predators. This was my inspiration for writing *Sunday Confessions,* a fictionalized conversation between a mother and daughter, based on actual events and people.

In *Sunday Confessions,* "Rachel Adamo" and her 22-year-old daughter "Jennifer," along with the rest of Rachel's family, are fictitious composites of women, men, and children I have known. I used my rape in 1982 as a starting point for Rachel's story, and wove the complexity of recovery from sexual victimization and the hidden stories of real survivors in and around it. Jennifer is representative of one of these less-talked-about stories, as well as a person in whom Rachel can confide. I have also used many of the environments – school and job – that are familiar to me personally. Indeed, these were the locations where I encountered the hidden stories. However, I have disguised the identities of the places and people involved. If the reader believes that s/he has identified the characters in the story, it is coincidence and not my intention.

I feel that it is important to add one more note of disclaimer. When it comes to sexual violence, the details of an assault, whether they pertain to the sexual acts, the words spoken, the feelings evoked, the assailant's appearance, the particular place or environment, the smells, the touches, or other particulars, are all significant and worthy of attention by the victim. If I were to include all these specifics, however, there is a danger that the story would resemble erotica or, worse, pornography. Clearly, that is not my objective here. I have tried to find a balance that includes enough detail to make the events "real" while avoiding the dangers previously mentioned. The reader will be the judge of whether or not I have succeeded.

My goals are threefold. First, I wanted to write a story that illuminated some of the hidden circumstances in which sexual victimization occurs and how it occurs. For in cases of rape, sexual abuse, or sexual harassment, there are almost never witnesses other than the victim and his or her victimizer. Nothing will change until there is public dialogue between people who have the power to change the circumstances or environment in which these hidden stories occur. Change requires a community who cares.

Second, I wanted to reveal some of the obstacles to recovery that justice-seeking cannot overcome by sharing the journey of a particular survivor. Anyone who has experienced sexual victimization can tell you that revealing the "truth" is only part of the recovery process, not the end of the journey. It is through intimate relationships with relatives, close friends, and lovers that recovery – with all of its ups and downs – takes place.

Finally, my hope is that *Sunday Confessions* provides information that aids the cause of preventing sexual violence and assisting survivors in the recovery process. Indeed, if this story helps *one* survivor of sexual victimization gather the courage to speak out, to release the shame, and to get the help s/he needs to recover, my writing endeavor will have been well worth the effort.

CHAPTER ONE
THE CHAPEL

On a warm mid-September Saturday, Rachel was running late. She had taken a long run before dawn so that she could drive her son, Henry, to a soccer game that started at 9 a.m. After the game, Henry was *starving*, so Rachel stopped at a convenience store, and that delayed her arrival back home to change for the memorial service.

Just as she suspected, the service had already begun when she entered Blake Chapel on the Austin University campus. Someone she did not recognize was reading scripture. Stepping into the university chapel, Rachel took in the architecture of this space she had not entered in almost thirty years. The building was constructed of granite blocks. Inside, the dark walnut walls, weathered with age, contrasted with the vibrant colors of the stained-glass windows, images based on stories from the Bible. The ceiling arched high above the floor. A large balcony, with seating for an additional two hundred people, also contained the large pipes of the massive organ that occupied the space behind the pulpit in front of the congregation.

Rachel scanned the congregation for family members. Not seeing them, she quietly climbed the stairs to the balcony. There they were. Her mom, dad, and sister, Sarah, sat on the front pew on the opposite side. Rachel bowed her head, crossed the expanse quickly, and squeezed herself into the pew beside her mother.

The memorial service was being held to honor and remember one of Rachel's theology school professors. Looking over the balcony's edge to the floor below, Rachel recognized many university faculty members and their spouses. She glanced at her parents, now in their 70s and 80s. She realized how lucky she felt that they were still with her.

As the service progressed, there was choir music, readings, hymns, reflections, and a homily. Three quarters of the way through the service, the congregation was asked to "pass the peace." Rachel stood with the others, turning left and right to shake hands and say, "Peace be with you" or to respond, "And also with you." She then turned to the row behind her and reflexively reached for the hand of the man standing there. She said, "Peace." But as the man repeated the greeting, Rachel's stomach tightened at the sound of his voice. She looked up and into his eyes. It was Jay.

Rachel turned away quickly, grateful it was time to sit again. With her back to Jay, she imagined she could feel the heat of his glare on the back of her neck. Glancing sideways, she sought the eyes of family members to see if they recognized him too. She wondered why it hadn't occurred to her that Jay would be at the service. He was a member of the theology school faculty. His colleague had died. Of course he would be there.

The service continued, but Rachel's mind was elsewhere. She asked herself: How do I look? Healthy? Young? Attractive? Damn him! It angered her that these questions flooded her consciousness after all these years. What difference did it make how she looked to him now? It *shouldn't* matter.

It was time for Communion. As the mourners lined up to move to one of the receiving stations, Rachel anticipated another opportunity to get a glimpse of Jay. There he was. He looked surprisingly ordinary. Jay's wife, Elizabeth, stood in line behind him. Rachel thought Elizabeth looked like a non-descript middle-aged woman now, and that pleased her.

After the service ended, Rachel hugged her parents. They were not staying for the reception. Then she grabbed her sister's arm and whispered, 'Sarah, did you see Jay?'

"What? Where?" Sarah exclaimed.

"He was right behind me. There he is. See him?"

"That old guy with gray hair?" Sarah responded.

"Yes. No facial hair. But it's him."

Sarah said, "Creepy. I never would have recognized him."

Rachel remembered the last time she talked to Jay – before she met her husband Kevin, before marriage and children. She shuddered at the memory of how they had parted. Rachel had returned to Austin from law school in San Francisco, California just a few months into her new academic program. Her express purpose had been to find Jay and confront him.

Jay had been a charismatic and brilliant professor who later became Rachel's romantic partner. Jay had promised to be her healer, her savior and secret confidant, but he had betrayed her over and over again. He had turned their relationship into something sick and twisted.

At his home in late 1988, Rachel had broken down. She had cried and cried until she was empty. The apology she sought, the resolution, never came. She left and returned to law school to continue wrestling with the demons of her past. It was so clear to Rachel now that her last meeting with Jay was but an early step in her journey to recovery. Healing was a long, slow process with steps forward and steps back.

A rape crisis counselor had once told Rachel: Rape is like a file in the file cabinet of your soul. The file never goes away. In the beginning, whenever you open the file cabinet, you go directly to the rape file. But, over time, you start to go to other files as well. Now and again, you happen upon the rape file and remember it is there. But it is no longer the dominant file. Seeing Jay that day at the memorial service had opened her file cabinet to the rape file again.

After the memorial service, Rachel drove home and went inside. She walked past her younger son, Sam, who was watching television. She heard Kevin and Henry outside discussing seasonal planting for the garden. But it was background noise as she rushed down to the basement and into the "magic closet," as her children had named it long ago. This was the room that housed the items Rachel bought to use as birthday and other special occasion gifts. Rachel also kept boxes with children's art and her own historical papers in the room. It was to one of these boxes she went. Blowing away the dust and peeling back the crumbling tape, Rachel pulled out a journal written in a simple, blue spiral-bound notebook and opened it to the first page.

It read:

June 24, 1982

I was raped this morning. God, was it just this morning? I'm still spinning. I feel... I don't know what I feel exactly. I did the right thing. I know that. I just hope that writing it all down will help me keep my balance...

Rachel continued reading from her journals in the basement late into the night, only making appearances to prepare and serve meals. Fortunately, her teenage and young adult children and husband had plans of their own. They hardly noticed Rachel's absence.

When she was finally done reading, Rachel considered her next move. She could put the box away and leave well enough alone. But was that really an alternative?

Rachel's mind lurched to thoughts of Jennifer, her oldest child who had graduated from college the previous May and was now living back at home. Something was wrong with Jennifer. She was disengaged from people unless circumstances forced her out of isolation. She was not the confidant girl that she had been while growing up, so much like her father. Rachel couldn't quite believe that the changes in Jennifer were all the result of her break-up with Chris, Jen's college boyfriend. Where had Jennifer's resilience gone? Jen had been a fighter, never down for long.

Rachel longed for the closeness she had once felt with Jennifer. She wondered now if sharing her own past heartbreak, crises, and recovery might help Jen conquer whatever was holding her back. To date, Jennifer had only known Rachel as an attorney and involved mother. But Jen was old enough now to know more. Rachel also hoped that confiding in Jennifer might provide the opportunity to establish a new kind of bond between them.

Telling came with risks. The story would change the way Jennifer saw Rachel. Was she prepared to be *that* woman to her daughter? And she needed to be sure she wasn't being selfish or self-indulgent. She would sleep on it, Rachel told herself. She would mull the decision over for a few days.

SUNDAY
OCTOBER 5, 2014

.

CHAPTER TWO
THE FAMILY

Jennifer turned the shower nozzle to the Off position. With her eyes still closed as the water ran off her face, she reached for the towel she had thrown over the top of the small shower stall. Her hand hit glass. It wasn't there. She wiped the water from her eyes and peered through the steam.

"Katie!" Jennifer exclaimed. The family dog was curled and napping on the towel that had dropped just outside the shower door. Katie blinked, lifted her head and looked in Jennifer's direction. She yawned and then nestled down again into the towel.

Katie was a mostly white, slim, mid-size dog with short hair and expressive floppy ears. Jennifer and her brothers had speculated about what breeds had combined to create Katie. But they would never know. Katie was the third mixed breed puppy her mom had adopted from the Humane Society during Jennifer's 22 years of life. Katie was Mom's running companion. But now that Jennifer had returned home "temporarily," she was Jen's running companion too.

Jennifer braced herself for the cold and opened the shower door to reach for another towel. As she dried her body and hair, and the steam subsided from the mirror, she looked at herself. She was pretty. Her thick, long auburn hair had been inherited from her maternal grandmother. Jen had the hazel green eyes of her grandmother too. Jennifer's brothers, by way of contrast, had darker features like their dad, Kevin Adamo, with his Italian ancestry.

Jennifer turned her head from side to side. Her complexion was clear with a sprinkle of freckles across her nose. In the summer, when she worked as a lifeguard or camp counselor, her freckles multiplied. She longed to have skin more like her brothers' – skin that tanned and didn't burn. Oh, well. Her nose and mouth were just right -- not too big and not too small. She was especially fond of the dimples that appeared each time she smiled.

Looking down, Jennifer thought, "I'm not fat, but my shape is boyish – small breasts and narrow hips." Suddenly, a wave of sadness interrupted her personal inventory. "What is it about me that Chris didn't like?"

Chris had been Jennifer's boyfriend for almost three years. They met in biology lab during their sophomore year. Chris was Pre-med, while Jennifer was just trying to fulfill her science requirement for graduation. She was a religion major. They hit it off immediately. They got each other's jokes. They liked the same music. They were compatible in bed. Jennifer had been to Vermont to meet Chris's family, and Chris had been to Texas to meet hers. It had all gone so smoothly until... *Until what?* Jennifer still wasn't sure what had gone wrong. During their last semester at Meriweather College in North Carolina, Jennifer had let herself believe they were headed toward marriage. In fact, she had stopped planning her own career and had hitched her wagon and her dreams to Chris's plans for medical school and beyond. She had thought she would go wherever he went.

Then, in March, over a plate of spaghetti and garlic bread, on the ceramic blue plates they had purchased together at a flea market, Chris had looked at Jennifer and said, "It's not your fault. You're great. You are beautiful and smart. It's just that, well, I'm going to Colorado to medical school and I want to go alone..." He continued speaking, but Jennifer had stopped hearing. The weeks that followed were filled with protests, numbness, anger, silence, sarcasm, and, finally, a resigned acceptance by Jennifer that this was the way it was going to be. She watched Chris accept his diploma and awards at graduation with a smile on his face that had nothing whatsoever to do with her.

Jennifer dressed hurriedly in baggy Meriweather College sweatpants, a white men's V-necked undershirt, and a "Ski Vermont" sweatshirt she had never returned to Chris. She slid her feet into a worn pair of flip-flops as she glanced at the clock by her bed. It was almost 10 a.m. She felt her stomach growl and realized she was hungry.

Jennifer opened the carriage house door and an unseasonably cool early October breeze caused her to wrap her arms around her middle. Katie appeared and scooted past her legs and out the door, racing toward a squirrel in the backyard. Jennifer descended the stairs quickly, crossed the yard scattered with dog toys, and reached for the back door of the house that opened into the family breakfast room and kitchen.

The smells of cooked bacon and coffee filled the room. Jennifer's mother, Rachel, was standing at the kitchen island, flipping pancakes on the griddle. Rachel looked up when she heard the door open, smiled, and greeted her daughter with a rousing, "Good morning, Sleepy Head!"

Rachel was dressed in loose-fitting Levi jeans and a light blue "Life is Good" t-shirt. Her long, curly, brown hair, color-treated to match her original shade before the gray began to take over, was pulled back into a ponytail. Jennifer observed that, other than the fine wrinkles that were mostly visible around her mother's bright blue eyes and thin-lipped mouth when she smiled, her pale skin was smooth and unblemished. Rachel rarely wore make-up. Jennifer knew that her mother was 56, but she looked younger because she was dedicated to exercise. She was tall, like Jennifer, and slender. In an unusual moment of expressed vanity, Rachel had remarked to Jennifer that she could still fit into clothes she bought thirty years ago.

Jennifer's two brothers, Henry and Sam, were sitting on stools at the kitchen island, while her father, Kevin, stood near the sink pouring himself a cup of coffee. Glasses of orange juice for five had been poured and were sitting on the counter. Bowls of scrambled eggs and bacon were set in front of the boys who waited for the go-ahead to fill their plates. Jennifer heard Henry and her father debating the likelihood that the local high school football team would make it to the regional play-offs while Sam sat quietly, typing something on his phone. It was a typical Sunday morning for her family, thought Jennifer.

Again, a feeling of sadness quickly followed her thoughts. She shouldn't be back home in Austin, Texas. She should have moved on. She didn't belong in this scene.

"Are you ready to eat?" Rachel asked generally as she turned toward Jennifer again. A chorus of "yes" and "I'm starving" followed from the male members of the family. Jennifer walked in and sat down at the breakfast table without responding.

"Do you want coffee this morning?" Kevin asked Jennifer.

"Sure," Jennifer responded without moving. Kevin moved to the cupboard and pulled out a mug. Jennifer thought how easy it was to let her parents take care of her the way they had always done. She sighed.

"Let's talk about plans for the day," Kevin said as he poured the coffee and added just the right amount of creamer he knew his daughter preferred.

Henry was the first to respond. "I have to work on a project with Seth at his house this afternoon."

Kevin and Rachel inquired about the specifics. What was the project? What was Henry's role in it? Did he need materials? How long would he be gone? Jennifer knew all the questions were necessary with Henry. He had been a difficult child, a child with learning differences who was prone to violent outbursts. Henry had had encounters with law enforcement for fighting, truancy, and shoplifting. Mom had been taking Henry to therapists, doctors, and specialists for years. He had been in four different schools before his parents found Munroe Academy to be the closest match for his needs. Eighteen-year-old Henry was finally a senior in high school, though Jennifer wasn't sure about the plan for Henry after he graduated.

Henry had some good things going for him. He had great hand-eye coordination and he was strong, so he had always been good at sports. He played soccer in the fall, basketball in the winter, and baseball in the spring. Her dad had trained Henry to do home repairs and to build things. Jennifer could imagine Henry doing construction or even specializing in a trade such as electrician or plumber. She knew her parents would see that Henry found employment. They had perfected their watchfulness, and Jennifer could not imagine that her parents would let Henry fail. Still, Jennifer wasn't sure her parents knew about Henry's pot smoking or his many "girlfriends."

Henry was tall, almost 6'2", and muscular. He had curly dark brown hair that never looked combed and a twinkle in his dark brown eyes. Jennifer thought Henry always looked mischievous. Girls who didn't know him did a double take when he passed by because he was strikingly good looking.

By way of contrast, sixteen-year-old Sam was shorter and slim with thick, straight brown hair he kept trimmed close to his head. His green-brown hazel eyes looked into your soul, Jennifer thought. There was no doubt that Sam was the "smart one" of the three siblings. He barely cracked a book and got straight As. But it was dance that lit a fire in Sam. He was a non-traditional boy in that way, and Henry often mocked him. Sam aspired to be famous with his dancing. He took tap, jazz, modern, and hip-hop dance classes, and performed in several ensemble groups. Sam also appeared in the occasional play, and there had been many dance recitals over the years. Sam had endless energy. Although he had many close female friends, he didn't have a particular girlfriend. Jennifer suspected Sam might be gay. It wouldn't matter to her or her parents. In any event, it wasn't something Sam had ever admitted. Time would tell.

Henry wolfed down his meal and headed for the door.

"Just a minute!" Kevin called after Henry. "You promised me some yard work this morning."

"Aw, Dad. I'm supposed to meet Jim over at the park to play basketball."

"Not until you cut the front yard grass and trim the bushes. Remember? We talked about this yesterday."

"I know. I know," Henry replied as he headed out the door a little more slowly this time.

Kevin was the voice of reason and rules in the family. His work, finding investors and overseeing historical renovation projects, required him to be flexible and think "outside the box." But, at home, he liked order. Jennifer was wired the same way. She made lists and kept schedules. Henry drove Kevin crazy with his messiness. Though Kevin was a sports-lover like Henry, he had an easier relationship with Sam, who pursued different interests, because Sam kept a neat room. Kevin was funny – or tried to be – and outspoken. Rachel said he was the extrovert to her introvert, and so they made a good team.

As Kevin followed Henry outside to the backyard to give further instructions about the yard work, Jennifer watched him. He was a couple of inches shorter than Henry and a few pounds heavier, but they looked so much alike that Jennifer could imagine her dad at Henry's age even if she hadn't seen pictures.

Rachel broke the silence. "Sam, what is on your schedule today?"

"I need to finish my Physics homework and an essay for Lit. After that, I have a rehearsal with the swing ensemble at two and then I'm going to help Stephanie with some of the new moves we learned in Jazz. She had mono and missed a bunch of classes."

"Do you need a ride? If so, what time? Maybe Jen can take you," Rachel replied.

"Thanks, Mom. Maybe I have plans too?" Jennifer interrupted.

"Do you?" Rachel asked.

Sadly, Jennifer thought, I do not. Before Jennifer could respond, Sam said, "I don't need a ride. Stephanie is picking me up."

"Well, okay. Listen, y'all. I need to get in a run before too much of the day is gone," Rachel said, and added, "I'll take Katie with me."

Jennifer then realized her mother had not been eating so she could exercise first. Her mother was so disciplined that way. Jennifer wished she had will power or a plan. Her mother was already scraping plates and loading the dishwasher as Jennifer sat glued in her chair, unable to move.

"I'd like us all to go to the 5 o'clock service at church today. Can we do that?" Rachel asked. Only Sam and Jennifer were left in the room to respond. "Yes," they spoke at once.

"I'll make sure your dad and Henry know what we are doing too," Rachel continued.

Jennifer knew that her mother would expect the boys to go to the church youth group fellowship and choir rehearsal after the service. Henry would protest, but eventually go because it was a family rule for which there was a consequence if he didn't. Sam was a willing participant and a strong tenor in the choir as well.

Jennifer also knew that her father would leave after the service to attend his weekly poker game at the Johnsons' house. This ritual had started years ago when Jennifer was just beginning in the youth group. A group of fathers of church youth had decided to have their own meeting on Sunday evenings to watch sports or play poker. It was never about the negligible amount of money exchanged. It had always been more about male bonding, Jennifer thought. Whether they would admit it or not, Jennifer knew it was a time the men could share parenting stories and get advice from one another. Jennifer had seen her father pull Mom aside on Sunday evenings, bursting with new ideas for family trips, managing Henry's behavior, or how to negotiate family disagreements. Mom always listened patiently until her dad was finished sharing his thoughts.

"What are you going to do today on your day off?" Rachel asked Jennifer.

"I really don't know, Mom," said Jennifer, as she let out an involuntary sigh.

Jennifer was working at Macy's department store, six days a week, stocking, pricing, and selling women's clothing. It filled her time and helped her pay her car loan and student debt, but it was dull work. She didn't know how long she could stand the job, but she didn't know what else she could do. Rachel read her daughter's mind.

"Tell you what. After I finish my run, let's talk. Between the yard work, basketball, schoolwork and dance, the boys are occupied until church. Let's spend some time together, just us."

Jennifer noticed that Sam had slipped out of the kitchen. She said, "Okay. I'll read until you get back."

"I have something important to share with you," Rachel said.

=====

Rachel changed into her running clothes, located Katie in the backyard and leashed her. She told Kevin that she was going running and opened the backyard gate. Katie was pulling forward, and Rachel commanded her to slow down. She knew her words wouldn't do much good until Katie began to tire.

Rachel's awareness of the beautiful October day faded as she entered her thoughts. How would she begin this conversation with Jennifer? Her story was about an ill-fated relationship and about being raped. But it was about so much more, she thought. That whole period of time in her life was connected and dependent, somehow, on the young woman she was *before*. But it was too much to ask of her daughter to sit through a history lesson on Rachel's whole life. She felt sure the important pieces would emerge as she shared the traumatic events. Still, she had to start somewhere.

Theology school, thought Rachel. She would tell Jennifer the kind of person she had been when she entered theology school. That was where she met Jay, six months before she was raped. Jay's involvement post-rape wouldn't make any sense if she didn't start with that relationship.

Katie was no longer pulling, but maintaining a pace and rhythm that allowed Rachel to stay deep in thought even as she wiped sweat from her eyes. She reflected on the autobiography she'd been required to write as part of her application to theology school. She had kept a copy and later placed it in her cardboard box of historical documents because it revealed so much about who she was *before*. In September, after seeing Jay at the chapel, Rachel had read that document again. She remembered the first lines now: "I will begin with love, and end with love, for love and the loss of love is the stuff that life is made of. Love gets me up in the morning and puts me to sleep at night. It is in my heart, my soul, and in everything worthwhile that I do. It is my motivation, my strength, and my reason for being." There was more that followed about her "loving family" and her extended family's connections to ministry. She had grimaced reading it this many years later. She sounded so naïve and trusting. Yet, Rachel knew, this innocence and worldview was precisely what Jennifer should know about her for any of the rest to make sense.

Rachel realized she was almost back home from her three-mile loop through the neighborhood. Katie had slowed some, but she would keep going for miles if Rachel let her.

=====

While Rachel showered and changed clothes, Jennifer sat in the carriage house in a recliner staring blankly at the book she had said she would be reading. Her mind wandered. Should she call a friend? Should she look for a different job? Should she open the computer and look up graduate schools? Stupid idea! She didn't even know what she wanted to study or who she wanted to be when she "grew up." She didn't want to think about Chris and how he had derailed her. She could get so angry at him. But her anger always dissolved into despair and depression. This was her day off and she didn't want to feel depressed.

Suddenly, the carriage house door opened and Rachel entered. She had a box in her hands, an old cardboard box.

"Hey. I have a story to tell you. Are you ready?" Rachel asked.

"I don't know what you mean by 'ready,' but I'm here and I can listen," said Jennifer. She had no idea why her mother was so insistent or what the old box could have to do with her story. Her mother's intensity and cargo reminded Jennifer of those early months during her senior year in high school when Mom carried around files on colleges Jennifer might attend and kept track of applications and which documents had been written, requested, or sent.

"That's all I ask. I thought I'd start by telling you about theology school and a man I met there. The man's name was Jay Winchester." Rachel settled herself in the other recliner and plopped the box down on the carpet.

Jennifer was intrigued. Mom had never spoken of theology school before. This could be interesting.

CHAPTER THREE
THE ATTRACTION

"I was close to your age when I first met Jay Winchester. I had graduated from college at Austin University where I had double majored in history and philosophy."

Jennifer smirked.

"Yes, I know. Without a plan for graduate school, teaching, or research, I was about where you are now. I sold building materials in a retail store for a year while I tried to figure out 'what next?' Sound familiar?"

Jennifer nodded.

"Although I can't tell you my future became clear to me, I will say that I began to consider ministry as a possible occupation. After all, my dad, your Papa, was and is a minister. Your Nanna is a minister's daughter. Your Aunt Sarah, Uncle Lucas, and I grew up in the church. Your Papa had been the man I most admired all my life, and he was so happy being a pastoral counselor. So, I decided to go to theology school and see where it led me. I was 23.

"I remember the first time I saw Dr. James Winchester. He was standing at the front of the lecture hall in an introductory New Testament class in January 1982, the beginning of my second semester in theology school. He wore a Hawaiian print shirt, faded blue jeans, and sneakers. His long, wispy, light-blond hair and tanned skin reminded me of a surfer. He was tall – probably 6'3", thin and angular. He paced back and forth, gesturing with his hands, passionate in his presentation. Even from the back of the room, I noticed the sparkle in his sea foam green eyes. I found him very attractive."

Jennifer noticed the way her mother glowed as she spoke of Jay. It was almost like listening to one of her girlfriends in college talk about a new boy she'd just met. But it was strange to hear the words coming from her mother's mouth.

"But it wasn't just the way he looked," Rachel continued. "His words captured my attention. He said that the 'great men' who shaped our interpretations of the Bible were *men* with faults, biases, jealousies, and loves of their own. They were 'embedded in culture,' and this shaped their questions and their theological conclusions. He said that understanding our own cultural and religious context was crucial to making knowledgeable choices about our futures and the future of our faith.

"My relationship with Jay – as he asked me to call him at our first meeting, started so innocently. One day, he was sitting at the back of the classroom near me listening to a guest lecturer. I leaned over and whispered a question to him about the lecture. I no longer remember specifically what I asked. I do remember that as I moved toward him, I felt light-headed, but remained composed. Jay invited me to come talk to him later in his office.

"That first meeting was conducted in a professional manner: teacher to student. We discussed theological issues. But there was an instant familiarity between us. I agreed with virtually every opinion Jay held. I was struggling with the theological doctrines and rituals of the church. Frankly, I was not sure what I believed in. But with Jay, I found an intellectual approach that challenged Christian traditions and gave me the freedom to do the same."

Rachel reached for the cardboard box. She said, "Wait just a minute," as she thumbed through a stack of lined pages covered in black or blue ink handwriting. "Here is an example of a note I wrote to Jay that semester."

I cannot imagine that a loving God would allow for the massive, incredibly overpowering amount of evil in the world. I think that we are committed to morals, religion and god (in various cultures) because they are the best we have been able to come up with to satisfy our inner longings for intellectual understanding, security in our lives and possessions, and inner peace. But when cold hard reality (sickness, injustice, etc.) comes down on us, we break our own rules to 'save' our lives. Thus we perpetuate evil and suffering, the very things we hoped to escape.

Even if there is a God, would human beings support the injunctions of religion if they were not *practical*? Maybe I'm looking for something that is unique about faith in God that would be an indication to me that God truly exists. Or perhaps I'm asking the wrong questions entirely. Could it be that it doesn't matter if God exists apart from human thought and experience?

I am not so foolish as to believe that these questions have not crossed your mind. And yet, for some reason you have committed your life to the study of the Bible and the making of ministers. You must have arrived at some sort of answer you can live with. I wish you would enlighten me.

"That's mighty serious sounding, Mom," remarked Jennifer.

"I was nothing if not serious about learning and probing the great mysteries of life," Rachel smiled, mocking herself. But her expression quickly shifted back to one of seriousness.

"At the same time that I was looking for answers to tough theological questions, I was also asking myself difficult personal ones. I felt no closer to finding a career than when I started college. As I mentioned earlier, I had worked selling building materials after college. I had also worked in the circulation department for the newspaper. I'll tell you more about that later. And I had begun but not completed a modeling course and pre-med classes! Going to theology school seemed like a reasonable and safe choice because the language of the church was familiar to me.

"However, by the second semester of theology school, I was already disillusioned. I was not sure I believed what I was being taught. I was tired of being compared to my father who was well known among the faculty. The prospect of identifying and claiming my separateness from Dad seemed possible after I met Jay. So that was part of his appeal to me too," said Rachel.

Jennifer knew her mother and Papa had a close relationship. But she had never thought of her mother as struggling to claim a separate identity from him. She guessed that maybe all children went through this struggle. She had certainly considered her mother's and father's past and present work when deciding to major in religion because that seemed so removed from their pursuits. How strange it was to be learning now that her mother had attended theology school! This separation business was more difficult than she had imagined.

Rachel continued, "The first meeting led to subsequent meetings in Jay's office. I'm not sure how and when it happened, but not long into our relationship, Jay began to ask me more personal questions about my family and love relationships. He shared his own stories as well. Jay took the position that the personal life of a scholar determines his or her perspective. Therefore, it made 'academic sense' to talk about our personal lives.

"Discussions turned to sexuality. Jay and I agreed that there was a lot of religious nonsense surrounding sex in the Christian faith, particularly the devaluing of the body in favor of the mind. I shared stories of crises with old boyfriends that continued to trouble me. Jay took it all in stride and I felt completely at ease revealing these most painful memories."

Jennifer interrupted, "You never mentioned crises with boyfriends to me."

"No," said Rachel. "It seems so distant now. Besides, your life was so different. You had a parade of teenage boys interested in you, and you handled it so well. During your senior year, you didn't even bother with boys. Sports and school and college applications kept you occupied. And then came Chris."

Jennifer felt her face flush, and she bit her bottom lip. She wanted to change the subject. "So, what happened then, Mom?"

"As I talked with Jay, I came to believe that my 'call' to ministry – if, in fact, it was a 'call' – had to do with helping others in crisis. Ministry wasn't about rituals and doctrines. It was about mucking around in the trenches with people who were hurting. Jay understood this. He had been there too. Jay told me about his past work in treatment centers with alcoholics. He also told me about a time when he intervened to prevent a rape in the inner city. Jay told stories of his confrontations with meaningless rituals and false holiness. I was inspired! This was exactly what I was looking for: ministry that involved the heart, mind, and body united in a common struggle for good over evil."

"Sounds like you," Jennifer interjected, remembering her mother's work with Legal Aid and many volunteer hours with a number of charities.

"Jay urged me to distance myself from the man I was then dating and to focus on my *own* needs. Jay did this very skillfully by validating my concern for the boyfriend, but also offering the perspective that his unhealthiness was not good for me. He said that I needed to be involved with a man who was more loving and nurturing. He spoke from personal experience and confided that he was in an unhappy, unhealthy marriage that was sapping all of his resources. I felt privileged to be chosen as his confidant."

Jennifer moved uncomfortably in her chair.

"As Jay and I continued to meet," Rachel said, "he began to talk to me about his writing projects. He said that it was very important to him to have someone as interested as I was to listen as he formulated and reworked his thoughts, especially since his wife no longer took an interest in his scholarly work.

"The winter months passed quickly. I felt all my senses turned on and engaged as I pursued my studies and looked forward to frequent, intellectually stimulating meetings with Jay.

"Jay and I passed notes in the back of the classroom on the days he wasn't lecturing. I found one of these exchanges in a class notebook, and I want you to hear it. Our communication reflects the intense pressures we were under and, at the same time, the insistence we both felt about spending time together."

Rachel pulled a worn piece of notebook paper from a folder in her box and read.

Jay: Thank you for your letter. I, too, was delighted that we talked. Tried to find you last night; scouted the library, but to no avail. I'm not the only one who is hard to find!

Rachel: I was in the undergraduate library trying to work on my exegesis paper, colloquy paper, and supervised ministry verbatim. The theology school library is too stuffy and theological. Allen...

Rachel stopped reading to explain, "Allen was the man I was dating at the time."

Allen found me about 8:30 and stayed with me until 2:00 a.m. when the library closed. Then we drank coffee for an hour until I had to go to work. Needless to say, I didn't get a whole lot done in the midst of explaining myself to him. He fluctuated from 'go to hell' to 'I love you. I'd marry you in a minute.'

Jennifer interrupted, "I'm so confused. Who is this Allen and why were you going to work at 2:00 a.m.?"

Rachel sighed. This was so complicated to explain. She had wanted to avoid dragging Jennifer through all her past relationships, but it was clear now that she would have to share more than she had planned to share. She said, "Can I tell you about Allen and my work after I finish introducing you to Jay? I'm realizing that you need to hear more about my past, but I'd like to finish this sequence first. Okay?"

Jennifer was puzzled, but she nodded 'yes.'

"Okay," said Rachel. "My note to Jay continued..."

With work and Allen and school I have managed to sleep 3 hours since Sunday. Oh, well.

Jay: Next time I'll look in the undergraduate library – even tried to call you! Hope the situation with Allen works out. I am not persuaded that you have to – or should – explain yourself to him – or anyone. That seems to me to put the burden on you *not only* to be you, *but also* to greet and hallow your special presence in the world. *That* however is for those of us in this world – not you – to do. Put differently, greeting and hallowing *you* is a form of grace given *to* and *not generated* by you. You need now to get some sleep.

"I'm sorry to interrupt again. But is that the way he always talked – 'greeting and hallowing'?" asked Jennifer.

Rachel smiled. "Yes. Pretty much. That's part of the reason I wanted you to hear this. His language was seductive to me... Then I respond with how crazy busy I am."

Rachel: I can't sleep yet. The exegesis is due tomorrow and I'm 'on call' at Austin University Hospital tonight. I made a deal with my boss to get tomorrow off from work with the agreement that I would work 22 hours this weekend. There goes Easter. What a great martyr I'd make! But, seriously, I will get some sleep soon. It's just that 'soon' may be tomorrow afternoon.

Jay: I'm not sure whose schedule is more absurd – yours or mine. Knowing and learning from one another – which is what I take to be the unspoken invitation we have been attempting to extend to one another – will doubtless be difficult under such circumstances. But perhaps I have misconstrued the situation – in which case, I apologize. If not, however, we might think about ways to keep the structures of schedules from blotting our times to talk.

Rachel: You understand the invitation correctly. In fact, it may be the most important thing to me right now. It seems that all of a sudden I lost control – got swamped. I can give you a schedule if it would help. On my better days, I am somewhat consistent. Really and truly – I do want to share with you; I'm excited about it.

Jay: Hot damn!

"That last part surprised me," said Jennifer.

"Yeah. It sounds funny, doesn't it? Jay was becoming more comfortable with me, more like a peer," said Rachel.

"That raises another question. How old was Jay?" asked Jennifer.

"He was fifteen years older than me," replied Rachel.

Jennifer gulped. "That's *old*, Mom."

"I'm sure it seems that way to you. But I had always been comfortable with people older than me – teachers, your grandparents' friends." Rachel realized that she had stumbled into another area where she and her daughter were different. She would need to come back to this 'difference.' But, first, she was determined to reveal the true nature of her relationship with Jay before she lost her nerve.

Rachel took a deep breath and said, "As Easter approached, fewer faculty and students remained on campus – drawn to their other duties related to this most sacred holiday in the Christian year. I was not working at a church, so I agreed to meet with Jay on Wednesday evening of Holy Week. I don't remember the details of our discussion, but after it was over, Jay walked me to the door, leaned over, and kissed me."

Jennifer swallowed hard.

"The kiss set me on fire! I had not allowed myself to think this might happen. Jay was *married*. And I didn't dare contemplate what might happen next. But I was overwhelmed with how good and right it felt to be touched by Jay. The kiss felt like an affirmation of our kindred spirits.

"The memory of that kiss replayed in my head again and again for the next two days. It was as if a powerful magnetic force controlled me now. And so it was that, on Good Friday, I found myself at the theology school at Jay's office once more. No one else was in the building. I don't remember what was said, but right away we started touching."

The words caught in Rachel's throat, but she pushed them out.

"We made love on Jay's office floor, over and over, all night long. It was, I thought then, the most splendid, perfect sex I had ever experienced."

Jennifer looked stunned and a little embarrassed, but Rachel continued.

"As dawn approached, and I knew our night of passion had come to an end, I uttered the truest words I had ever spoken: 'I love you.' I couldn't help myself, Jennifer. I could not hold the words back. Jay smiled, but his eyes betrayed him. He was not at liberty to speak so freely. I knew that. His reassuring touch spoke for him. It said: 'We must move slowly. Don't ask for more than I can give.'"

CHAPTER FOUR
BEFORE JAY

Rachel took another deep breath. She looked at Jennifer who had an expression on her face that Rachel couldn't read. Becoming aware of her mother's gaze, Jennifer dropped her head and noticed her clenched hands and white knuckles. She loosened her grip and looked up again.

"But *why*, Mom? I understand the stuff about Jay being an expert, having answers you were looking for, and all that. But didn't it seem creepy to be with a man so much older than you? A married man? He sounds so different from Dad."

"He was." And is, Rachel thought to herself. What is love? What makes a person fall in love? I could describe all the physical and emotional characteristics of Jay in greater detail to Jennifer and it still wouldn't explain something so heart-felt and soul-full. People fall in love with the wrong person all the time. And no matter how often outsiders point out what's wrong with the love, nothing changes until the heart changes. A critic just makes the lover feel worse, if she values the critic's opinion at all. It is the beloved who will change the lover's heart if it is to change. Despite all the bad externals related to Jay, he loved me back for a very long time. And my heart could not deny him.

Rachel sighed. "This is where I need to back up and tell you more about my past. I hope this will help you understand 'why Jay.'

"When I was in high school, I was not your typical flirtatious girl. For one thing, I was athletic. I was serious and shy. I probably came off as aloof to many of my peers. That wasn't at all the way I *felt*. I worried about having the right answer or response, and I rehearsed everything in my head before I spoke because I was so afraid of saying something stupid or the wrong thing.

"I was also a feminist at a time – the 1970s - and in a place – the South - where that was a very new thing. It made a lot of people uncomfortable. When I was middle school age, there was a group of women at my church who met and discussed how to change language in hymns and liturgy to make it more inclusive. This won't sound so unusual to you, but it was new then. They talked about God as Creator or Mother instead of, or in addition to, God as Him or Father. They talked about using human and humankind instead of man or mankind. They were a consciousness-raising group. Is that term familiar to you?"

"Sort of," responded Jennifer. "But can you explain what you mean?"

"During the 1960s, a host of movements for equality emerged. Many of these were not new movements but new *waves.* As you know from studying history, the Civil Rights Act was passed in 1964 as a result of the Civil Rights Movement. The climate was also right for women to make headway in the march toward equality with men. This is probably not the time to give a history lesson on the women's rights movements," smiled Rachel. "Suffice it to say that when I was a tween and teen, women in the suburbs who had been isolated in their homes, raising their children and taking care of their working husbands, began to meet or gather in each other's homes and share their stories. They noticed that women who worked did not receive equal pay for the same work that men did. They realized that men were treated preferentially in many other ways as well. These groups of women were called consciousness-raising groups... Does that help?"

"Yes, it does," said Jennifer.

"The point is, I attended some of these meetings at church. I also attended meetings of the National Organization of Women. I got pumped-up about discrimination against girls and women, and I wanted to do something to change it. One of the first things I did to fight discrimination was try to join an all male club at my high school. Members had to have a B average and letter in two sports. I qualified, so I applied. But I was a female, so my application was rejected. Word got around about my actions and I was labeled."

"What kind of label?" asked Jennifer.

"I can't remember now what words were used. Maybe 'queer'? The point being made was that I liked women and didn't like men. You know, Jen, I didn't think I knew anyone who was a homosexual at that time. I was wrong, of course. But it was a time of hiding for most members of the LGBTQ community. All I knew then was that the label was bad and that it made me unapproachable by my male peers.

"I think I told you that I never dated in high school. It wasn't because I wasn't interested. Now you know part of the reason 'why.'"

Rachel paused, remembering her unnecessary suffering born of ignorance and idealism.

"It was hard, Jennifer, harder than I let myself believe at the time. I was committed to women's liberation! But I felt unattractive and unlovable. The only people who complemented me on my beauty or intelligence or commitment to doing the right thing were your grandparents, their adult peers, and my teachers. I was deemed 'mature for my age.'

"But when I went to college at Austin University, I had the opportunity to recreate myself. I wanted to know what it was like to have a boyfriend, and that trumped all my feminist inclinations. I learned to flirt and to dress a little more femininely – to use a sexist term." Rachel smiled again. "But I was still shy and serious. I had learned how to communicate with adults better than I had learned how to communicate with men my own age. I'd never been to parties, drunk alcohol, or smoked pot. I was a young woman who would rather exercise and play sports."

Jennifer thought about how similar she was to her mother in that way. She had been passionate about soccer and swimming. She had gone to the occasional party, but parties were never her focus.

Rachel continued, "My first love was a graduate student and teaching assistant in biology named Nathan. He had his own apartment, car, and a motorcycle we took on a road trip during spring break. He taught me to cook. He taught me how to make love. As I think about it now, he was my *teacher*. We weren't two kids fumbling through it, trying to figure it out. He was the expert and I was the novice."

Jennifer tried to imagine her mother as a young woman in love "fumbling through it." This was hard. As soon as she understood what the concept "sex" meant, she had resisted thinking of her mother as someone who had sex. But Mom was forcing her now to think about it. It shouldn't surprise her, she thought. Mom had always been so open and graphic when it came to sex – embarrassingly so!

Jennifer remembered that when she was eleven, Mom told her it was time to learn about puberty, bodily changes, and sex. She didn't want to listen, so Mom gave her a book to read instead. They had a standing date on Wednesday afternoons after school to discuss what Jennifer had read or was *supposed to* have read in the book that week. Mom would come into her bedroom and sit down in Jennifer's desk chair. Jennifer would sit on her bed but pivot to turn her back to Mom while Mom asked questions to see if she understood the material. It was torture! She hated Mom then. She couldn't understand why her mother would not respect her privacy and modesty.

And it didn't end there. Mom talked to her brothers about sex too. Shouldn't that have been Dad's job? He seemed to disappear whenever Mom, while mashing potatoes for dinner or folding clothes, matter-of-factly brought up erections and wet dreams. It was gross! But the boys didn't seem to mind. In fact, they taunted Jennifer because of her modesty. There had been times, driving in the van to a practice or event, when Henry or Sam yelled, "Tell us some more about penises, Mom!" Jen would cover her ears and start to hum to drown out the conversation while her brothers laughed and punched each other playfully. Mom *never* took her side. She just answered the questions the boys asked or brought up some new disgusting information.

When Jennifer got to high school, however, she was glad her mother had been so open. The girls who whispered about sex or, in a moment of passion, went further with a boy than they wanted to go, seemed immature and foolish. Her mother's methods did not seem so outrageous then. Jennifer understood all the basic biology and the potential consequences of different sexual acts before she ever needed to make decisions out of ignorance. Sure, the Internet had changed the way she and her friends learned about sex. But there was so much information out there. Who knew what was right or wrong, normal or on the fringes? Whether she wanted to or not, Jennifer had to admit that her mother was someone she could go to if she had questions pertaining to sex. So, it wasn't really surprising that her mother was being so forthcoming now.

Jennifer thought about her own first sexual experiences. They had come much earlier for her than for her mother, with a boy she'd known since kindergarten, a playmate turned groper when adolescence hit. They hadn't gone all the way because Jennifer put a stop to it. She had been scared. She knew she wasn't ready.

But then, when she was fifteen, there was Robbie, a first-string striker on the boys' varsity soccer team, a handsome boy with steel blue eyes and curly brown hair. Jennifer had gone to a party at Delia's house after their respective soccer games. She drank a punch laced with alcohol. Robbie approached her and, relaxed by the alcohol, she flirted shamelessly with this accomplished, popular senior boy. Robbie offered to drive her home, and she accepted.

Jennifer remembered the moment in his car when Robbie reached across and put his hand on her thigh. She was electrified. She put her hand on top of his. He turned and asked, "You wanna go somewhere else first?" She knew what that meant, and nodded "yes." Her stomach was filled with butterflies as Robbie changed directions and made his way toward the darkened end of a large church parking lot, empty of cars on a Saturday night. When he stopped the car, Robbie leaned over to kiss her and then gently directed her into the backseat.

It happened so quickly. Their shirts came off. His mouth was on her mouth, her neck, and then her breasts. He unzipped her jeans and tugged them to the floor. Robbie took a condom from his pocket, unzipped his own jeans, and pulled them down below his knees. He tore the packet open with his teeth and slid the condom effortlessly over his erect penis. When he entered her, she felt a sharp pain that soon subsided as he moved up and down on her. When it was over, his weight fell on her. He mumbled, "Oh my God. You are so sexy." That was it.

A few minutes later, they were dressed and driving toward Jennifer's house again. There was a palpable awkwardness between them. Robbie glanced her way and smiled. But she recognized the falseness of it. She felt the wetness in her underpants – her blood.

When Robbie pulled up to the curb in front of Jennifer's house, she paused momentarily to see if he would get out to open her door. He didn't. Instead, Robbie leaned across the expanse between them and lightly kissed her on the lips. Then he reached further to pull the door handle so the door popped open on her side. "That was nice," Robbie said. "I'll see you at school." Then he repositioned himself to drive away, and Jennifer knew that was her cue to leave.

She had a key to her house, and quietly unlocked the door. She glanced back once toward the street, but Robbie was gone. As soon as the door creaked open, Jennifer heard the distinctive sound of her father's movement in his recliner in the family room at the back of the house. She knew he had been waiting up until she got home.

"Have a nice time at the party?" Dad called out. Jennifer could hear him rising from his seat.

"Yes. It was fun. I'm tired. I'm going to bed," she responded, as she started up the stairs. She wanted to avoid confronting him now. What if he smelled alcohol on her breath – or something else? What if Dad saw something in her expression or dress that gave away her secret? "I'll see you in the morning," she added as she reached the top step.

Jennifer dashed down the hall to her bedroom, opened the door, and shut it behind her. She let out a sigh of relief. She suspected Dad would not attempt to invade her private space so late at night. She moved quickly into the adjoining bathroom and shut that door behind her too. She turned and raised her gaze to the mirror over her sink. She searched her face for signs that she was different now. If anything had changed, it wasn't visible on the parts of her she exposed to the world, she thought.

Over the next few days, Jennifer waited expectantly for Robbie to call or text. When she saw him at school, he never took the opportunity to move closer to her or to acknowledge her presence. It was as if nothing at all had transpired between them. She might have been angry or hurt. Instead, Jennifer discovered that she felt relieved. She knew there was no future for her with Robbie. They were too different. He had done her a favor, actually. He had liberated her from her status as a virgin. The mystery was no longer a mystery. In an unexpected way, she now felt more relaxed. The burden of wondering when, how, and with whom was gone. Now she could and would make choices with new knowledge and understanding she didn't have before.

Rachel was speaking, and Jennifer tuned in again. "We dated for nine months. Nathan met my family and became like a big brother to Lucas. I fantasized marriage and kids with Nathan. When he dumped me, my heart was broken."

Jennifer wanted to ask why it ended, but her mother continued talking.

"That relationship was significant in another way," said Rachel. "During the summer when we were still dating, Nathan had a job in Boston and he wanted me to come visit him. I didn't have the money to get there. So, I took a job that summer when I was 20 as a newspaper carrier for the Austin Daily News to make enough money to buy my plane ticket. Little did I know that working for the newspaper would become my staple income for the next few years, my fallback job."

Jennifer yawned.

"Are you getting bored?" Rachel asked.

"No, Mom. But is all this going to have something to do with my original question about Jay?"

"Yes. And I'm sorry it's taking so long to explain. All these pieces fit together to make the 'perfect storm.'..."

"A 'perfect storm'?" asked Jennifer, puzzled by the expression.

"A 'perfect storm' is an expression that describes an event where a rare combination of circumstances or forces come together to drastically aggravate a situation. You know, Jay was right about at least one thing. We only perceive, believe, and plan through our own limited personal experience. Everything that had happened to me before influenced the way I responded to Jay when we met," explained Rachel.

Jennifer nodded and her mother continued.

"Okay. So, once I started working for the newspaper, I discovered it was a great way to make the money I needed to support myself in a short period of time. Plus, the hours 3 a.m. to 6:30 a.m. didn't interfere with my class schedule."

Jen's jaw dropped. "You worked in the middle of the night? Is that what you were doing when you wrote about going to work at 2 a.m.?"

"Yes, it was. As you know, I'm a 'morning person' by nature. It wasn't so hard to get up as long as I took a nap during the day or went to bed early. Not exactly a college student's hours, but it worked for me. I kept right on delivering newspapers through the rest of my college years and then, later, in theology school.

"As you might suspect, I was a hard worker who showed up on time and rarely, if ever, made mistakes in my deliveries. The managers noticed me because of my strong work ethic – or so I thought. Frankly, I was oblivious that my youth and attractiveness also brought attention. One manager in particular, named Jason, took a special interest in me. Jason was tall and strong and good-looking in that bad boy kind of way. He had a great sense of humor. He seemed to intimidate most people, but he intrigued me.

"Jason offered me additional hours delivering missed papers that were called in by customers after the 6:30 a.m. deadline. For that job, I came back to the branch warehouse after delivering my route and waited around with the district managers who were on duty. They drank coffee, chain-smoked cigarettes, and made crude jokes – mostly about women and sex. Jason protected me from the crassness of the other men by taking me out for breakfast or in his car to check on some issue with a paper route.

"For months, we talked and worked and shared bits and pieces of our histories. He had been married before and had two daughters who lived with their mother. He was Vietnam War veteran. He was a recovering alcoholic. He could take apart a car and put it back together again. I hope it makes sense for me to say that my fascination with all his differences from me was a big part of the attraction."

That was *so* Mom, Jennifer thought. She was always pushing her kids to try new activities, clubs, books, and ideas. She read articles or heard stories on the radio that she shared with Jennifer and her brothers, prompting them to respond to questions and challenging their opinions. Sometimes Dad had to intervene when she wouldn't let go of a subject. Jen remembered the time their church youth group was going to make sandwiches to take to an area of Austin where many homeless people hung out. The idea was for the youth to personally offer the sandwiches and conversation to homeless individuals. Henry didn't want to go. "It was boring," he said. Mom became animated, telling Henry this would be a new, good experience for him. "Just because you haven't done something before, just because it's a little scary, doesn't mean its 'boring' or something you shouldn't try!"

Rachel continued her story. "Then, the summer before my senior year in college, on the morning before Jason left for vacation, while we were sitting in his car, he leaned over and kissed me. I kissed him back. That was the beginning of a romance that lasted a year and a half."

"He must have been old," suggested Jennifer.

"He was in his mid-30s," said Rachel.

"That's *old*," said Jennifer.

"Your grandparents were not thrilled," Rachel replied, remembering how cold her dad had been toward Jason.

"Basically, I worked, went to school, played on sports' teams, and hung out with Jason. I had very little contact with the college community otherwise. I lived in an apartment off campus and dated an older, previously married man with children who had an interesting past."

"In other words," Jennifer interrupted, "this theology guy wasn't the first older man."

"Right," said Rachel.

"What ended the relationship with Jason?"

"I graduated from college and met Allen at my new job at the building materials store." Rachel paused before continuing. "This isn't going to sound like a very sensitive or caring response, Jen. But, I think, even though I couldn't articulate what I was feeling to Jason, I just knew in my gut that he wouldn't fit in my future. I couldn't see us together forever."

Jennifer involuntarily sucked in her breath. She felt like she'd been punched in the stomach. Mom sounded like *Chris*. Was it really that easy to toss away someone you loved? Maybe Chris had *never* loved her. Maybe Mom had just been using Jason for "the experience."

Rachel could see that her daughter was far away, thinking about something or someone else, probably Chris.

"Hey, Jen. Just so you know, I loved Jason. But I think he loved me more. I think I wasn't ready to settle for this one man. After all, it had taken me twenty years before I went on a first date. After I recovered from the break-up with Nathan, I knew L-O-V-E wasn't like the Disney movies – all happily ever after. I resolved to have adventures with men rather then look for one I could hitch my trailer to. I wanted to know passion. But more than that, I wanted to learn *everything* about *everything*. Does that make sense?"

Jennifer nodded, wondering if Chris had felt the same.

Without waiting for Jennifer's response, Rachel continued. "Jason had exposed me to so many things I knew nothing about before him. I wanted more of that. I was looking for answers to life's mysteries. My decision to go to theology school was as much about answering questions like: Does God exist? Why do bad things happen to good people? Why is the church so punitive and restrictive? – as it was about establishing a career. I hadn't been "called" the way some people describe their decision to enter the ministry. I thought I believed in a loving God. I knew church members had nurtured me. But I wasn't sure about much else."

Rachel uncrossed her legs and stood up. She reached into the dusty cardboard box and grabbed the spiral bound notebook on top. "Let's go walk Katie. You want to?"

Jennifer kept her seat. She said, "I'm guessing Allen was an older man too."

"He was."

"So what you are saying is that you were already predisposed to date older men. You felt comfortable with them. And you were looking for adventures and answers, as well as passion," concluded Jennifer.

"People talk about being attracted to 'types,'" Rachel continued. "My 'type' was never primarily about the physical. The primary thing that attracted me to men was *new experiences*. I seemed always to be drawn to men who had lived lives outside my sheltered experience."

Rachel paused and turned serious again. "There's another factor, Jen. It's a factor that has less to do with me, personally, than with students of theology generally. The people who go to theology school tend to fall into one of two camps. In one camp are the dogmatists – the students who are there because they need the degree to get the job they want. They think they already know what they need to know, and they make their education fit their beliefs. They tend to be close-minded and impenetrable. This is an exaggeration, of course," Rachel smiled. "At least I hope it is.

"In the other camp are students like me – students who are searching, trusting, vulnerable, and open. We believe in the goodness of God, the power of Love, and we are trying to make sense of evil, death, illness, and suffering. Our openness makes us easier 'prey' to persuasive logic, charismatic speech, or, unfortunately, to those persons who do not have our best interests at heart – consciously or unconsciously."

Jennifer felt her cheeks flush, but her mother did not seem to notice.

Rachel slapped her thigh. "Now, come on. Let's go."

CHAPTER FIVE
THE FIRST RAPE

"Where are we going?" Jennifer asked as she rose slowly from the recliner.

"I need to move." It was more than that, Rachel thought. It would be hard to face Jennifer telling the next part of her story. She knew, from experience as a parent, that older kids often spoke more freely in a car when they were beside or behind her than when they were confronted with questions face-to-face. This time, Rachel was the one who needed the freedom that walking side-by-side would give her.

Jennifer followed her mother to the garage where Rachel grabbed a leash off its hook and attached it to the collar of Katie, who had instantly appeared as soon as she heard Rachel's and Jennifer's footsteps on the carriage house stairs. Rachel opened the backyard gate, holding Katie's leash firmly as she lunged forward, and waited for Jen to follow. The women walked down the driveway past the men in the front yard. Henry was pushing the lawnmower, earphones attached to his head, and Kevin was aggressively pulling weeds. At the sidewalk, Rachel, Jennifer, and Katie turned left, in the direction of the Austin University campus.

Rachel broke the silence. "I need to tell you about a particular important day in my life – one I haven't shared with you before. Okay?"

Jennifer was worried, but she said, "Okay."

"First, let me set the stage. During my first year in theology school, I was again working for the Austin Daily News delivering papers in the early morning hours before classes. This time around, I was working out of the Midtown Branch. I sometimes witnessed drunks staggering home in the early morning hours, prostitutes at work, and homeless people rummaging through dumpsters or looking for a place to rest. Your grandparents worried about my safety, and even I started to think it might be safer to have a dog in the car while I worked – a discouragement to anyone who might view me as an easy target. The more I thought about a dog, the more I liked the idea. I lived alone in an apartment, and a dog would be good company, both at home and at work.

"On June 23, 1982, I visited the Austin Humane Society with adoption in mind. I found a young puppy - a German shepherd mix with long ears and expressive brown eyes. I filled out the paperwork, paid the fee, and took him home. I still wasn't sure what I would name him when I left for work with the puppy on the morning of June 24th."

Rachel and Jennifer had reached the Austin University main campus which was a short walk from their home. Rachel directed Jennifer to sit on a nearby bench and let go of Katie's leash. The dog immediately sped off in the direction of a squirrel. From experience, Rachel knew that Katie would wear herself out chasing birds and small rodents, but never stray too far from her owners. On a Sunday afternoon, when the campus was mostly deserted, Rachel was not likely to be reprimanded for letting the dog off leash.

Rachel sat beside Jennifer and opened the notebook she had tucked under her arm for the walk. "Let me read to you from the journal entry I wrote on June 24, 1982."

... I arrived at the branch office at 3 a.m. I made sure that all the newspaper carriers in my area showed up for work before I set out to deliver 300 newspapers on an open route. I loaded the papers I had bagged into my car and left the warehouse around 4:15 a.m. This particular route is in a mixed commercial and residential area. There are more apartments on the route than houses. Most of the apartments have internal doors, so I have to park my car and go inside the buildings to drop newspapers at each customer's door.

Fifteen deliveries into the route on a major road, quiet at this time of night, I noticed a car with its flashers on parked a few feet up the road from where I parked in a driveway to go into an apartment building to make deliveries. When I came out, the stalled car was still there. I could hear the driver revving the engine. I walked over to my car and got in. As I began to back out of the driveway, the driver of the car opened his door and ran toward my car window.

"Can you help me move my car off the street?" he asked. "There is something wrong with my transmission."

I don't know much about cars or engines. I noticed that the man was driving some sort of sports car on oversized tires. My car is a 1972 Chevy Vega, low to the ground. It was clear to me that I could not push him off the street.

"Our bumpers won't connect," I said.

"But what am I going to do? Please help me."

I studied the driver. He was a clean-shaven, nice-looking black man, dressed in a patterned close-fitting shirt made of slinky synthetic material and dark slacks. He was dressed like someone who had been out on a date.

I thought about his request. In two hours, this road would be jammed with rush-hour traffic. His car could not stay where it was.

"Could you take me to the gas station up the street?" he asked.

"No, it isn't open yet," I replied.

"My brother can help me. He is at my house. Can you drive me to Eastside?"

Eastside was only five miles away. If all I had to do was deliver this man to his brother, I would still have time to complete my paper deliveries before the 6:30 a.m. deadline.

I knew I was supposed to be wary of strangers. But strangers had helped *me* solve car problems on many occasions. This was my fourth old car in five years. Strangers had helped me change tires when lug nuts were too tight. Strangers had taken me to gas stations for fuel and service. Once, I even had a transmission problem that sounded exactly the way this man's car sounded. I knew that those strangers were not people my parents would have approved of, but they turned out to be Good Samaritans. And I had been raised to help others in need.

"Okay. I'll do it. But we have to get your car off the street first. Can you move it into the Midtown Retirement Towers parking lot across the street?"

The driver ran back and jumped into his car. He moved it, by fits and starts, into a parking place in the back of the L-shaped lot. I pulled my car in behind him. The man helped me move the newspapers and puppy to the back seats. He climbed into the seat and we began our journey to Eastside.

I suddenly realized that we had not even introduced ourselves. The stranger must have been thinking the same thing.

He said, "My name is Barry. What's your name?"

"Rachel."

"How old are you? I'm 29."

"Twenty-four."

"Where do you live?"

The question seemed a little too personal to me. I was happy to help him with his car, but I wasn't going to let him in on my life. I had been around enough inappropriate comments and questions from young men on the prowl to be bothered by his query.

"Not far from here," was my calculated response.

"I was out dancing at Disco Heaven. My car was driving fine. It just started stalling a few minutes before you arrived... Hey, do you know where you are?"

I had never been to Disco Heaven, but I knew of it by reputation. It was a popular dance club. As Barry spoke, I was just passing the Eastside city limit sign.

"Sure. I've been to Eastside many times."

"Turn here," Barry said, directing me south of downtown Eastside. "Do you still know where you are?" I wondered why he repeated the question.

"Not really," I said. "Just give me the directions to your home."

There was a pause in the conversation. "Do you have a boyfriend?" Barry asked.

"Yes," I said - because it was the safest response. This question was more disturbing to me than his last personal question, and it annoyed me.

"How do you feel about black men?"

I *really* didn't like the sound of this question. I am a white woman. Barry is a black man. I started worrying that he was coming on to me. I wanted to answer in a way that would not create a conflict between us.

So, I said, "If you are asking how I feel about interracial dating, I think it's fine. But I'm not interested."

Barry leaned toward me. "I could show you a few things."

He *was* coming on to me.

"How close are we to your home?" I asked. I wanted to get Barry out of my car right away. I was uncomfortable. I started looking for street signs to try and figure out where I was.

"Stop the car," Barry announced abruptly.

Thank goodness, I thought. I pulled over to the curb. But Barry continued to sit in my car.

"Is this your house?" I asked.

"Yes."

Now, I was angry. Barry had been rude to me and I was beginning to worry that I would be late delivering the newspapers.

"Please get out," I said.

"I just want to talk to you for ten minutes."

"I don't have time. I have to get back to Midtown and deliver the newspapers." I didn't know why he was ignoring my request.

"You have nice hair. Can I kiss you?"

Oh, my God! I thought. I was scared now. I told myself to stay calm and not to act scared.

"No. You need to get out of my car right now," I demanded.

"I have to sit here until you kiss me."

"No! Get out," I said.

Before I knew what was happening, Barry reached across from the passenger seat and put both of his hands on my upper arms and pressed me firmly against my seat. I was trapped. I pushed against him, but he would not budge.

I stated, calmly, "You need to let go of me and get out of my car. I'm not kidding."

Barry grinned and kept his hands firmly pressed against my upper arms. I twisted in the seat, struggling to loosen his grip. I had not expected this behavior at all. I felt like an idiot. Why hadn't I seen this coming? I took a breath and told myself to keep talking calmly. I thought, surely, he would come to his senses and leave.

But each time I struggled, Barry met my resistance with greater pressure. Suddenly, Barry lifted one hand and grabbed my cheek. He started biting my neck. He forced his mouth against mine. I smelled and tasted his mouth. He smelled like sex! I concluded he must have been with another woman that night, but I didn't know what to make of the information. My stomach tightened.

My mind was racing. I couldn't believe this was happening. The smell of his skin overwhelmed me. What was wrong with him? Why didn't he listen? Had I done something to provoke this behavior?

"Get out of my car! Stop this! Go home!" I blurted out.

Barry loosened his grip on my arms and reached for my breasts. In that split second, I crossed my arms across my chest.

"Move your hands or I'll cut them off!" Barry demanded. He started to reach in his pocket.

Jennifer suddenly let out a loud rush of air. Rachel turned to her, and Jen realized she had been holding her breath. "You okay?" Rachel asked.

"I guess so," was the only thing Jennifer could think to say. Uncharacteristically for Rachel, she turned back to the journal without dwelling on her daughter's reaction.

Abruptly, memories of rape crisis training flooded my mind. I had trained to be a rape crisis counselor at Downtown Community Hospital when I was a college student. What had the director said about weapons? Then I remembered: *A weapon is more likely to be used if it is exposed.* In that instant, I prayed that Barry would not remove a knife from his pocket. I thought that if I relaxed, maybe he would calm down. I willed some of the tension out of my body. Barry removed his empty hand from the pocket.

He grabbed my crossed arms and jerked them away from my chest. He yanked up my t-shirt and bra, and began sucking roughly on a breast. I felt myself drifting away from my body. I was watching a man I didn't know perform an intimate act on *what seemed like* a stranger's body. I tensed again. I tried to move, but could not budge him. My struggling was useless.

Suddenly, Barry stopped. He said, "Start the car."

I asked, "Where are we going?"

"Just shut up and do what I tell you to do."

I felt dizzy, but I started the car. Barry instructed me to turn around a curve and then to the right. I searched the dark for landmarks or a means of escape. But what could I do? This was *my* car. Where could I run? I didn't know where I was.

The car's headlights hit a street sign. I memorized the name: Cherry Lane. My mind was still racing with thoughts about what I'd been taught during rape crisis training. I needed to remember everything that was happening. All at once, my thoughts crystallized around the obvious: *Barry is going to rape me*. This couldn't be happening. I have to stop it. I knew I needed to stay calm and not panic. I tried to think what to do.

Barry interrupted my thoughts with another demand, "Stop the car here."

I observed that the car was parked beside a telephone pole with ivy growing on it. I was rigid with fear by this point. Barry grabbed me again, climbed over me, and forced me into to the passenger seat where he had been sitting. I was on my back, pressed up against the door. I felt fuzzyheaded. While holding me down with one arm, Barry removed his pants and loosened the string holding up my sweat pants so that he could pull them down as well.

And then it was happening. Barry forced his penis into my dry vagina with a shove. It was like I drifted away and watched what was happening to my body. I thought about the smell of his sweat. I stared at the steam on the windshield. I observed the armrest and console pressed into my back and shoulders. I told myself, "This is only sex, and I know about sex. I am not a virgin." I floated out into the darkness beyond the car.

With a snap, my mind returned to the scene. *This was a rape*. I needed evidence. I needed semen. Barry was pumping up and down on me for what seemed like an eternity. I wondered if he had any semen to leave if he had sex with someone earlier that night. I became a criminal investigator. I needed evidence to prove what Barry was doing to me. I knew I could get through this if he would only leave evidence.

My body hurt all over. I tried to move into a less painful position and my hand swung past the glove compartment. Barry screamed, "Get your hand away from there!"

I was startled, but my mind began to race again. Why the outburst? Does he think I have a weapon in there? Why is he so afraid that I have a weapon? He knows that what he is doing is wrong. He's done this before and he knows what to watch out for. What did he do with his other victims? A new panic set in: A rapist would not want a witness around to report him. Will he kill me? Stay calm. Stay calm. One thing at a time. First I need evidence.

It was at that moment that I made a decision I knew I would never reveal to another soul: *I will help him reach orgasm*. I concentrated on relaxing my stomach muscles. Under the great weight of Barry's body, I tried to move in a rhythmic way. I watched his face for signs that he was almost there. At last, it happened.

Barry pulled out quickly and began to straighten himself up. I told myself not to think about dying. I had to get Barry out of my car. I wanted to keep him calm and act as if nothing of consequence had just happened. If he thinks I don't know I've just been raped, maybe he won't have to hurt me anymore.

I quickly pulled my clothes back on. Barry looked nervous, more nervous than I had seen him look. That wasn't a good sign. He had appeared confident before.

Barry spoke, "I have a confession to make." He tried to grin. "I have to go back to my car."

I decided to play along and said, "What do you mean? This isn't your house?"

"No. I need to get back to my car."

That didn't make any sense. His car was not working. But I wasn't going to argue. I wanted my own car back. I opened the passenger door and walked purposefully around the car to the driver's side. Barry was yelling, but I ignored him. I was aware that it was just beginning to get light, but I refrained from looking around out of fear that this would alarm Barry more.

I opened the driver's door and said, "I don't like anybody to drive my car. Tell me how to get back." Barry seemed to relax at these words. He moved over into the passenger seat again.

The drive back to Midtown began. I was aware that Barry was agitated, but I pretended not to notice. I wanted him to think that my only concern was about being late with my paper route. Barry threatened me several times, saying: "Don't hassle me about this or I'll get you."

It was clear to me that Barry knew he had done something wrong, but the closer we got to the Midtown Retirement Towers, the more optimistic I felt. My mind was working quickly again. If I was going to report him, I had to be able to identify him. I needed to get his license plate number. I stifled my joy as I realized that Barry was parked in a lot with only one-way in and out. If I parked near this exit, I might be able to get his tag number when he drove out – assuming he really did get his car started.

By the time we arrived at the Towers, it was light outside. I stopped near the entrance to the Towers and began to unload the newspapers in pretense of continuing the deliveries. I heard Barry start his car and wondered if the stalling had been fake and calculated to lure me into picking him up. But I didn't have time to dwell on these thoughts. As Barry drove past me, I focused on memorizing the license plate number. As soon as he was out of sight, I walked to the entrance of the building, rang the bell, and said to the doorman, "Please let me use your phone. I've just been raped."

CHAPTER SIX
THE IMMEDIATE AFTERMATH

"*You escaped!*" Jennifer exploded without thinking, and broke her mother's concentration. As Rachel raised her head from the notebook, Jennifer observed her mother's faraway look. She also became aware of the tension in her own body. She took a couple of deep breaths and tried to relax.

"I did," said Rachel. "Amazingly, I did. Listen to what happened next," she said, turning again to her writings.

The doorman paused for a second and then responded, "Where are my newspapers?"

For the first time in several hours, I breathed a sigh of relief. I almost laughed. I was back in a familiar world where words like "rape" didn't make sense. I collected myself. I knew that I had better conserve my energy.

"I will bring the papers to you in just a moment if you will only allow me to call the police first," I said.

Without further protest, the doorman moved aside and let me enter the building. I picked up a card at the desk and wrote "Barry" and GB14629. I called my boss, Tony, at the newspaper first.

"Tony, you need to come to the Midtown Retirement Towers. The papers aren't delivered. They are in my car..."

Before Tony could protest, I added, "I was raped."

There was a pause. Then Tony said, "We'll be there shortly to get the papers."

"And, Tony, could you call the police?"

I knew there would be many service calls that morning from angry customers who had not received their morning paper. I felt guilty about causing extra work for others.

I briefly thought about calling my parents, but I knew I would fall apart if I did. I knew from rape crisis training that there was a long day ahead of me. I needed to be rational, not emotional. I would not be going home until I had been seen at the Downtown Community Hospital and spoken to police officers.

I picked up the phone again and dialed Jay's home number. It was risky to call his house because his wife might answer the phone. But this wasn't just any call. I knew Jay would explain the critical nature of this early morning interruption to his wife. After all, Julie knew me. I was a trusted babysitter for their son.

Jennifer interrupted, "Mom, I... I don't know what to say first. Is this why you told me about Jay? Because you called him when you were... raped?"

Rachel paused before answering. "I needed you to know who he was before I told you about this day. There's more... about Jay. Just listen for now." Rachel began to read again.

Then I waited. Surprising myself, I felt excited and anxious to talk to the police. I had been smart enough to find a way to identify my attacker. The police would like that. I had been savvy enough to think about collecting physical evidence that the doctors could use. I was alive! I had lived through the impossible. I played the details of the past three hours over and over in my mind, knowing this would be very important in prosecuting the rapist.

My puppy comforted me as we waited for the police to arrive. He had been in the back of my car with the newspapers during the ordeal. He was completely quiet and must have been sleeping. I needed him now more than ever. He was my only "witness." He was warm and soft and felt so good to hold. I was grateful that Barry had paid so little attention to him.

The police officer and the circulation department men from the newspaper arrived at about the same time. The newspaper men ignored me and gathered the newspapers for delivery. I felt guilty again about not getting my job done. I wondered if they would understand or blame me.

The police officer asked me to get into the police car. He seemed disgruntled. Then he said, "My shift was almost over when your call came through." I started to apologize for the inconvenience. He took a brief report and called in the license number that I gave him. I hoped that his irritation at not getting off work promptly would not reflect poorly on me. When he said nothing about the hospital, I asked him to take me there.

The bright whiteness of the lights in the emergency room made me squint as I came through the automatic doors into the hospital with the police officer. He had a conversation with medical personnel that I could not hear, calls were made, and then he left. The person behind the desk handed me some papers to fill out. Then I was escorted by a nurse to an exam room and given a rough cotton gown to change into. The nurse was cordial and matter-of-fact.

After the nurse closed the door behind me, I began to undress. I pulled the t-shirt over my head and unhooked my bra. I noticed my soreness and stiffness for the first time. The gray, cut-off sweatpants dropped noiselessly to my ankles as I untied the string that had kept them up. It's funny that I remember that. I stepped out of them. My underpants stuck to my skin with sweat and – I suppose - other secretions, but I peeled them off, never looking down. I would not allow myself to get emotional now. Each time my mind began to travel back to the last time my clothes were removed, I jerked back to the present.

I redirected my thoughts to rape crisis training. I knew which samples would be taken. I told myself that this would be an exam in stirrups like any annual visit to my OBGYN. There was nothing to fear.

A knock. Then a youngish woman in a white coat with her hair pulled back in a long brown ponytail entered the room, followed by an assistant – another woman. The first woman identified herself as Dr. Fox. I could tell she was working hard to find a balance between professional and sympathetic. She made only fleeting eye contact with me. Mostly she asked questions and made notes in a chart.

"When did you have your last period?"

"A week ago."

"When was the last time you had consensual sexual intercourse?"

"Two days ago."

"Are you on birth control?"

"Yes. The pill."

With help from the assistant, I climbed up on the table and into the stirrups. The doctor's first touch made me jump. It hurt. With reassuring words, Dr. Fox inserted the speculum and examined me. I watched the assistant tear open a rape kit and remove items. The doctor used the materials to retrieve samples from inside me and around my vagina. She also plucked pubic hair and head hair and put the samples in containers provided by the rape kit. I knew the samples could be used to determine if someone else's hair or secretions were on me or in me.

Dr. Fox made an examination of the rest of my body. She pointed out bruises on my back and scratches on my face, and made notes in my chart. I was a little surprised that these physical marks existed. That was a good thing for the case, right? It was evidence of force. But I shuddered as I realized again that I could have been injured much more severely.

The doctor explained that she was giving me a morning after pill to prevent the possibility of an unwanted pregnancy. I swallowed the pill with water the nurse handed me, unwilling or unable to really think about what pregnancy might mean if it happened as a result of this attack.

With the exam completed, I was asked to change back into my clothes. The rape crisis counselor had arrived. She asked me how I was feeling. I didn't want to talk. I simply responded: "Can I see my puppy?" The counselor took me to the location outside the hospital doors where another person dressed in scrubs held the puppy's leash. The counselor told me that a sex crimes detective was coming to meet me, but continued to press me to talk about my feelings. I just held the puppy closer.

A few minutes later, the sex crimes detective arrived. She explained that she had been called to help me locate the place where the "crime" had taken place. Since I couldn't give an exact address, the detective would help me retrace my movements earlier that morning.

We started the drive back toward Eastside to find "Cherry Lane."

The detective's use of the word "crime" empowered and comforted me. I felt safe with her as we retraced my movements earlier that day. It looked so different in the light. What if I couldn't find the spot? But there it was: the ivy-covered pole. I was very excited, but didn't let on. The pieces were falling into place. The detective called in the closest house address over her radio. A couple minutes later, the dispatcher reported back. Barry's car was registered to that address!

I was startled. The rapist had taken me to his house to assault me! What did that mean about him? I was puzzled and confused.

The detective then told me that she was transferring me to a different police department because the rape had occurred in a different county than the one where the car ride began. A new officer came to pick me up and transport me to Barfield County Police Headquarters.

At the station, there was a lot of activity going on. The new detective assigned to my case, Detective Dallas, was working on a robbery. He seemed disinterested in me. He led me to an empty room with large glass windows and left me there.

It was now early afternoon. I hadn't eaten and I wasn't clean. Exhaustion overwhelmed me. I just wanted this to be over soon.

The detective entered the room and handed me a pen and paper. He instructed me to write down my version of the events. I very carefully described the events of the early morning -- leaving aside my subjective states for the most part, and eliminating any references to thoughts I had about collecting semen or my suspicion that the rapist had been sexually active earlier in the evening.

After I was done writing, Detective Dallas brought in a set of pictures and wanted me to identify my assailant, if I could. As the detective lowered pictures of several men to the table, in what seemed to be slow motion, a new panic set in. What if I had already forgotten what "Barry" looked like? What *did* he look like? I couldn't remember. Slowly my eyes began to focus on the pictures. There he was. I recognized him immediately. But why did the police department have a picture of him? The only reasonable answer was that Barry had been arrested previously for another crime. Detective Dallas left to seek a warrant for Isaiah Barry's arrest.

Alone again, I thought: "The stranger who I was trying to help just a few hours earlier is soon going to be imprisoned because of what I said he did to me." It was so bizarre, so TV drama-like. Would he be angry with me? I would, if it was in his shoes. Would I be in danger? I didn't have the energy to think about that right now.

My duties were done. The weight of the world fell in on me as I realized it was time to tell my family. I wasn't sure I could do it, but I knew that my mother was the one to tell. Eleanor Morris was the most nurturing person I knew. Mom could tell the rest of the family. I thought about my parents, grandmothers, brother and sister, aunts, uncles, and cousins. I couldn't possibly tell each one what had happened. I imagined their sad faces and efforts to find something comforting to say. I imagined having to explain what happened over and over to friends and strangers alike. I felt exhausted from thinking about it and held my puppy closer.

I called Mom at work. She listened as I recounted the details of the last ten hours. As I had anticipated, she did not pass judgment – at least not verbally. As I talked, I was aware of feeling dirty and on the verge of tears. My body began to ache again. Mom promised to tell my father and suggested that I call my sister, Sarah, to pick me up from the police station.

As I waited for Sarah outside in the bright sunshine, I couldn't hold myself up any longer. My legs felt like jelly, so I slumped to the curb. I desperately wanted to shower and to crawl between cool sheets, though I suspected I wouldn't sleep. When Sarah arrived, I was grateful to see her. But I also knew, when I looked at my sister's beautiful face, a face that radiated only compassion - even Sarah could not help me feel safe again.

Rachel stopped reading and slowly raised her head in the direction of Jennifer. Jennifer sat, stunned and silent. She thought her mother must be waiting for a response, but she didn't know what to say. Suddenly, the words came rushing out.

"Mom. I am *soooo* sorry. I had no idea."

"How could you, sweetie? It happened so long ago. I wrote about what happened for the police. But when I got home, I wrote about all the things I was thinking and feeling that I instinctively withheld from the police report. I was glad to have all this detail later when I began to work on my recovery," said Rachel.

"You were strong when it mattered," said Jennifer, marveling at her mother's survival skills.

"Thank you for saying that," said Rachel. She remembered thinking she was strong in the immediate aftermath of that rape. But, over time, the judgments and perceptions of others had changed the way she viewed herself. Technically speaking, she was powerless with Isaiah Barry. But in the days, weeks, and months to come, she became *less* powerful, yet appeared to be in control.

Katie was back, panting, by the bench. "Ready to go home?" Rachel asked.

Jennifer wasn't sure if she was ready or not. "Mom, what happened? Did they catch him? Is there more to the story?"

"They did, Jen. I was involved in the prosecution and conviction of Isaiah Barry for most of a year. I kept a journal about that year. Actually, I kept lots of journals or notebooks that year and later years. They are all in the cardboard box. I want to share what I wrote with you when we have more time. It's pretty intense and I don't want to overwhelm you with too much too soon."

Jennifer chuckled, "Yeah, like what you just read wasn't overwhelming?"

Rachel smiled. "I know. That sounds crazy, right? Trust me on this. I want to give you some time to 'process' what I'm sharing with you. I think it will be easier on both of us that way. Can we, maybe, have a standing Sunday morning date?"

Jennifer didn't understand why her mother needed a 'standing date,' but she was intrigued. She said, "Okay. It's not like all my Sunday mornings are booked right now... I'm *really, really* sorry you had to go through this. And I appreciate it that you feel comfortable telling me now."

Rachel smiled again. "Thank you for trusting me." Katie whined. "Let's go home!" Rachel said as she picked up the leash and squeezed her daughter's arm.

Jennifer's mind was spinning with images of her mother on the night she was raped. She had seen pictures of her mother at that age – tall and thin with waist-length dark hair. She dressed in the dated clothes of the 1980s, but in much the same way Jennifer dressed now – athletic shorts or jeans, t-shirts, and workout clothes. Jennifer wondered if she would have picked up a nice-looking stranger in the middle of the night. Probably not. Her parents had always danced a fine line between counseling her to "be kind to others" but "be wary of strangers." Jennifer suspected now that her mother's rape had influenced what she taught her children.

On the walk back home, Rachel completely changed the subject. She asked about Jennifer's work. She asked what meals and snacks Jen preferred to have the upcoming week because she was making a shopping list. Rachel followed Jen up the stairs to the carriage house and retrieved her cardboard box. What was her mother afraid she would see?

When her mother left, Jennifer picked up the book she had said she was reading, but her mind drifted back to Chris. She had followed his lead the way Mom followed Jay's lead. She had been the eternal optimist like her mother too. There were signs that her relationship with Chris was rocky, but she had ignored them. As time wore on, her needs became secondary to his. The food they ate, the movies they watched, the nights they made love… all of these things and more were decided by Chris. On second thought, maybe she *would* have picked up a stranger in need. Maybe she *would* have assumed that he was an honest, fair man…

The Adamo men had deserted the yard and house by the time Rachel reentered the kitchen with her box. She wanted to drop it on the kitchen table, but she knew the memories of that time pained Kevin. So she took it downstairs to the magic closet again.

Rachel thought about what she would share with Jennifer next. There had been a public accounting of her physical and mental state that June night in 1982. There had been a trial. Rachel had purchased a copy of the trial transcript from the State Archives in 1988. It was in the box of historic documents too. Before closing the box to store it, Rachel found the transcript and opened it to the defense attorney's cross-examination of her and read:

"Would you tell us what your physical condition was at the time you arrived at the hospital?" the defense attorney asked.

"I never saw myself. I had been grabbed, my cheek and my neck. I never saw a mirror, so I don't know at that point. My back was bruised. It was sore. I was aching all over, but I don't know how much of that was scared [sic] and how much was bruises," Rachel had replied.

"Could you explain your mental condition?"

"That's hard. I mean, I was told that I was in a state of shock, but I was -- I was scared. I mean, I was still scared but I knew that I had to do certain things before I could quit, before I could cry, before anything. There were things I had to do."

=====

That night, Jennifer fell into a deep but fitful sleep. And she dreamed. She dreamed that she was in a big room with gray concrete walls. There were four snakes, the size of boa constrictors, but of different colors. One snake was pink, another green, another yellow, and the fourth was blue. Jennifer was terrified of snakes. But in the dream, she taunted and coaxed them out of their sleep toward the middle of the room where they converged on her dog, Katie. All four snakes had a piece of Katie in their mouths until it looked as if Katie would be consumed. Jennifer stood paralyzed, watching. Then, suddenly, she raced forward, pulling the snakes off the dead or severely injured dog. She wasn't sure which. The snakes turned on her, biting and pulling chunks of her flesh. She was covered with blood. Was she dead or alive?

Jennifer jerked awake. Her pajamas were soaked and she was shaking. The memory of the dream assaulted her and she began to cry, first in a whimper, but soon she was sobbing loudly with her arms wrapped around her knees, pulling them to her chest, and rocking uncontrollably.

Jennifer opened her eyes to the dimly lit darkness of her bedroom. She was safe here. Jennifer silenced her sobs and looked around the room. A laundry basket of folded clean clothes sat beside her bed. Her desk was stacked high with college textbooks that she had yet to find a place for, gathering dust. Pictures of friends and special times hung on her walls. The graying teddy bear she had loved and slept with since she was a baby lay at the foot of her bed, a bed covered by the quilt her mother had commissioned. It was made of fabric scraps from her favorite t-shirts and other clothing she treasured in childhood. Jennifer felt her heartbeat slow as she breathed deeply.

She dragged herself up from bed, beginning to shake again, this time from the damp of her skin and clothes in the cool room. She pulled off the pajamas and reached for a dry t-shirt and shorts on top of the laundry basket. Once she had changed, she went to her bathroom and drank a tall cup of water from the sink. She looked up into the mirror and was reassured to see that she was still there, still the same Jennifer. She returned to her bedroom, turned on the light by her bed, grabbed her teddy bear and the novel she had been reading, and snuggled back under the sheet and quilt to read.

SUNDAY
OCTOBER 12, 2014

CHAPTER SEVEN
SHOCK AND VULNERABILITY

The following Sunday, Rachel and Jennifer sat down together again after brunch and Rachel's run.

Jennifer said, "I've been thinking about the rape all week. I've been thinking about all the women I knew in college who said, at one time or another, that they had been forced to have sex or were too drunk to stop it."

Rachel replied, "When I was in law school and graduate school, I learned that we live in a 'rape culture' that permits the sexualization and exploitation of women and girls. I was taught that one out of every three or four females experiences rape or attempted rape in their lifetime. But in 1982, I only knew that my presence made everyone around me uncomfortable. The doorman at Midtown Retirement Towers, the newspaper people, and even my family responded as if rape was *unusual* -- so extraordinary as to be completely foreign. I assumed that criminal prosecution would vindicate me and make me 'normal' again. No one said I should be proud that I survived. No one told me it wasn't my fault.

"Let me read to you from the journal I kept. This was written about a month after I was raped."

June 27, 1982

I have been moving about in a blur for the last few days, repeating the appropriate details to various people who seem to need to know what has happened to me. I encounter a variety of responses, including disbelief, anger, sympathy, and avoidance. I try to understand what each response means about me. Some people tell me to suspend my normal activities and take time to "recuperate." What does that mean? I know these memories will not fade in a few days.

I feel like a stranger to my own body. I see myself interacting with others as if I am suspended above the ground. At times I want to scream. At other times I want to be left alone. I want to forget...

Rachel stopped reading, looked up and said, "For many weeks after I was raped, I repeatedly experienced the sensation of my mind and body being separated from each other. I knew it was a sensation that paralleled my reaction during the rape. I needed to know that it was okay for me to inhabit my body, but I didn't know how to ask for that affirmation. Early on, my emotions were volatile. I later learned that this response to sexual assault is normal, but I didn't understand it then. My emotional outbursts alarmed me, disrupted my daily routine and disturbed others. To appease everyone, I learned to suppress my anger and tears, and to bury them deep inside.

"I was afraid to return to work, but I did not want to appear fearful. I asked my teenage brother, Lucas, to go with me on the same paper route where I had agreed to help Isaiah Barry, on the next day, June 25th. It was sweet how protective he was of me. I felt safe with him. I got 'back up on the horse,' as they say. But once the paper route was complete, I didn't want to do it again."

"You had to do the same paper route the very next day?!" asked Jennifer.

"It sounds crazy, doesn't it?" responded Rachel. "I think that is pretty indicative of the mindset of the people I was surrounded by at work. My being raped on the job just wasn't taken very seriously. I remember that I returned to the branch office after Lucas and I were done delivering papers to fill-out an 'accident report.' I sat down with my immediate supervisor, Tony. He asked, 'When did you stop delivering papers?

"'At approximately 4:30 a.m.,' I responded.

"'What was the reason?' Tony asked.

"'I was raped.'

"Tony blushed and quickly bowed his head to the form in front of him. I knew he wasn't going to talk about what happened to me. And what would I have said? Filling out an 'accident report' made me feel foolish. But I didn't feel safe delivering papers in that neighborhood anymore. So, I asked to be moved to another branch office or to be given a different position that did not require me to be on the streets at night in Midtown.

"Tony said, 'There isn't another job available.'

"I could feel the anger rising in me and I blurted out: 'But that's not fair! You know I can't be out there. Not now.'

"Tony responded, 'Then you have no job."

"That's unbelievable, Mom!" Jennifer interrupted.

Rachel continued, "But I 'got it.' This was a business. It didn't matter how I *felt*. I composed myself and pleaded my case to him. I told him I knew I was creating a problem, and I was sorry about that. But he knew I was a good worker, and I promised to stay out of trouble if he would just let me work somewhere else. I acknowledged that this dilemma was *my* fault.

"Taking the blame worked. Tony responded, 'I'll see what I can do.'

"I went home to wait, panicked that I would not have enough money to pay my bills. But two days later, the ADN offered me a position as a receptionist and bookkeeper at the Midtown branch. It was a day job, and because it was summer and I was not in school, it was a job I could take. I was told that I could work at that job until a paper route in another part of town became available.

"I was relieved. Being raped had not dampened my independent nature. I did not want to become a burden to my family. Paying my own way, even when I was a student, had been a source of pride to me. Between scholarships, money inherited from a relative, and work, I had been able to pay for college. I owed no one."

Jennifer said, "But it wasn't your *fault* that you were raped, Mom."

"No, it wasn't my fault that I was raped. I'm glad you can see that. But it was my decision to help Barry when I should have been delivering papers, and that led to my being raped. It was hard, even for me, to separate the two things. And the more I felt blamed from the outside world, the more I accepted responsibility for what had happened to me," said Rachel.

Jennifer thought about the Women's Center at Meriweather College. She'd never been there. But she had heard of women using the center to get support after sexual assaults. The school newspaper periodically included stories of alleged assaults on campus and a judicial counsel response. She asked, "Mom, what did you do for support?"

"That's a good question. I liked being at work because it preoccupied my mind. When I was home, I had too much time to reflect. I was *different* now -- though I didn't really understand how. My optimism was gone. I wondered who would understand me.

"I went through the list of close relatives in my head. One of my grandmothers was a rule follower, and I admired her discipline. But I had broken the rules, so I feared her judgment. My other grandmother was more of an adventurer and do-gooder like me, but she had the tendency to try to transform all suffering into blessing. The idea of transforming rape into a blessing seemed ludicrous to me. I felt like I couldn't confide in either of them.

"I considered my siblings. Sarah was in turmoil about work and relationships. I had always helped *her*. I couldn't imagine how she could help *me*. And Lucas was only a teenager. I didn't think that either one had time for me, or could possibly understand what I was feeling.

"Your Papa, as you know, was a pastoral counselor. I had been afraid that he would be angry because I gave a stranger a ride. But, instead, he was very emotional about his personal feelings of hurt and pain. I was grateful that he didn't blame me for being raped, but his intensity of feeling overwhelmed me. I knew that everything in his training and experience was telling him to let his feelings out. But when he did, his feelings took up all the available space in the room. I could not imagine sharing how *I* felt for fear of making him even more emotional.

"That summer, as I recall, Papa canceled counseling appointments because he said he couldn't concentrate on his work. He hired an attorney of his own so that he could discuss my case with a professional. He took care of himself, which was good. I wanted to protect him from any more pain.

"Your Nanna was the backbone of our family – a good listener, loving and supportive. She was the obvious person for me to turn to. But shortly after I was raped, Jay warned my mother that she would have difficulty understanding what I was going through, and that he was the best person to be my confidant."

"Wait a minute," interjected Jennifer. "How would Nanna know Jay?"

"Oh," said Rachel. "I forgot to mention that Nanna had taken a job at the theology school as an administrative assistant – or maybe they were still called 'secretaries' in those days. That was years before I enrolled as a student. Nanna knew the faculty."

Jennifer nodded. "So Nanna saw Jay as an authority too."

"I guess that's right," Rachel replied. "Mom and I both believed Jay when he said he was the one to help me recover."

Jennifer rolled her eyes, "So Jay was still in the picture. I don't get it, Mom. What happened between Easter and June? Didn't it ever occur to you that the relationship could not continue?" Jennifer knew she was coming on strong, but Jay's marital status *really bothered* her.

"I'm glad you asked. I need to fill in that period of time for you," said Rachel.

"In the aftermath of that first night of passionate love-making with Jay, when I was alone again, I realized that I had violated my own moral code. Adultery was wrong. I never considered it possible that I would have sexual intercourse with a married man. But these thoughts were overshadowed by my belief that Jay was the perfect man for me. This wasn't a fling for me. I wanted to be part of his life, to share everything. I rationalized that Jay's marriage would simply mean I had to be patient while he arranged for a divorce. I did not doubt that we would someday be together.

"I was so naïve," said Rachel, shaking her head. "I had no idea that I had opened Pandora's box like so many others have done. There was nothing simple about committing adultery except the sex. But for a short while I was able to focus only on those moments and the way they seemed to bring together two halves of a singular whole. I will never know if Jay could have been the 'man of my dreams,' the man I wished him to be, because I will never be able to uncomplicate the situation we found ourselves in. Would he have been attracted to me if he were *not* married? Were his words and actions calculated or tailored specifically to capture *my* attention, or would any student have served his purposes?"

Jennifer had wondered those same things. But this was her mother's story, and she wouldn't think about her own right now.

"In the days that followed, and under the circumstances, I spent more time thinking about Jay than actually being with him," continued Rachel. "He was beautiful, loving, intelligent and perceptive. Jay came to my apartment when he could to discuss the news of the day, but primarily to make passionate love before he returned to his family."

Rachel dug around in her box of historic papers again for another book – a diary she kept in those days before the rape. She read some of the sappy words she had penned so long ago to Jennifer.

Jay and I are so 'real,' so 'at home' with each other that we are the limits that create possibilities. With Jay I am able to claim all of me and therefore I am able to truly be with him and love him as I have never loved another human being.

He tells me that I give meaning and concrete substantiation to the ideas expressed in his writing. For me, Jay is a total mystery, a total reality, a total pleasure, both consuming and liberating. I will love him and challenge him and care for him and continually greet him with open arms. I need him. I want him. And I will be with him and for him and for us forever.

Jennifer pantomimed sticking her finger down her throat.

Rachel said, "I know. The words sicken me now, but that was how I felt then. In the beginning, Jay was just as anxious to be in my presence as I was to be in his. Shortly after our initial sexual encounters, Jay hired me as the new babysitter for his two-year-old son, Ben. Each babysitting assignment meant we would at least see each other before and after the job. I loved Jay's son. He had his father's golden hair that surrounded his face in ringlets and the large deep blue eyes of his mother. Ben was innocent, playful, and completely trusting.

"This was a double-edged sword – this time with Ben. On the one hand, it brought me further into Jay's world. Ben was always going to be part of it; and I wanted a close relationship with this precious child. On the other hand, Ben was a stark reminder of my complicity in the potential destruction of this family. Indeed, the more time that spring of 1982 that I spent with Ben, the harder it was to ignore the shame of my illicit affair.

"Then there was Mary, Jay's wife. Jay presented her as cold and uncaring. But my experience with her painted a different picture. She was a beautiful, intelligent woman. There was something anxious and unsettled about her that I didn't understand, but I felt compassion for her. She was a *real* person that I could not ignore.

"Here is more of the diary, " said Rachel and read again.

I am torn between my love for Jay and my conviction that we cannot go on forever this way. The most difficult part of our relationship has to do with knowing Jay's wonderful little boy, the possible impact of the discovery of our relationship on him, and a growing sense that if Jay and I are to have a future together, he should go back to his wife and figure out how to end it. He says he isn't ready for change. Jay says, 'Fidelity is being faithful to the other person's way of being in the world.' He says that because his wife no longer expects sexual intimacy with him, making love to me is not being unfaithful to her. Sex is not a part of her 'way of being in the world' with him. I want to believe him, but I don't know.

"That is such bullshit, Mom!" exploded Jennifer.

"I know you're right. I remember that excuse – coached as 'reasoning' - so clearly: *Fidelity is being faithful to the other person's way of being in the world*. It made sense in my head but not in my gut. I should have paid more attention to my gut. I didn't tell anyone about my relationship with Jay for years because I knew, to the outside world, it was wrong.

"Over the years, I've asked myself, again and again, why I let myself cross the line. I think I have at least a partial understanding now." Rachel paused. "Before I ever engaged in sexual relations with Jay, he had seduced me through the use and power of theological language. Jay convinced me that there was a more enlightened morality that made our sexual relationship admirable instead of dirty.

"Jay fed so many of my cravings. His non-traditional ideas about theology appealed to the part of me that sought a separate identity from my more traditional parents, yet his status as a scholar and theologian made him acceptable to the part of me that wanted my father's approval. The focus on sexuality in our discussions fed my craving for a more realistic assessment of the role of sexuality in everyday life. The fact that my family had always attempted to be honest about feelings meant that honest discussion about sexuality appealed to me as well. I was primed for consent. Yet, the part of me that believed in commitment, as I had learned from my mother and father, could not engage in a sexual relationship with Jay and leave it at that. From the beginning, I was always pushing for more and meeting Jay's resistance.

"With the advantage of 20/20 hindsight, I know I would have ended the affair had I not been raped. Jay's wife, his young son, the conservative theological community, and my own conscience all weighed against continuing the relationship. But being raped *changed me*. The rules I had relied on: who to trust and how to behave – were gone. In a way, I had to rebuild my moral framework to incorporate the reality of the unthinkable, the unbelievable -- my rape.

"And – the truth is – I had weaknesses. My two biggest weaknesses were excellent teachers and blind trust. I was attracted to knowledge and those who dispensed it well. And I trusted that people were basically good at heart. I was attracted to Jay's wealth of knowledge, but I also trusted that he, as a professor of religion, knew – better than I - right from wrong."

Rachel scratched her head. "You know, there's another factor, another aspect that is particular to rape that prevented me from leaving Jay. Before I was raped, I thought I knew that rape was about taking away someone else's *power*. 'It's not about sex,' I remember hearing at the rape crisis center. But they were wrong. 'Power' wasn't the whole story. Rape is a violent act that affects sexuality. It is important for a survivor of sexual assault to feel safe to talk about *sex*. Most of the families I knew did not talk about sex openly, including my own. But Jay offered me a place where I could explore the meaning of rape for my sexual self. This was a good thing – in the beginning..."

"So the affair continued. Then you were raped. Jay stepped in to help you because you trusted him," said Jennifer.

CHAPTER EIGHT
PURSUING JUSTICE

"*Right*. Now I want to tell you about what was going on *legally*," Rachel said. She put down the diary and picked up the journal again. "Listen to this," she said.

July 14, 1982

I had my first court appearance today for the prosecution in the case of *State v. Barry*. It was a preliminary hearing and I testified against Isaiah Barry while he watched in the courtroom. They said I made a good witness. I gave a clear and precise account of what happened. I feel fortunate that Barry violated his parole in addition to violating me because, once the judge determined there was "probable cause" that the crime of rape had been committed, I knew Barry would remain in prison until the trial.

"That was a scary time, Jennifer. I'm sure I must have been prepped for the courtroom, but it was still difficult to face the man who had raped me. I didn't make eye contact with him except when I identified him for the Court. It was a lucky coincidence that Barry had been on parole at the time he raped me. This 'alleged rape' was a violation of parole that allowed the judge to keep Barry in jail. If this had been Barry's first alleged crime, he might have been freed on bail until the trial. Having Barry behind bars alleviated my fears of imminent retribution. But the crazy thing was, I felt *bad* for him. It was my words – *my words* – that put another human being behind bars."

"That was the rescuer, caretaker part of you speaking, Mom," responded Jennifer.

"Yep. It was hard to reconcile the church girl who had been taught that God loves and forgives us all, in spite of our imperfections, with the justice-seeking girl who knew a crime had been committed and should not go unpunished.

"During those summer months of 1982, I had a lot of time to reevaluate my actions as I waited for news from the prosecutor's office. In my college years, I had been trained as a rape crisis volunteer. In fact, the *only* Rape Crisis Center in Austin at that time was in the hospital where I was examined after I was raped. I knew when I asked the police officer to take me to the hospital that I was also being taken to the place where a rape crisis volunteer would be notified.

"When I was trained as a volunteer in college, I decided what *I* would do if *I* was ever raped. Although many women do not formally report sexual assaults, I believed I had the family and community resources to get me through a crisis if it happened. I would report. I respected the police and the difficult job they had. I believed that no man had a right to force sex on a woman against her will, and I put my faith in government institutions to enforce that claim. But now that I had set the process in motion, I realized that I had not anticipated how exhausting it would be. And the process had only just begun!

"I was working for the Austin Daily News, babysitting for Ben, worrying about the legal proceedings, and trying to let Jay help me feel 'normal' again. Meanwhile, I had very disturbing thoughts I couldn't control. Listen to this." Rachel read from her journal again.

August 14, 1982

Jay continues to be my comforter, friend, and lover. I have spent a lot of time this summer with Jay, his wife, and his son. He is remodeling a portion of his house and I am helping in the construction. He understands that I need physical projects to take my mind off continuous thoughts about the rape. Jay told me that I was in shock for the first few days. I don't remember that, but I know I still feel tortured. I have feelings I can't say out loud.

Sometimes my body, my whole being, feels like an irritation. I want to scratch and tear at it, but it does no good. I imagine my fingernails digging at my flesh, scraping away the meat on my bones; the irritation is further inflamed - red - raw. I pull away chunks of skin, the blood begins to ooze - at first a trickle, but slowly becoming a constant stream - and still I cannot be soothed. I cannot reach the source of my discomfort.

I feel as if I am in a cloud. I look at my hand, distanced from my body. I could calmly and methodically drive a rusty nail through it. There is some pleasure derived from the sound of cracking bones, and flesh that gives way to the spewing of blood, and later the gnawing ache that is somehow numb - as if the focusing of pain on a particular gruesome sight and the streaks of blood poisoning that shoot out from it, gives meaning to my life. It tells me where I hurt. The excruciating character of such a torture at times causes blackouts, escape... My thoughts and feelings scare me.

Jay allows me to babysit for Ben. I love spending time with Ben because everything is simple to him at two-years-old. He wants hugs, play, and laughter. I can provide all that he asks and, at the same time, escape my own misery.

"What a contrast of images. You talk about all these feelings of being tortured and then you jump into a discussion of babysitting," said Jennifer. "Did you see, at the time, how weird that was?"

"Honestly? No. I lived in two simultaneous worlds. Those images of hurting myself were very real. There was a hurting deep inside that I couldn't reach. I wanted to get at it and carve it out like a cancerous tumor. Now, when I see women hurting themselves through cutting, anorexia, self-medicating with drugs and alcohol, or other self-inflicted hurts, I know they too have emotional damage that is beyond their reach, and I empathize.

"But I couldn't *live* in that tortured world. I escaped it at work and at play," said Rachel.

"There's more about Jay that I want you to hear. I know you don't like him, but I need you to hear more about why *I* did." Rachel flipped back a few pages in her journal and read.

August 9, 1982

My puppy, Gustav, was not gaining weight. I took him to a vet and learned to my horror that he had distemper. The doctor told me that I should take him back to the Humane Society and exchange him for another puppy. The thought of returning him and the thought that he might be put to sleep rather than cured was unbearable. No. I would keep him and take my chances. The vet gave me a regimen of pills, a special diet, and a grim picture of what to expect: I had to make him eat or he would die. I took him home and began the heart-breaking ordeal of trying to save his life. I called my family and I called Jay. I did a lot of crying.

About midnight, I felt a hand on my shoulder. It was Jay who had crept in to comfort me. He should have been with his family, but he had come because he knew how badly I hurt. I will always remember this night and remember Jay as gentle, compassionate, and unselfish. He senses the times when I am in deepest despair.

Rachel looked up from the journal. "Jay was amazing when Gustav was sick. I give him credit for that. He really understood what I needed. There were other times he understood me too. That is part of what makes this history so difficult to 'summarize.' Jay was good to me at times. He was caring. There was gentleness about him that touched my soul. I'll never know for sure what was in his head during those early months, but I truly believed in the 'magic' of us. We were the quiet or calm in the middle of a storm that swirled in chaos all around. I never wanted Jay to leave me alone with the storm. *We* were the only thing that made sense to me.

"Standing back from that time, I can see how our early months were a set up for something akin to the 'battered woman's syndrome.' The relationship starts out loving. The man or partner abuses the beloved, but then returns to apologize and to bestow affection and kindness, promising never to hurt his/her beloved again. The abused one, remembering the love that brought them together, forgives and trusts again – until the next beating... But I'm getting ahead of myself."

Jennifer was confused again. "What abuse are you talking about? The affair?"

"No. You will come to understand what I mean," said Rachel.

"If you say so," said Jennifer, still confused, but willing to let her mother control the course of the conversation. "Well, can you tell me what happened to Gustav?"

"He survived! He was with me through all of the legal proceedings and then... well, he helped me survive all of that." There would be more to say about Gustav, thought Rachel. But that could wait.

"Thank goodness!" said Jennifer.

"Soooo," Rachel segued back to her story. "Just remember that image of a comforting Jay because a few days later I wrote this...

During the times when Jay and I are alone, he pays close attention to my personal suffering. We discuss how I am feeling about the legal process, but most of all, we discuss how I am feeling sexually. My mind and body still feel separated. I watch and think about what I am doing sexually instead of 'being there.' Jay is trying to help me bring my mind and body back together again. He talks to me about how we are touching and tries to get me to talk about it. Jay says I don't know my sexual-self. I need a manager, and he is the one for the job. He says that I could be the perfect lover if only I would let go and trust him to catch me. I feel dirty or contaminated sometimes, but I know it is not his fault that I feel this way.

Yesterday, we took my therapy a step further. Jay thought that it would be good for me to re-experience the rape while he played the role of the rapist.

Rachel glanced up at Jennifer to see if she was listening. Jennifer's wrinkled brow let Rachel know that she was.

...I didn't understand at first. He told me that when I recognized *him* as my assailant, I would recover some of my former strength. Jay's hypothesis was that this reenactment would allow me to regain the sense of power or control I had lost during the rape. My visualization of the rapist, Isaiah Barry, would disappear and be replaced by an image of the man I loved. I agreed to participate. As the drama began, it was like a nightmare to watch someone I loved turn into my enemy. Jay grabbed my arms and pushed me down. He said and did all the things that Barry had done to me. But when I stopped screaming and crying, Jay held me. He assured me I would be better now.

"Oh my God, Mom! You let him *rape* you?!" exclaimed Jennifer.

"It doesn't make much sense to me either this many years later," said Rachel. "I wish I had recorded the words Jay used to convince me to go along with his plan. Jay was a master of persuasion – at least, with me.

"During that time between rape and trial, I was developing the ability to be two different people at the same time. Outwardly, I was strong and courageous. Inwardly, my self-hatred and sense of powerlessness increased. I was divided between the composed self I showed the criminal justice system and the shattered self I confronted alone at home. I never knew when I was going to cry, become angry, or suddenly feel fear. I was also divided between the public appearance of celibacy and the private experience of being a mistress. And I continued to sense a division between my rational mind and irrational body.

"So, when Jay said he could 'heal' me and bring together these divisions, I wanted to believe him. I believed that Jay understood the feeling of being out of control because he had shared examples of women in his life who had used sex to manipulate him...

"What do you mean?" asked Jennifer.

"There were several stories he told me. The one that left the biggest mark on him, though, was a relationship he had in graduate school with one of *his* professors. She flirted with and teased him and, ultimately, broke his heart. She was very controlling and he obeyed her every request. If I had been in my right mind, I might have seen that Jay was repeating this same behavior with me, but calling it something else.

"This feeling of being out of control was something I knew that all rape victims experienced because the assault was beyond their control. I knew that regaining a realistic sense of control over my life was extremely important. What I didn't understand was how destructive Jay's helping methods were. And I didn't really comprehend how disturbed *he* was by my rape.

"Later on, through therapy, I would come to realize that Jay was not helping me regain control. Instead, he was trying to transfer the rapist's control over me to *himself*. Jay believed I *enjoyed* being raped. He saw it as an expression of my sexual wildness or sexual otherness over which he had no control. His actions were based on the assumption that I needed *some* man to control me sexually, and he wanted to be that man."

"That makes sense," nodded Jennifer.

"There must have been some part of me that resisted because the very next day I wrote this..."

August 18, 1982

I can't help it -- I like Jay's wife Mary. I have decided I have to push Jay away and back to Mary to see if they can work things out. Besides, I know my relationship with him is not going to change until he deals directly with the problems in his marriage. I will tell him that we can't continue to seal ourselves off from the rest of the world. I will tell him to think about Ben. How long before Ben notices the love in our eyes that should be somewhere else?

What is at once so 'good' for us becomes so 'bad' as soon as it operates in the rest of our lives. What Jay can say to me or share with me becomes something he can't say to Mary. No matter how much I give him or how often or how hard I try to love him, ultimately I take away more from him by not giving him the chance to make his marriage work -- if that is what he wants. And he needs to find out. We all do: Jay, me, Mary, Ben. It hurts us all when Jay is split in pieces trying to love each of us in different ways and never fully being able to do so.

"So your conscience kicked in when you spent time outside your bubble with Jay. That was it then? You ended it?" asked Jennifer.

"Oh, Jen. I wish that I could say 'yes,' sighed Rachel. "I had the thoughts, but I didn't have the strength to make good on them when Jay insisted we continue our hidden romance.

"Let's take a break. I need some water," said Rachel, rising from her seat.

Rachel and Jennifer descended the stairs as Katie scooted by them and beat them to the kitchen door. Jennifer reached for a Diet Coke and Rachel grabbed a Vitamin Water from the refrigerator. They could hear Kevin and Henry groan together in the family room. A football game was playing on the TV, no doubt.

"Where's Sam?" Rachel called out to Kevin.

"Dance practice. What else?" replied Kevin.

"Okay. We're still talking over in the carriage house if you need me," said Rachel.

Henry replied this time. "Football all afternoon, Mom. We're good."

Back in the carriage house, settled with their drinks, Rachel resumed her story. "The summer was over. School was back in session, and I was beginning my second year in theology school. Again, I was confronted with the reality that I was a student and Jay was a professor. I wrote…"

September 2, 1982

I wish I could play the secrecy game as well as Jay does. At school, we are not equals. He is an authority and I am one of many students. He treats me like any other student. Although I understand why he does it, it hurts inside. Jay is afraid I will let my feelings show in public, so we have agreed not to meet in public places except as necessary. I know that means our isolation will grow.

Rachel said, "Jay was right to be cautious. I couldn't see the long-term. I was stuck in the moment. I couldn't comprehend the harm.

"As a parent, I liken my predicament to the way kids and teenagers get fixated on 'what I want now is what matters.' My metaphorical legs had been knocked out from under me and I was something less than an independent adult at this point."

"It goes back to what you were saying about the world not making sense the way it used to make sense, right? I mean, you were more like a child, dependent on others," said Jennifer.

"That's a fair assessment, I think," replied Rachel. "But, unlike a child, I had some very adult responsibilities to attend to. The wheels of justice continued to turn, and I needed to play my part. I wrote…"

September 13, 1982

I was subpoenaed to testify before the grand jury - a group of about two-dozen citizens who sit to hear evidence from the District Attorney's office about alleged crimes and vote to either issue an indictment or drop the charges. My stomach was in knots during the days before. I worried that I would stumble, forget things, or fail to convince my audience. But the grand jury did believe me, and they issued the indictment.

Rachel turned to Jennifer and said, "I was on my own. No one, not even Jay, could be in this with me. It was another area where I felt out of control. It didn't matter that I had the truth on my side. What mattered was whether or not a group of strangers believed me."

Rachel turned back to her journal again.

October 8, 1982

I testified as a witness at Isaiah Barry's probation revocation hearing today. This hearing, not always a part of criminal procedure in rape cases, was held because it was alleged that Barry had violated the terms of his probation. An attorney told me that Barry was on probation for an earlier drug conviction. As a result of my testimony at the hearing, the Judge reinstated Barry's fifteen-year jail sentence.

I started attending a rape survivors' support group led by the director of the Rape Crisis Center. It is an "open group." That is, survivors can come and go as they need support. The group focuses on the feelings of women who are trying to cope with the effects of rape on their relationships and careers. I haven't met a survivor who is involved in a court case yet. Most rapes are not reported, so I am in a somewhat unique position. I told the group members about the results of the probation revocation hearing and they were pleased for me.

Rachel stopped reading. "I never felt completely comfortable in that group. Most of the women who shared their stories of sexual assault had been in situations that could never be prosecuted successfully. They were angry, but helpless in terms of pursuing 'justice.' I was on a different path that required steady nerves, rational thinking, and singularity of purpose: conviction. My feelings would have to wait."

Jennifer asked, "What do you mean when you say they couldn't prosecute successfully?"

"Think of some of the sexual assault stories you heard about women at your college. A woman might say she was at a party, maybe she had too much to drink, maybe she didn't, and a guy had sex with her when she didn't want to have sex. She says it was forced or that she didn't consent. He says she was a willing participant. There are no other witnesses to corroborate either of their stories. An experienced attorney is not likely to take that case because the burden of proof in many rape scenarios cannot be met.

"In a criminal case, the prosecution must show 'beyond a reasonable doubt' that a crime occurred and that the defendant is the one who committed that crime. That's a very high standard. If a juror can imagine another reasonable explanation for what happened that does not involve the defendant committing a crime, that juror is instructed to vote 'not guilty.' In other words, the sexual assault may *have* occurred, but there is not enough evidence in *legal* terms to convict," said Rachel.

"Okay. I get it now."

"The legal process is tricky, and it can vary from state to state. The process I am going to describe applied to my case, in our state, at a particular point in time. Listen to this," continued Rachel.

October 15, 1982

The Assistant District Attorney who is assigned to my case called me into her office a couple of days ago. I thought we would be discussing my upcoming trial, but, instead, she told me I could choose not to continue the prosecution. I was surprised and confused. I asked her why I would not want Barry to go on trial for rape. She said the probation revocation hearing took Barry off the streets. If we went to trial and lost, the hearing judge would probably reinstate Barry's probation, and he would be out again. It was up to me to decide if I wanted to risk it all.

I asked, "Don't we have a good case? Wasn't it better to convict him of rape? What had changed in these few days?" I pushed the ADA to tell me more. She paused and then told me that she had just lost an aggravated sodomy case. That jury believed that a nineteen-year-old girl had consented to anal sex despite ample evidence of the physical harm that resulted. She said, "You never know with juries." She has given me a few days to decide if I want to proceed with my case.

I know what I want to do. I want to go to trial. It will vindicate me. Everybody is counting on it. But am I being selfish? If we lost, it would mean that other women would be in jeopardy with this rapist. I know he raped me. Don't I deserve my day in court? Isn't that the only way to put this thing behind me?

I am amazed at the number of acquaintances who sympathize with the ADA's position. I am more amazed at the number of survivors in the support group who advise me to take what I have and run. Jay says they are all scared. I put together a list of pros and cons, but I cannot shake my conviction that I have to go to trial. I will tell the ADA that I want a trial. But I know I am gambling, not only with my own safety, but also with the safety of women in my community.

Rachel spoke to Jennifer again. "It took this dilemma of whether or not to continue the prosecution of Barry for rape to make me realize that I was *counting* on the legal system to legitimize the trauma I had experienced. And I had confidence – most of the time – that I would win.

"I guess I need to explain something else about my case. My case had credible evidence. My report of the assault immediately after it occurred and the physical evidence collected at the hospital worked in my favor. *And* my rape was similar to mythic notions about rape: Black stranger rapes innocent white girl. This *is* a myth, you know. Most rapes occur between people of the same race. I wasn't 'proud' that this racist stereotype helped me. But I was wise enough to know that it did. Also, taking part in the criminal justice process channeled and focused my energy. And it felt good to be believed by the professionals working on my case.

"I didn't realize at the time that there were negative consequences of entering the criminal justice process as well. My emotional recovery was put on hold. I should have had a counselor, but I didn't think I needed one. Others observed that I was doing well, and because I had not reconnected to my feelings, I took all my cues from the outside and agreed with their assessment."

"So you were going to trial," concluded Jennifer.

"I was going to trial… eventually," affirmed Rachel.

CHAPTER NINE
STRANGER SEX

"*M*eanwhile, back at home…" Rachel forced a smile and picked up her journal to read.

October 21, 1982

I did something last night that I still can't quite believe. Jay has been worried about me because I continue to be depressed and because he senses my unwillingness to completely let go during sexual intercourse. He came up with a plan. He thought that if I could go out and seduce someone, I would have a new sense of power and control. He is right that I feel powerless. He said that such a conquest would reassure me that I am desirable rather than dirty. I want Jay, and I want him to want only me. I didn't want to do this thing, but I don't want to lose Jay.

Jay convinced me that I should pick up a man in a bar, have sex with him, and return to Jay so that we could have sex as well. The whole thing seemed impossible and crazy to me. In the first place, I didn't really believe I knew how to pick up someone for sex and nothing else. Sex has always been part of an on-going relationship for me. In the second place, I didn't want to have sex with a stranger. But after several debates with Jay, I realized that the only way he would be happy was for me to pursue this. I couldn't ignore his excitement when he talked about what I should do. I wanted that excitement directed toward me.

Jay dressed me. He made suggestions about what turned men on. I wore a pair of tight jeans and a skimpy vest with no shirt. The outfit showed off my curves and flat stomach.

I went to a crowded, noisy dance bar and ordered a drink. I waited. On my second drink, a young man approached and asked if I wanted to dance. I said, "No." The young man then said, "I like your tits. Want to fuck?" I was amazed. Was it this simple? My stomach jumped into my throat, but I squeaked out a "Yes." He left me to find his companion and obtain car keys. I couldn't believe this was happening. I actually thought, "Jay is going to be so proud of me!"

When the man returned, I followed him out into the parking lot and climbed into the back seat of a large car. We undressed and had sex. All I thought about during the sweaty act was how happy Jay would be with me. When we stumbled out of the car to rearrange our clothes, a group of people stood by clapping and cheering. My companion took a bow. I stood there, silent. He invited me back inside for another drink, but I quickly declined. I had to get back to Jay. I knew he would be waiting for me. We had arranged a timetable so that he would only need to be out of his house for a limited time to meet me. I knew it was luck that I managed to keep the schedule.

I was very excited as I drove home. I had done it! I had done the impossible, and Jay would be happy with me. When I entered my apartment I had a big grin on my face. I watched Jay's face change from an expression of concern to one of delight – but there was a trace of pain that remained. He grabbed me and voraciously made love to me. He wanted details, every detail of what had happened at the bar, in the car, how it felt. I could describe the events at the bar, but I had more difficulty describing the actual sex. I hadn't really paid attention. Jay was insistent, so I manufactured details. In the back of my mind, I realized that I had done something similar to what I had done when I was raped. I had mentally removed myself from the situation and had observed or thought about other things.

As our sexual encounter was ending, Jay asked, "Am I the better lover?" I was surprised by the question, but responded, "Of course." He wanted more. He wanted to hear that he was the best lover. I told him he was. He wanted to know why. He wanted more details. In my mind, Jay was the only lover I had been with that night. Jay told me how proud he was of me and left to go home.

It was a strange evening. I don't know quite what to make of it. I felt the glow from Jay's admiration of me, and I was also, strangely, proud of myself. It doesn't make sense that I should feel "good" about doing this intensely personal act with a stranger. It was too easy. There were no real feelings involved -- just actions. I wonder what it means about me.

When Rachel looked up from her journal, Jen was staring, her mouth slightly open.

"It's disturbing, isn't it?" asked Rachel. "That's not how you see your mother."

Jennifer snapped out of her trance and said, "No, it's not. I have to remind myself that you are telling me about someone who is close to my age."

Jennifer thought about the time in her first year of college when she had let a guy she barely knew have sex with her. Although it was consensual, it was so different from other sexual experiences because there was no *relationship*. It was just sex. She had wanted to be held and appreciated in this new place, so far from home. She saw the guy around campus from time to time after that, though they never spoke again. She had tried not to think about it. In the aftermath, she had felt the opposite of the way she had wanted to feel – not appreciated, but devalued. What her mother had done was something else, something extreme and dangerous.

"Mom, you could have been hurt. You could have gotten some sexually transmitted disease or worse!" Jennifer said.

"You're right. I didn't think about any of those things. I didn't really believe the sex was going to happen. I had no idea how easy it was to find a man to have sex and *only sex* with! All of my previous experience with intimacy had come after establishing a relationship of trust with a man I cared about. It had been *emotionally* risky. This other way was risky to my safety and health, but I was oblivious. I was so focused on gaining Jay's approval. I was completing an assignment for the good professor!

"I was shocked when Jay asked for details. It was as if I had misread the question on the exam. And then I was mad at myself because it appeared that I wasn't going to get a good grade after all. So, for the first time in my life, I cheated. I made up the details that I wasn't sure were true to get a better grade. I wasn't sure because I hadn't really been 'present.' But Jay didn't know any better. In retrospect, I wish I had never learned the 'skill' of lying about sex." Rachel thought, but did not say aloud – "It got easier every subsequent time I did it."

"Jay may not have intended to use my attraction to him to manipulate me, but he succeeded in doing so. I had lost the ability to tap my feelings and convictions that might have enabled me to stand up to him. But no matter how bad Jay's life or past may have been, he was not justified in abusing my blind trust."

"You kept the relationship going?" asked Jennifer.

"I kept the relationship going. Yet, a part of me rebelled, as you will hear..."

November 12, 1982

I can't stand it. I miss Jay so much. He is never around when I want or need to talk to him. I can't call. I can't show him how much I love him in the principle place where we see each other -- school. When he is with me I never know for sure when I will see him again. It is tearing me up.

I tried having a relationship with someone else. Frank Evans is a friend and classmate. He is my age, smart, funny, and compassionate. We can talk about almost anything, and I knew he was attracted to me. I saw in him the possibility of a "real relationship." Part of me thought that if I could transfer my feelings of affection to a man I could date openly, my depression would end.

Frank and I spent a night together. What I remember most about that night was how wonderful it felt to wake up next to the person I went to bed with. In the morning, I made coffee, and we sat around talking. Out of the blue, for some unknown reason, I said, "I'm a nice girl to have sex with, but you wouldn't want to marry me, would you?" Frank paused for a moment and then said, "No, I wouldn't." I was mortified, but I hid my feelings from him and laughed instead.

Jay sensed I had been with someone else and prodded me until I confessed. He says this is more evidence of the power of my sexuality. It will rule me unless I understand its dimensions by exploring it with him. I feel ashamed.

Rachel turned to Jennifer and said, "Jay wanted me to be his secret mistress. Jay pushed me away to have sex with a stranger. I didn't like those things, so I sought out a better, more 'normal' relationship with Frank. Frank was a great friend and fellow theology student. We shared a passion for social justice. I must have known this would hurt Jay, or maybe I thought it would bring him to the realization that he could only have me under different circumstances. But I wasn't strong enough to really pull away. Jay was always able to bring me back with his persuasive words – his 'I know you like no one else knows you.'"

"What happened to Frank?" asked Jennifer.

"We went back to being friends. But – I should tell you - a few years later, I called him to talk about what happened between us. Frank said he responded the way he thought I *wanted* him to respond. Jennifer, what Frank said helped me realize that everything about my public behavior at that time cried: 'Leave me alone. I'm dealing with this and I don't need your help.' None of my friends knew how to treat a rape survivor, particularly one who tried to act as if everything was under control."

Jennifer nodded. She understood exactly what her mother was saying. She knew how to pretend that everything was under control even when it wasn't.

"The trial was coming up in January," continued Rachel, "and I was scared. After the semester ended in early December, Jay left with his family to spend Christmas vacation in Seattle. I felt abandoned. What happened next is a longer section of my journal. I hope you have some patience left," smiled Rachel.

"Before I read this, let me explain that back in the 1980s, the Austin Daily News had two editions – a morning paper and an afternoon one. As you know, with the growing availability of online news sources, many traditional newspapers have gone out of business or, like our paper, cut back to one edition. In 1982, when this chapter of my story occurred, I was delivering the afternoon newspaper. But, on weekends, the two editions combined and were delivered in the early morning hours."

December 20, 1982

The most amazing thing happened to me today. First, the background... For the past few weeks, I have been working additional hours at the newspaper. For the afternoon paper delivery, I go into work at 2:00 p.m. and finish by 5:00 p.m. I work for Tom Sears, the district manager, and his assistant, Deborah. The three of us have become friends and often go to Paul's Tavern after work to drink 25-cent beers.

"Twenty-five cent beer?!" exclaimed Jennifer.
"A sign of the times, my dear," said Rachel.

...Through our conversations, I learned that Tom and Deborah are both unhappily married. They are having an affair with each other.

When Deborah went out of town with her family a few days ago, Tom asked me to be his assistant while she was gone. It was our job to deliver the "open routes" for which there were no paper carriers. Sometimes we split the papers and went our separate ways. Other times, we worked together, one of us reading the route list and the other throwing the papers. As we were delivering a route together two days ago, Tom leaned over and kissed me.

Today, Saturday morning at 3:00 a.m., Tom and I arrived at work and helped other paper carriers get their routes bagged and out of the warehouse. Several people didn't show up, so we were stuck delivering hundreds of newspapers ourselves. We divided them and hurried to beat the clock. The one thing I have always loved about delivering newspapers is the "high" I get from the physical exertion and the challenge of beating my own best time. I pushed myself and it was sheer exhilaration. Jay would never understand this feeling. Tom and I agreed to meet at my apartment after the papers were delivered.

We were both tired, sweaty, and proud of our efforts when we met. We shared the same feeling of contentment about a job well done. We made love gently and quietly. Being with Tom made me realize how tired I am of talking about and analyzing sex. We showered and sat back in bed relaxing. Tom turned to me and asked, "Do you want to run?" Running is something else that Tom and I share a passion for that Jay does not. We changed back into our clothes and took a leisurely five-mile run to Midtown Park, around it, and back. We showered again and walked to a local pub, arriving just as it opened. We drank a couple of beers and then Tom had to go. As we walked out into the sun at 11:00 a.m., I felt as if I owned the world.

I didn't have to think or act a certain way. All I had to do was feel. And what I felt and feel is "in tune" with my body and its rhythms. Sex can be part of the flow of life, not a beginning or ending, but somewhere in the middle, congruent with other aspects of the sensual. Maybe I am also trying to hurt Jay -- to get back at him for being unavailable or for trying to control my sexuality. I don't know. I don't want to think about Jay or Deborah or the three marriages involved. This was an oasis.

"Mom…" interrupted Jennifer.
"Hear this first," Rachel responded.

December 27, 1982

Jay returned from Seattle prematurely. He appeared at my door while Tom and I were in my bedroom making love. I went to answer the door. When I saw Jay, I was suddenly angry at him for intruding without warning me. He was shocked. He said he had come to deliver a Christmas present, but I sent him away. He came back later and told me that I "smelled like sex." He said he couldn't believe I would become involved with a married man who already had a mistress. How "selfless" could I be?

My anger was gone. I felt dirty and stupid. Deborah would be back, of course. I hadn't really intended for this affair to be long lasting. I defended myself by saying that I was already having an affair with an unavailable man. What difference did it make? Jay saw a big difference. He reminded me that he understands me like no one else does. I can't disagree with that. I promised Jay that from then on, Tom and I would be work associates only.

I feel guilty and ashamed and sad. Jay is wallowing in self-pity. He says he can't trust me. He says he doesn't know if we can go on. I feel particularly bad because I know that other women have betrayed him. I don't know if Jay will ever forgive me. Still, I can't help but remember how good it felt to share that time with Tom. It is something I can't explain to Jay. Tom made no demands. Yes, I put myself in another impossible situation, but it didn't feel that way. Neither Tom nor I ever expected any more than what we received. In a way, it was so uncluttered.

Rachel looked up in anticipation of Jennifer's response. This time, Jennifer didn't look shocked. She looked mad.

"Maybe I'm starting to catch your craziness, but I get it! I get how Tom was appealing after all you'd been through. I get that having a mutually agreed upon sexual relationship was better than being raped or controlled by Jay's agenda," stated Jennifer.

"Wow," replied Rachel. "I'm surprised. I wasn't sure how this would translate to you. I had veered so far from 'normal' that Tom's having a wife and mistress didn't matter nearly as much to me as feeling *free* in the moment. Tom offered something very important that Jay could never give me. He offered minutes away from thoughts about and preparations for a rape trial. He didn't try to control me. He didn't plan for my future. I desperately needed that respite. The stress was enormous. But I set myself up for an emotional battering by Jay that I was not strong enough to resist. It was a pattern we would repeat many more times.

"I also want you to remember that I was angry and hurt because I couldn't have what I wanted. By this point, I'd learned that I could separate sex from relationships. In later years, I would learn that rape victims who have not recovered typically have one of two responses to men after rape -- abstinence or indiscriminate sex. I fell into the latter category. Still, I wonder if I would have responded differently if Jay had not been in the picture, prodding me to 'own my sexuality,' as he often said.

Rachel took a deep breath. "We need to stop here. I have a meeting at church. If I'm remembering correctly, you have an appointment with some of your old friends from high school."

Her mother was right. In the proceeding week, Jennifer had managed to muster the energy to contact a couple of friends who, like her, had moved back to Austin after college. It seemed strange that her mother's tragic story had bolstered her confidence. For weeks, she had spent all of her non-work and non-family time alone. Suddenly, she wanted contact with people her own age. She hoped the time with Louise and Cheryl would be the beginning of a new chapter in her life.

CHAPTER TEN
HUSBAND KEVIN

That night, when Kevin returned from his men's group, Rachel noticed that he wasn't energized and talkative as he usually was. Kevin had grabbed his basket of clean clothes from the laundry room and was now sorting the items into piles: underwear, socks, t-shirts, and so forth, before opening drawers or placing neat stacks on the shelves in his closet. The silence felt eerie to Rachel.

"Honey, is there something wrong? Did something happened at your meeting?" she asked.

Kevin was quiet for a few seconds, then turned and faced his wife. "Do you have to tell Jennifer about your past?" His brow was furrowed. Rachel sensed his anger.

"We talked about this. I think it will help our relationship. I already feel closer to her. She's old enough now to know what happened to me. She's a young woman."

"Like *you* were?" Kevin blurted out. "She's *not* like you were then."

"Not now. Not yet," Rachel ventured.

"Not *yet?!*" Kevin exclaimed. "That *asshole* will never be part of Jennifer's life."

"I know that. You know I know that," protested Rachel. "But she's searching like I was. She's vulnerable. Her heart is broken and she wants to be loved. And there's something else going on with her. I can't put my finger on it…" Rachel trailed off.

Was Kevin right? Was this too much for Jennifer? Rachel remembered how resistant Jennifer had been to the sex education she tried to provide to her young daughter. And she remembered their conversation right before Jennifer's 14th birthday. Jen had requested her own computer. Rachel responded that there were three computers in the office for kids to use. Jennifer had groaned. She said, 'You think I'm stupid! You think I'm going to some place bad!' Rachel countered that she didn't think Jennifer would *intentionally* go some place 'bad.' But she knew that predators found kids by masquerading as peers, using information that kids innocently provided about themselves, and then lured kids to locations where they could prey on them. Jennifer had responded, 'You are scaring me. I hate it when you talk.' Rachel had been amused by the latter statement. But now she wondered about the first. Jennifer was sensitive. Was she giving her too much information now? Was she scaring her in an unhealthy way?

On the other hand, Jennifer's sensitivity was an asset. It was a part of her personality that made her so open and accepting of others. Rachel remembered the time she had chaperoned a field trip with Jennifer's second grade class to a Native American cultural event. Before the trip, Jennifer had announced that she had a new best friend at school named Alana. Most of the second graders came on one bus. But the children in wheelchairs like Alana came on a separate bus and arrived later than the rest of the class because it took so long to load and unload each wheelchair. As soon as Jennifer saw Alana approach, she ran to greet her. For the next few hours Rachel watched Jennifer talk to, stroke, feed, and hold hands with this beautiful, blind, African-American girl confined to a wheelchair. They smiled and laughed with each other. It had touched Rachel deeply. Jennifer, Rachel thought now, was capable of understanding what Rachel had to tell her if she took her time, let Jennifer ask questions, and paid attention to Jennifer's emotional state.

"She's *fine*, Rache" said Kevin, interrupting Rachel's thoughts. "Dragging Jennifer into your unhappy past is only going to upset her. It will make her afraid of men – of *everything!*"

"There's nothing wrong with a healthy bit of fear," Rachel replied. "There are dangers for her as a woman that I'm not sure you understand." As soon as the words were out of her mouth, she regretted them.

"Not *understand?*" Kevin said sarcastically. "Didn't I let you tell me your story? Didn't I accept it as truth? Didn't I love you anyway?" Kevin's voice was louder now.

"You *did*. But you also said something along the lines of 'Now I've heard the story. The past is the past. Let's leave it there,'" said Rachel.

Kevin struggled to find the right response. "I thought you wanted to leave the past in the past too." Rachel glimpsed the sadness in his eyes.

She paused to consider how best to reply. She wanted Kevin to know how much she loved him. "I know the story was hard for you to hear because you love me so much. It hurts you to know that I was hurt. I don't think I ever could have found another man as sensitive and caring as you. I understand why you'd prefer we never spoke of rape or of Jay again.

"But... and please don't take this the wrong way..." Rachel could see Kevin's back stiffen. "You are really good at showing a happy face to the 'public.'"

Kevin started to interrupt, but Rachel waved him off. "Let me finish.

"You see the cup half-full when others – myself included – are paralyzed by the cup half-empty. That's why you are so good at business development and turning unsatisfied clients into satisfied ones. And it's not because you are dishonest. You are anything but. You just want to see the best in people and the best in situations. It's a great quality and one that I admire."

Kevin had calmed down. He was listening to her now.

"How many times have I wanted to rush Henry to a doctor, or find a therapist for Sam, or call a meeting of concerned parents? And you stopped me from jumping to the worst conclusion before we did more research or considered alternative explanations." Rachel smiled at her husband, and he, grudgingly, smiled back.

"On many occasions we've talked about how we complement each other. Right? We approach situations and people differently. And, usually, between our two perspectives, we find a compromise that makes sense," said Rachel.

Her expression changed to one of grave seriousness. "I am who I am because those things happened to me. And you love *this me*."

Kevin sighed. "I do. I just don't see how telling Jennifer will help her in her life. She will see you completely differently, and I'm not sure that is a good thing."

Rachel realized that the initial tension in their conversation had now dissipated. She said, "I will admit, I have that fear too." She rushed to add, "But my stronger sense is that there is so much more to gain. Being a woman in this world – even with all the progress we've made – is fraught with dangers and complications that I am in a peculiar position to know because I experienced some of them. She's my daughter. If I can't help her navigate the rocky waters, who *can* I help?"

Kevin sighed again. He knew he would lose this disagreement. He didn't like what his wife was doing. He didn't want to be reminded of her past himself. Their life together was so different than the stories Rachel had shared with him about the "time before" he met her. But he trusted her. He had always trusted her. So many times when he'd had his doubts about a "need," Rachel had proved him wrong. Henry's need for mental health intervention or Sam's need for adult involvement because he was being bullied... Kevin would have let his boys suffer longer had Rachel not had her intuitions. He did love the woman she had become – because of her past and in spite of her past.

"Just tell me when it's over," Kevin shook his head. "Oh, and tell me if Jen has any particular bad reaction that I need to be aware of... I guess this is like telling the kids about sex. You do the work, but I'll back you up."

Rachel smiled broadly and moved forward to wrap her arms around her amazing husband.

CHAPTER ELEVEN
THE TEACHER

That night, Jennifer jerked awake, eyes staring at darkness. Her pajamas were drenched in sweat again. What was going on with her? This was the second time in just over a week. She must have had a nightmare, she thought. As her head cleared, the memory of her dream came into focus and she shuddered.

It was David. Coach Reese was what the other students called him. But he had asked her to call him David when they were alone.

Jennifer raised herself up on her elbows. She had to get out of her wet clothes. She was freezing. Her mother's stories had stirred something in her, memories of events she thought she had put behind her, sealed away and forgotten, too painful to remember.

"Jennifer," Mr. Reese had said, "if you come here after school today, I can help you with the problems." The bell had rung, and Jennifer was the last person left in her Trigonometry class. She was still filing her notes and packing up her backpack to move on to third period. She looked up at him and his smile greeted her. She felt her cheeks flush, so she bent to her belongings as she responded, "Okay." When she dared look up at him again, she thought she saw him wink at her.

Mr. Reese was a math teacher at her high school of 2000 students, but he was also the wrestling and track coach. He was less than 6' tall, but muscular and fit. He had thick, dark brown hair and dazzling green eyes. Jennifer sometimes overheard other girls talk about how handsome he was in whispers and giggles. He was younger than most of the other teachers. But until he winked at her that March day of her senior year… Was it a wink?... she had never thought of him in any way except as her teacher.

Throughout the remainder of the day, Jennifer found herself thinking about Mr. Reese off and on. He was good-looking. How old was he, really? What was he like? She'd seen him in the gym with his wrestlers and on the track with his team. He commanded authority. He walked with an air of confidence and spoke with conviction as he slapped a player's back or joked with a group in the hall between classes.

Jennifer wondered what he did after school and practices. Did he have a girlfriend? A wife? Why was she thinking this way?

She almost didn't go to his classroom that day. It felt awkward somehow. She'd been to teachers' rooms before for tutoring or to ask a question about an assignment. Those other times had been fine, she told herself now. She might as well go. Mr. Reese knew she had struggled with the equations in class today. And she had said she would be there.

As she entered the room, Mr. Reese was typing something on his computer. But he must have heard her because he closed the laptop, looked up and smiled at her again. She felt herself blushing once more and wished she could turn around.

"No practice today," he said, raising his hands in a gesture of 'freedom.' "I saw you doing a lot of erasing and crumpling of paper today," he smirked. "Those problems on page 169 giving you trouble?"

Jennifer began to relax. She was here for math. That's all. "I guess so. I didn't understand..." She couldn't remember now what the assignment had been. But she remembered that Mr. Reese had gotten up and brought a chair closer to his desk and motioned for her to sit down beside him. He had reached across her paper to show her how to work the problems and she had smelled his aftershave. He had been so close.

Once she understood the work, he sat back and asked her how school was going and what her plans were for next year. They talked about the track team. He shared his opinions on several competitors and his assessment that the team would do well this Spring. He wanted to know if she ever came to meets. He asked about the girls' soccer team she played on. He was easy to talk to. They laughed about some of her classmates, but not in a hurtful way, she thought. Finally, he looked at his watch and said he needed to go. The time had passed so quickly. Jennifer couldn't believe it was already 5 o'clock. Mr. Reese said she could come by any time. He had enjoyed their conversation. She agreed.

The next day, as she was dressing for school, she thought about what to wear – what looked best on her? Mr. Reese came to mind. Why was she being so silly about this? He was her *teacher*. She couldn't have a crush on him!

During math class that day, Jennifer had a hard time staying focused. When class ended, she realized she didn't understand the homework assignment. She hadn't paid enough attention. She took her time packing her backpack until no other students were left in the room. Mr. Reese broke the silence. "Do you need help again?" he asked. Jennifer looked into his beautiful green eyes and nodded.

"I'm coaching this afternoon, but we'll be done by five. Is that too late for you to come to my office?"

Jennifer thought about her schedule. Soccer practice would end at 4:30 today. She could stick around school. Who knows what would be going on at home? Henry was out of control. Just last week, he'd been caught shoplifting at CVS *again*. The cops were called. Her parents were distraught. She heard them talking behind their bedroom door at night: "What are we going to do about Henry?" "Do we need to find a new school?" "His peer group is the problem." Henry was disrespectful to her parents and downright mean to Sam. She tried to steer clear of him as much as possible. What with their different extracurricular activities, they hardly sat down for family dinners anymore. If she was late coming home, her parents would hardly miss her.

"That's okay," Jennifer said.

"I'll be in the coaches' office. Can you come there?"

"Sure. I guess," she said hesitantly.

"Bring your book and notes, okay?" Mr. Reese smiled again, and Jennifer lost herself in his smile. Suddenly, she realized she was about to be late to her next class.

"See you this afternoon," she said, and hurried off to class. Her armpits were damp. Why was she reacting this way? "Get over yourself!" she scolded silently.

At 5 o'clock on the nose, Jennifer was waiting outside the gym, preparing herself to enter the building where the coaches' offices were located. Just then, the doors exploded open and out walked Coach Smith and Coach Nesbitt, two of the other coaches. They were talking and didn't even seem to notice she was there. She slipped into the building behind them, found the stairs to the basement and descended. Mr. Reese was rifling through a notebook when she came in the door.

"Oh, good," Reese said. "You're here. Did you bring your math book?"

Once again, the mention of 'math' settled Jennifer, and she approached the desk, nodding her head. They worked on problems for thirty minutes before Mr. Reese reached over the six inches between them and squeezed her hand. "I think you've got it!" he said and smiled into Jennifer's eyes. There was a hesitation, and then he leaned closer and gently kissed her lips. He pulled back slowly, measuring her reaction.

Jennifer was momentarily frozen. What had he just done? Why had it felt so good? Shouldn't she be frightened? She felt nothing but warm. A smile grew on her lips.

Reese leaned in again, but this time he parted her lips with his tongue for a long, hot, wet kiss that made Jennifer hunger for more. She felt wet between her legs and involuntarily parted her knees. His hand was on her knee now, moving slowly up her thigh...

Jennifer shivered and the motion brought her back to the present. She still hadn't changed her clothes. She jumped out of the bed, tore off the nightgown, and grabbed the closest t-shirt and pair of shorts on her floor.

She couldn't think about this now. She looked at the clock. It was almost 2 a.m. She had work in seven hours. She had to get some sleep. Jennifer crawled under the covers, put her earphones

on, and maneuvered the iPhone to her favorite playlist. She sang
to herself and drifted off to sleep.

SUNDAY
OCTOBER 19, 2014

CHAPTER TWELVE
THE TRIAL

The meeting at the coffee shop with Louise and Cheryl had been more fun than Jennifer had imagined. The young women reminisced about different events and people from high school and gossiped about what some of those classmates were doing now. At times, Jennifer laughed so hard, she almost cried. They told stories about their experiences in their respective colleges, sharing challenges and heartaches, successes and pivotal moments. It was hard to believe how easy their conversation flowed. All the barriers that had kept them emotionally distant before seemed to have fallen down. No longer were they trying to prove how attractive or smart or talented they were – while privately doubting any of it was true. No longer were they pitted against each other in contests for the best boyfriend, the highest grade, or the most awards. The three women left their two and a half hour get-together with plans to meet again very soon. Jennifer thought that if anything terrible ever happened to her, like it had to her mother, she would have these friends as a support system.

Jennifer's workweek passed uneventfully. But as she closed out her register at Macy's on Saturday evening, she recognized her growing anticipation to hear the next chapters in her mother's story. When Rachel arrived in the carriage house with her box of documents on Sunday morning, Jennifer was perched in her usual recliner, ready to listen.

"I want to start with the trial," said Rachel. "I wrote about it in so much detail, I think I'd rather read to you so I don't forget anything important."

"Okay," said Jennifer.

January 10, 1983

   My trial started today. I woke-up early and dressed in a skirt, vest, and blazer sewn by my mother. I hoped that the suit would meet with the approval of my attorney and that the love and care my mother put into these garments would carry me through the day. I was very nervous. The outcome of this trial will determine many things -- my credibility, my reputation, my sense of self-worth, and my future safety. I know that a conviction will not erase all of my fears about strangers, but I expect some relief.

   I have learned a lot about the criminal justice system over the last seven months. For instance, I have learned that the crime of rape is a crime against the State. Although the act at issue was an intensely personal experience for me, this is not "my" case. I am merely a witness for the State. Potentially, I could report everything as factually as it happened, but if the other witnesses fail to do their jobs according to legal standards, or if the chain of evidence has been broken, or if the jury doesn't find me or other witnesses credible, the jury will declare that a crime has not been committed. Although I have more to lose than anybody else on the prosecution's side, I am dependent on people and events over which I have no control.

   I am also aware that whatever happens in court will have significant effects on all of the people I love. My father, mother, brother, and sister were all in the courtroom today when the trial started. Their feelings and, perhaps, their reputations are also on the line. This rape has not just happened to me; it has happened to them as well. And there are others -- relatives and friends -- who will also be affected by a conviction or acquittal. As I waited to be called as a witness today, I fantasized the worst scenarios: being shunned and called a liar or losing the respect of those closest to me.

The Assistant District Attorney (ADA) prepared me as best as she could for trial. We had been over my testimony and the possible questions the defense attorneys could ask. I had been given suggestions on how to dress and how much emotion to show as I spoke. I felt as if I was about to go on stage, and I was.

When I arrived at the courthouse with my family, I was asked to sit outside the courtroom throughout the trial except for during my testimony and the closing arguments. This is called "invoking the rule." It is a means of preventing witnesses from hearing each other's testimony and corroborating each other's stories. My family promised to be my eyes and ears.

I was the first witness called after the jury was selected and all preliminary motions were heard. After I was sworn in, the ADA asked me questions regarding my residence, my employment status, and my standing in school. Then I reported the events leading up to the rape.

During the course of my testimony, I was interrupted by three small boys who rushed into the courtroom with their mother. It turned out that these were Isaiah Barry's children. They called out to their father, "Daddy! Daddy!" The Judge asked the mother to remove them, but the point had been made that the man on trial was a father, not merely an alleged rapist. I am sure the defense attorneys planned this interruption. I was rattled, but not unduly. I think I was on automatic pilot.

I spoke clearly and rationally. At the same time, I knew the jury needed to see some emotion, to see some of my hurt. I worried that I could not control it. Could I give them just enough without opening the floodgates? I tried as best as I could to balance composure with vulnerability.

After my direct examination, one of Barry's attorneys cross-examined me. He went over much of the same testimony I had already given, including a description of my 1972 Vega. It seemed as if he was trying to prove that I wasn't concerned about getting the papers out on time, and that I had initiated the drive to Eastside as well as the sex. He implied that no one in his or her right mind, including Isaiah Barry, would choose to have sex in that small car unless it was a mutual affair. He also questioned me about the fact that I had not seen a weapon, about the fact that I did not run away when I got out of the car to return to the driver's seat, and about the fact that I voluntarily drove Barry back to his car. He questioned me about my previous training at the Rape Crisis Center as if to suggest that I was a vengeful feminist using my knowledge from the training to cover for my lack of morals.

When I finished testifying, I left the courtroom and sat in the hall outside. Every ounce of me was tense, but I was relieved that it was over. I had been warned that I might be recalled, so I couldn't completely relax yet.

From my seat in the hall, I heard the next witness being called -- my former boss, Tony Hall. Tony had received my initial call from the Midtown Retirement Towers asking that he call the police and come pick up the undelivered papers. Tony hadn't arrived at court yet, so Jay was then called to the stand as the other person I had called that morning. Jay and I had previously discussed the need to slightly alter the truth about why I called. We agreed that we would say I was calling to cancel a breakfast appointment.

Next, Tony Hall was called again. He still had not arrived. The State moved on to medical testimony as I waited outside. There was evidence that I had scratches and bruises on my neck and arms in addition to evidence of semen in my vagina.

Tony arrived during the lunch break when my family was outside in the corridor with me. As they were comforting me and telling me how well I'd done, I was paying attention to Tony. Something was wrong. He was nervous, but there was something else. I got closer. Then I knew -- he was stoned! His red eyes gave him away. I didn't say anything. I didn't want my parents to see or know. I asked my brother to talk with Tony and test my theory. Lucas agreed with me. Inside I was panicking. What if Tony got on the stand and the jury figured it out too? What if the attorneys figured it out? I imagined their expressions when it dawned on them. I imagined the jury reacting to those expressions. I imagined Tony forgetting what he was supposed to say or being rattled by strong cross-examination. How could he be so selfish? He knew how important this was. God, there was so much that was out of my control! Tony's testimony could discredit me entirely if anyone figured out that he was stoned. It wasn't fair. What had I ever done to deserve this kind of treatment from him?

I didn't have to find out how Tony's testimony would affect the jury because he disappeared before court resumed. Maybe he knew at some level that he could destroy me and wanted to avoid that. Maybe he was just more frightened of taking the stand than anyone had imagined, and the marijuana couldn't cure that fear. Whatever the reason, he never came back and he was not called again.

My family told me that a doctor and several police officers testified to establish the chain of medical evidence, the investigation, and the arrest procedure. Everything had to be done by the book or the case could be dismissed on procedural grounds. Apparently, the court was satisfied. The court recessed until the next day.

January 11, 1983

When the trial resumed today, Barry took the stand and testified to his version of the events that had occurred on June 24th. Family members told me that he said that he had a job and that he was a deacon in his church. He tried to establish that his car had indeed been in need of repair on the night he met me. Barry testified that I insisted on driving him home. He said he told me that he was married. He said I told him that I had a boyfriend who occasionally came over to spend the night. In this imagined conversation, I also told him that I was going to college and needed all the money I could get. Then, we apparently talked about sex for a while. When we reached his neighborhood, we started kissing and touching each other. He offered to help pay my bills and we had sex. I got upset because he promised me $75, but he only had $50. Then I took him back to his car. He got his car home, but could not get it to work. I was shocked! He had invented a story that made me out to be a prostitute!

Under cross-examination, Barry testified that he had been working up until the day of the alleged rape. At a later point in the trial, the State brought in the defendant's old employer who testified that he had been discharged on June 21, 1982, for excessive absenteeism.

After all the testimony had been given, I was allowed to reenter the courtroom to hear the closing arguments. I sat beside my father and watched his hand open and close into a fist. I finally grabbed his hand and held it tightly. He was scared and so was I. The ADA said I was "dumb" to give the defendant a ride. I cringed at the word, but I knew she was right, in a sense. I hoped the jury could distinguish between consent to give a stranger a ride and consent to sex.

The jury was dismissed to deliberate, and my family and I went outside the courtroom to wait. I was nervous, but I couldn't convince myself the jury would believe Barry's preposterous story after hearing all the evidence that contradicted him. We didn't wait long. Much to my relief, the jury came back with a verdict of GUILTY within a couple of hours.

The lawyers and my family congratulated me. I am proud of myself, but I also want to put this behind me. The only thing left is the sentencing, which will occur in a month or so. Before that can happen, there has to be a pre-sentence investigation to determine if there are aggravating or mitigating factors to be considered. Barry's sentence could be lengthened or shortened depending on his dangerousness to society.

Rachel sat up and stretched. She realized her stomach was in knots. Jennifer was momentarily frozen.

"Wow. That was so intense... and so *interesting*. I mean, the way the legal system works. That's why you wanted to go to law school, I bet. I never thought to ask you 'why' before," said Jennifer.

Her daughter was more focused on the process than on the emotional aspects of the trial, Rachel realized. This was a lot for her to take in. She would cut Jennifer some slack.

"That's part of the reason," Rachel replied. "That decision to attend law school would come later, and we'll get to that. At the time, my attention was on this specific trial and all the people involved.

"I was a good witness. I did everything the attorneys asked of me. But what I remember most about the trial was worrying about my family and how desperately I wanted Barry to be convicted so that *they* would be okay. I think my sense of responsibility for others during the trial stemmed partly from the way rape trials are conducted. The State was, in essence, required to prove my *innocence* before it could prove Barry's guilt. I had to demonstrate to the jury that I had resisted enough for my assailant to know he was *forcing* me to do something I did not want to do. But how could I prove that was the case? Only the two of us were in my car. Legally, it was *not* something I could prove alone. However, the medical testimony of cuts and bruises and my statements to police officers immediately after the alleged crime bolstered my claim. Still, I felt the heaviness of the burden. Before I was raped, I was presumed virtuous. But once I became involved in a seedy sexual matter in the public spotlight, I *needed* a conviction to restore my reputation."

Rachel reached in the cardboard box, picked up the trial transcript, flipped it open to the beginning, and gestured with it in Jennifer's direction.

"'Innocence' can be a tricky thing to prove. What I didn't know at the time of the trial, but later learned by reading the transcript, is that a large part of the preliminary discussion between the lawyers and the judge concerned the admissibility of my sexual history. I had reported to the doctor who examined me at the hospital that I had had sex two days earlier. Barry's defense attorneys wanted to use the doctor's written report of this fact as a reason to discuss my sexual behavior generally. The judge wouldn't allow it because of a state Rape Shield law that protected the sexual history of most victims."

"I don't understand what you mean," interjected Jennifer.

"A Rape Shield law makes it impermissible, in a criminal case, to admit evidence of a victim's past sexual history to undermine her – or his – credibility. So, for example, the defense can't call a witness to testify that the victim has a history or reputation of blaming sexual encounters on others, crying 'rape,' or sleeping around. The defense can't call a witness to testify about a victim's past sexual partners because that doesn't have anything to do, directly, with the alleged sexual assault.

However, there are some exceptions to the rule. Past sexual behavior with the *defendant*, or sexual acts with another person that might show the rape was *not committed* by the defendant, might be relevant.

"Thinking about this now, I feel lucky that the judge in my case ruled the way he did. Imagine what could have happened if I'd had to testify about the sex I told the doctor I had two days before the assault – sex with *Jay*!"

"You would have been outed!" exclaimed Jennifer.

And that might have been a good thing, thought Rachel. But she said, "It could have opened the whole can of worms."

"I didn't comprehend the defense's trial strategy at the time, but it is now clear to me that Isaiah Barry was instructed to say many of the things he said. Some of his comments cut to the core of the legal elements of rape. He attacked the consent issue. He claimed that I initiated our meeting, the car ride, and the sex. He made me sound immoral because I, supposedly, knew he was married. All mention of force, coercion, or threats about using a weapon were removed from his version of the events. I became the threatening one: a prostitute with a vengeful agenda. The sick nature of choosing to rape someone in front of his family's home was translated into a matter of convenience for me. The 'broken' car justified his getting in the car with me in the first place *and* his inability to get to work."

"All very clever," said Jennifer.

"Yes. But, once the verdict was in, I thought I had heard the last of Barry. I hadn't," said Rachel.

Chapter Thirteen
Post-Trial

*P*icking up her journal again, Rachel began to read aloud.

January 15, 1983

As I was sitting at home alone last night, the phone rang. I picked it up and said, "Hello." I heard a voice that I couldn't identify at first. It sounded vaguely familiar. Suddenly I realized it was Isaiah Barry. I panicked: Where was he? I asked, "What do you want?" He replied, "Don't let them kill me. Please don't let them kill me." I felt disoriented. What was I supposed to do in these circumstances? I wasn't supposed to be talking to him, was I? I said, "I can't talk to you." I hung up.

I started to shake. What had happened? How had he gotten my phone number? How could he be calling me? Wasn't he supposed to be in jail? Was I safe? And then another set of emotions hit me. This was a living, breathing human being who was begging me for his life. What had I to do with determining life and death? That was too much. I saw his face and heard again the words he had spoken that night -- the lies, the coercion, the threats, and the anger. I didn't want to think about him as a person. I didn't want that responsibility. I wanted justice. I wanted to be safe. I wanted others to be safe. I didn't want to think about this man as a man. It is easier if he stays a "rapist." He is a rapist!

I called Dad and told him what had happened. He was outraged. I shouldn't have called Dad. I still can't handle his intensity. We agreed I would call the District Attorney's office in the morning. I told Dad to calm down, that it would be all right. The ADA was surprised when I told her about the phone call. She said she would investigate and get back to me. Later she called and said that no one knew how Barry had gotten to a phone or where he got the number. Yes, he was still in jail. It wouldn't happen again because the phones would not be left on.

Dad wants me to move from my apartment immediately. I don't want to move. This is my home, and I don't want this stranger taking over more of my life than he already has. But, after more discussion, I told Dad I would find out if I could move to another apartment in the same complex. I will get an unlisted phone number.

"I've never heard you talk about Papa being an angry man. He's never been like that around me," said Jennifer.

"That's because he isn't your *Dad*. Think about the way *your* dad gets when he believes you are being treated unfairly..." Rachel was remembering the times her husband had stormed around in their bedroom, cursing one coach or another, because he didn't believe his daughter was getting enough playing time.

"...or when he thinks I'm not 'living up to my potential,'" Jennifer interrupted.

Rachel smiled at her daughter's sarcasm, remembering how many times Kevin had used that phrase. "Fathers want to protect their daughters. My situation was an extreme case, and Papa had no more control over the process than I did. So he was angry and sad and frustrated.

"You see Papa's emotions in the way he plays his music on the piano, the clarinet, or one of his saxophones. That's his outlet these days. When he was younger, and as his child, I saw a more emotional man. He worked hard listening to other people's crises and emotions all day as a pastoral counselor. Then he came home to find peace and got a band of rowdy kids instead. Sarah, Lucas, and I learned to give Papa some space to decompress when he got home *before* bombarding him with requests and demands. We knew that if we didn't give him time, "NO" would be the answer to our questions." Rachel smiled.

"But let me tell you a story about my emotional dad that may help you see how his sensitivity was also a good thing.

"When I was middle school age, our cat had kittens. There were three of them. We knew we would have to give them away when they were old enough, so we gave them temporary names. We named them after ourselves: Rachel, Sarah, and Lucas. It was summer in Texas and it was hot. Our old house didn't have air conditioning then. But we did have an attic fan that we turned on at night to suck the cooler air in and through the house. Of course, that meant the windows needed to be open, so all our windows had screens. We also had a screened porch. That was where the kittens stayed. Papa, wanting to bring more cool air into the house, propped a folded card table in the doorway to the screened porch to keep the kittens *out* of the house, but to let the fresh air *in*.

"One summer morning, I woke up and hurried downstairs to play with the kittens. To my shock and horror, the card table had fallen – presumably because the kittens had tried to climb it – and baby Rachel had been crushed and lay dead on the tile floor."

"Oh, my God!" Jennifer gasped.

"I was devastated and grief stricken," Rachel continued. "And then I got angry. My dad was teaching summer school to ministers at the theology school. I jumped on my bicycle, tears streaming down my face, and peddled as fast as I could to the school to find my father. I found him, standing in front of a classroom full of students and stood in the doorway until he saw me. He excused himself and led me down the hall and into a stairwell where we stopped. I screamed at him. 'You are a murderer! You killed my baby! I hate you!' I went on and on, pounding his chest with my fists, screaming and crying until I was exhausted. When my fury was spent, his arms gathered me in. He held me gently, but firmly, while I wept.

"Jennifer, I don't remember that he said *anything*. He didn't make excuses. He didn't try to explain. But his embrace told me that he loved me, told me that he understood and accepted my pain, told me that he would be there for me no matter what happened, no matter how bad it got.

"Later on, when I was a Youth Minister..."

"You were a Youth Minister?" Jennifer interjected. There was so much she didn't know about her mother.

"Yes. And I'll get to that part of the story too. When I was a Youth Minister, I preached a sermon about that event that the youth group members called 'the dead kitten story.'" Rachel smiled at the remembering. "My point was that I learned about God's love through my father. God doesn't always stop the painful things from happening or give us explanations that take away our pain. But God is there to hold us and love us and be with us in the midst of it all. And that means something, that matters."

Jennifer was touched by the story. "I'm glad you told me. I've never thought much about Papa as your Dad."

"He has mellowed with age. Grandparents get to keep some distance from the drama of their grandchildren's lives. They did their time raising their own kids. But, even though I was an adult at the time of these events I am sharing with you, I was still Papa's baby, just like you are my baby," Rachel said as she reached out and squeezed Jennifer's hand. "I would do everything in my power to protect you from harm."

Jennifer thought about this. "Mom, in some ways you sound so *unemotional* in this journal compared to Papa. But it happened to *you*."

"It's strange, isn't it? I was thinking the same thing. I sound more like a reporter of events that aren't personal to me. The only explanation I can provide is that I was holding it together to present a calm, collected persona to the outside world... Let's read some more of the journal," said Rachel.

February 22, 1983

I received a phone call from the DA's office three days ago. The attorney told me that Isaiah Barry had been sentenced to twenty years. Ironically, just minutes before the call, I was out in the parking lot helping a stranger jump-start his car. I laughed and told myself I haven't really changed much since I was raped. I feel defiant. I will show everyone that survival is a matter of will power.

"I see what you mean," interrupted Jennifer.

"Good triumphs over evil, I thought. Meanwhile, I was going about my business, defying that anything was different, by helping another stranger. I truly thought I could wipe my hands of the whole matter and return to life as usual." Rachel continued reading.

Today, Gustav disappeared. I let him out as usual. He is always good about doing his business and coming back home right away. I began to get concerned when he didn't come to the door after a few minutes. I called and searched for him, but he was nowhere to be found. If he doesn't show up soon, I will put up posters, check the animal shelters in both nearby counties, and put an ad in the newspaper.

Rachel said, "As if to prove how wrong I was, the fates dealt me a devastating blow the same day with the disappearance of Gustav." Rachel's eyes met Jennifer's. She noted the innocent anticipation. She hated telling her daughter what came next because Jennifer was such an animal lover. It was bizarre, Rachel thought, that she felt so protective of Jennifer in *this* way and less protective when it came to telling her about the ways that she had been hurt.

Resigned to keep going, Rachel read again.

March 1, 1983

I feel sick. I have followed several leads from calls I received about dogs fitting Gustav's description. Nothing. I was fearful for him. We met the day before I was raped. He was with me when it happened. We lived through his distemper together. We lived through my months of court proceedings. We were survivors. And now, mysteriously, he disappeared just when it was all over.

Today I received a phone call from someone who identified himself as having read my newspaper ad. He described Gustav, and I became excited. I said, "Yes. That sounds like him. When can I see him?" The man on the other end of the phone line responded, "Well, the reason I called was just to tell you that he is alright. But you can't have him back." I was startled, "What do you mean 'I can't have him back'?" He replied, "I'm an older man -- a homosexual; and my lover recently died. I'm not going back to the bars to find someone else." There was a pause. Then he said, "Did you know your dog likes sex?"

I became hysterical. I started shaking and screaming, "You can't do that! He's my dog; and you can't have him. Please, please, please give him back!" He said, "I'm sorry, but you can't have him back," and he hung up the phone.

Rachel stopped reading to say, "I had used my parents' phone number in the ad. Dad was still concerned about my safety, so that seemed like the thing to do." She returned to the journal.

I was in my parents' house, but my sister was the only other person there. I was screaming and crying hysterically. She rushed in and I told her what had just happened. She did what she could to calm me down, saying sick people make calls like that just to get a reaction like mine.

I cried for Gustav, but I also cried for myself. Gustav is being raped! My baby is being raped, and I am absolutely powerless to do anything about it. Today I realized what it must have felt like to my family when I told them I was raped. I have not been able to cry for myself about being raped, but now I am crying buckets.

"Oh, Mom…That would have killed me," Jennifer sighed, her eyes wet with unshed tears.

"It felt like the deepest wound yet to lose Gustav in that way. I was *his* parent, and I had the reaction of a parent. But my stuff, my emotions that had been locked inside, were triggered too.

"Listen. Just so I'm sure you are understand. Homosexuality and bestiality – sex between a human and an animal – have *nothing* to do with each. You know that, right? This was some crazy person trying to get a rise out of me." Rachel said.

"Yes, I know," said Jennifer, a little indignantly.

Rachel thought about how accepting and learned her daughter was regarding sexuality. She had been very limited in her knowledge at the same age.

"Did you ever find Gustav?" asked Jennifer.

"Listen," responded Rachel.

March 13, 1983

I continue to hope that Gustav will miraculously reappear. A secretary at work who studies Eastern religions told me that she thinks Gustav might have been "sent" to get me through that one period in my life. Either Gustav or I had some lesson to learn that was complete when the trial and sentencing were over. I have held on to that hope, and other possible explanations, while making almost daily trips to one or more of the three places where Gustav might be if someone turned him in to Animal Control.

Today I made my last trip to the Austin Humane Society, hoping Gustav would be there. He wasn't. But I saw a puppy who is a lovely ball of gray, black, tan, and white fur. She looks a lot like Gustav did as a puppy, except that this little girl has the most expressive eyebrows, and a black patch over her lip. I adopted her. Jay helped me name her Adagio. I will face the future with her by my side.

Rachel said, "I don't believe in 'God's will' when it is used to explain away a catastrophe. Still, I clung to the words of assurance by my coworker that Gustav's abbreviated life with me served a preordained purpose. And, I have to admit, if Gustav had not disappeared, I would not have met Adagio. Adagio was my constant companion, love-of-my-life, for almost fifteen years. She was a candle flickering in the darkness on so many occasions. She came to me because of loss, but loss didn't define her or our relationship. Adagio went to work with me. She sat outside the theology school and waited for me. She sat under my desk in law school. I like to think she helped me choose my husband and care for my children because she taught me how to love by example - by giving her love so freely to me."

Jennifer said, "I loved Adagio too."

"I know you did, sweetie. She was the best."

Katie lifted her head off the floor and looked at Rachel. "I think you've insulted Katie, Mom," laughed Jennifer.

Rachel reached down to stroke Katie's neck and ears. "I love you too, little one," she cooed.

CHAPTER FOURTEEN
SELF-BLAME

Straightening herself, Rachel said to Jennifer, "I want to try to get through the Spring and Summer of that first year post-rape. You with me?"

"Yeah," said Jennifer.

"I need to warn you. I read through this the other night, and I was struck at how I sounded like a reporter rather than an affected human being to whom all of this was happening. Don't assume I wasn't affected. It's just that I wasn't 'connected' in a feeling way to these events. You'll see what I mean…"

April 4, 1983

The theology school is hosting an international event this year: The New Testament Revisited (NTR). Scholars from all parts of the globe are coming to speak at Austin University later this month. Jay is one of the principle people in charge of making arrangements for this major event. Accordingly, I am spending less time with him. He has also become more concerned that Mary will discover our relationship.

In the meantime, I have been working longer hours for the newspaper to pay my bills. Financial independence remains a top priority for me. I also have a lot of schoolwork to catch up on because I was not able to concentrate on academics at the beginning of the semester while I was actively involved in my court case. Fortunately, my professors have been understanding.

Several of my classmates would like to go out with me. To them I appear unattached, and I can't say otherwise. I am not interested in any of them, but Jay is still jealous. I feel like I am always on the defensive with him.

Jay is insistent that we each describe our past relationships with lovers. He says we will then be able to "claim those sexual experiences as our own." I know that Jay is afraid I will drift away from him because we were spending less time together. But his demand for detailed descriptions makes me very uncomfortable. I am never quite sure how he will react. Will I hurt him or excite him? I love him so much. The last thing I want is to hurt him.

Jay also wants us to use slang names to talk about sex. He says that moving away from the language we learned to describe sexual experience -- the old, moralistic categories -- will push us to a new level of awareness. Making love is "fucking." Penis is "dick" or "cock" and vagina is "cunt" or "pussy." I hate using the words, but I can't tell Jay that talking about body parts as if they are unconnected to our souls reminds me of Barry. Plus, Jay must believe I was partially at fault for being raped because he keeps trying to get me to say that I enjoyed the sex.

Rachel said, "Whenever Jay felt stressed, like he did during the preparation for NTR, I received some new sexual demand that made me uncomfortable. This time the demand was to describe sexual acts by using slang words. He always provided a reasonable rationale for his requests. But to this day, I cannot call a penis a "cock" or a vagina a "pussy" without feeling ill. Sometimes I wonder if those words can ever be used with love or if they are always outward signs that there is something fundamentally wrong in a relationship."

Jennifer tensed. She, too, had known a man who wanted her to 'talk dirty.' She, too, had felt ill at ease. She pushed the thoughts away and tried to refocus on her mother.

"There's more," said Rachel.

April 24, 1983

I am angry about being shut out of Jay's life while he receives praise for his work with NTR. But I can't tell him. I know that if I showed anger, he would accuse me of being another manipulative, demanding woman in his life. I have to remain silent.

My primary role is to babysit Ben -- free of charge -- foregoing paid hours at the newspaper while Jay and Mary, as well as his assistant, Elizabeth Nash, take part in the festivities. I am holding onto the hope that this success will carry him closer to tenure – which is his ultimate goal. Jay has promised me we will marry and have a family once he achieves tenure.

I am in trouble with my family now too. I have been eating less and smoking more. I know I smoke cigarettes instead of eating meals. I can see most of my ribs. But putting on clothes that are now baggy makes me feel good. My weight is something I can control. But today I got caught. I met my mother at the university pool. She took one look at me and declared that I would not be swimming because she was going to take me home and feed me! It's crazy, but in that instant, I felt very loved.

Rachel stopped reading and said, "I need to back up and tell you that I started smoking when I dated Jason. He smoked, and I wanted to know what it was like since I'd always been a good girl. He warned me not to do it, that it was addictive. He was right. I was a closeted, intermittent smoker for a couple of years *until I was raped*. Afterward, smoking became a comfort. Besides, Jay, who didn't smoke cigarettes publicly, smoked with me. He relied on me to have the cigarettes. It was another one of our secrets."

Jennifer had known that her mother once smoked. But now the smoking had a context that made sense.

"I was not dealing with my emotional baggage," said Rachel. "I wasn't trying to diet. But 'skinny' is linked to beautiful women in our culture, as you know. And not eating was something I could control. Yet, I was not a true anorexic. I really did love it when my mother wanted to feed me."

"I know what you mean, Mom. I've never smoked, but I went through a period in high school of not eating like I should," said Jennifer.

"Your senior year?"

"Yeah."

"I noticed, but I figured it was stress from college applications, AP classes, and being the first to leave home," said Rachel.

Jennifer took a deep breath before responding. "Umm. Yeah, that was mostly it."

"I watched, you know? I would have intervened if I thought you were in danger," said Rachel.

I was *in danger!* Jennifer's mind screamed. But she said, "It was a lot of stress. I got through it."

"I'm so glad you did," Rachel smiled. "*My* stress came to the surface in different ways – like smoking and not eating, and in dreams…"

April 26, 1983

I had a dream last night. The characters were my father, my sister Sarah, and I. Sarah had just acquired a magnificent fishing rod - an enormous one - painted and elaborately designed. But the lure on the line was not a lure at all. It was a huge bird with feathers and many bright colors. We were standing outside near my grandmother's old house. I begged Sarah to let me play with her toy. She finally consented, admonishing me to be careful with it. I cast the line way up into the sky. The fishing rod became a beautiful kite. The bird-kite soared and ruffled its feathers in the wind. Just then a big gust of wind caught the bird and line and wrapped them around a telephone pole, which had not been there a minute before. The toy was ruined.

In that instant many thoughts flashed through my head. I knew Sarah would blame me for this. And I knew that - though the wind had caused the disaster - I would be the one held responsible. I did not want to listen to her accusations. My rage was mounting. I did not want to apologize. I did not want to deal with her calmly and sensibly. But I knew my father would step in to mediate our inevitable quarrel. And I knew that at his hands we would reach some compromise after pain-staking conversation. I knew I would lose. In that instant, I turned on Sarah and began pounding her, in full fury. But I felt guilty as hell for beating her up this way.

As I reflect on the dream, I realize it is packed with symbols of what I am still experiencing months after the trial. I am the kite soaring beautifully in the air until a sudden event, my rape, destroys me. I feel responsible for that destruction of beauty. I know I will be blamed though I see that forces beyond my control are operating. I don't want to "talk about it" -- the way lawyers talk about rape in their "reasonable" language, the way my father sat us down at the kitchen table as children to talk through our angry emotions. I feel rage; and in this dream I can express it. But the only way I know to express anger is as a child with fists. I'm afraid my rage at being raped is so strong that it will become the uncontrollable anger of a child if it is expressed.

Rachel paused from reading and said, "When we were young, there was a time when I knocked Sarah off of a table in a fit of anger. She received a concussion and the family went to the hospital. I remember watching her walk up and down a straight line at the doctor's request and praying to God that if God would only let her be all right, I would never hurt her again. Because I was older and bigger than my siblings, I was told that I had the greater part of responsibility to prevent fighting. Over time, my feelings of anger became equated with guilt about not being able to control that anger. In this dream, I was aware that anger at my family only leads to more guilt."

Jennifer thought about her own childhood and sibling quarrels. She, too, was the oldest. She remembered being able to push Henry around when they were very young. She remembered getting in trouble because she was older. But by the time they were seven and three, Henry's violence toward baby Sam had become the focus of her parents' disciplinary efforts. She spent more time playing peacefully with other little girls her age and avoided the drama at home, if she could.

Jennifer remembered feeling abandoned sometimes. She fantasized that she was a princess with all the privileges. Or, she fantasized that she was a courageous orphan who could take care of herself.

She realized that she was different than her mother when it came to family relationships. Her mother jumped in with both feet. She engaged and wrestled. Jennifer, on the contrary, backed away from controversy or charged conversations. "If I had broken my sister's kite," she thought, "I would have run away. I wouldn't have stayed to fight. And I wouldn't have felt guilt. I would have felt *hurt*." It was strange the way her mother's stories prompted her to be so introspective about her own life.

Rachel was continuing to read, and Jennifer tuned back in.

Then I had a second dream. This dream took place in my present apartment. Many people came and went. I do not remember them all. But I do remember the sense of being in a small place with many bodies and yet feeling swallowed up by loneliness. At the end of the dream, my baby Gustav comes limping through the front door. His fur is matted with clumps of blood and dirt. His paw is torn open. His eyes are full of both sorrow and joy. His nose is wet with life. I rush over to him and we embrace. He looks up into my eyes and says, 'Mama, I'm never going to run away again. It's scary out there.' We cry.

I think the people in the apartment represented those who participated in some aspect of the aftermath of my rape. The trauma in this dream is Gustav's disappearance. In spite of all the people present, I felt isolated. Rape is not an experience easily shared or understood. Gustav's dirt and blood were my dirt and blood. His torn paw was my torn and bruised body. Gustav blamed himself for making the decision to run away just as I blamed myself for choosing to be out in the middle of the night delivering papers and helping a stranger. The world is a scary place.

"In spite of everything you'd done to get 'justice' and move on, your emotional pain continued," suggested Jennifer.

"Right. And there's more…"

April 30, 1983

My neighbor, Roy -- a college student who had witnessed the comings and goings of Jay, Tom, and Frank -- asked to come over to my new apartment. He brought a bottle of wine which we shared while we talked. We were both a little tipsy when he started to come on to me. Before I knew what was happening, I was pressed up against a wall and he was muttering things about what he could or would do to my body sexually. I suddenly froze. Then I regained my composure and began pushing him away. I reminded him that he was "just my friend." He backed off, turned, and left without another word. I feel awful. I didn't mean to hurt him. The only explanation I can come up with for what happened is that there is something about me, some uncontrollable seductive power, that brings out these responses in men -- at least that is what Jay says it is.

"You were blaming yourself again," said Jennifer.

"Yes. I was stuck in self-blame. But here's the other important thing – I was a beautiful young woman, like you are. I needed to *know* that, really *know* that, and then act accordingly. I was going to attract attention. But as long as I accepted the explanation Jay gave me – that I had uncontrollable seductive power – I wasn't taking responsibility for my own safety. I felt powerless."

"You were brainwashed," said Jennifer.

"Funny you should use that word. It was a word I later landed on to explain what happened to me during those years. But I certainly didn't see it at the time." Changing the subject, Rachel said, "One more dream…"

May 5, 1983

Yesterday Jay asked that we "separate" while he focuses on determining what is going to happen to his marriage. This could be good for us, but since the future is unknown, I am also afraid. Then last night I had a powerful and disturbing dream: I am in a room full of male theology students and Jay. I am the lone woman. Frank is at one end of the room and Jay at the other. I wanted to be with Jay, but I couldn't let anyone know of my attraction, so I stayed on the opposite end of the room. Jay is talking to a group of men about the Bible. He begins to rub his crotch. I am getting hotter and hotter watching him. Frank, at the other end of the room, is loud, telling jokes, leaning back in his chair. Jay finally unzips his pants, removes his penis, and begins to stroke it pleasurably. The two men closest are watching and listening as he continues to talk. The two men pull their penises out and stroke each other. Men around the room begin repeating this ritual, pairing up or masturbating alone. I am now beside Jay watching. He is not paying any attention to me. I clutch his leg. Suddenly, I realize that Frank is angry at Jay for taking control of the room. Frank is also aware that my eyes are fixed on Jay's cock. Frank says, 'Just because you have the biggest cock, it's no reason to shame the rest of us by pulling it out.' He then bids me to come to him, laughs at Jay who is helpless to defend me, and pushes me down to suck on his cock. I dare not look at Jay and betray our secret. I am ashamed. I close my eyes and begin.

Rachel saw that Jennifer was blushing. "I'm sorry if this embarrasses you – listening to your mother talk about cocks, masturbation, and fellatio. I'm asking a lot of you. If it gets to be too much, you have to be able to tell me to stop. Okay?"

As she spoke the words, Rachel wondered if Jennifer was *capable* of telling her to stop. It dawned on her that there was an imbalance of power in their relationship because she was an authority figure to Jen. She reminded herself to use her authority with compassion. Rachel had an agenda, but she knew she shouldn't impose it on Jennifer if harm might come to her. There was a line between standing up for what one needed and wanted and imposing those needs and wants on another in an abusive way. She, of all people, should understand that. But finding the "line" wasn't always easy.

She had to remember that her goals were to help Jennifer manage her own life and to rebuild their mother-daughter relationship. She did not want Jennifer to think she needed to heal her mother's wounds for her. Nor did she mean to add baggage to the heavy load Jennifer seemed to carry these days. Rachel told herself: "Tread lightly and listen carefully."

Jennifer *was* embarrassed, but her mother's admonition reminded her that she was also flattered that Mom trusted her enough to share this very painful story with her. "I'm okay," she said. It was hard to know what else to say.

Rachel continued, "The dreams were so vivid. I can't remember another time in my life when I woke from sleep with such clear and complete memories of my dreams. After the trial was over, I should have been free to focus on my emotional recovery. I was no longer obliged to keep my feelings in check to do a good job as a witness. Energies that had been directed outward should have been turned inward toward healing. Instead, in the Spring of 1983, I continued to follow Jay's directions for how I ought to conduct my life. I had been the victim of male sexuality turned toward abusive ends, and nothing really changed after the trial. Nightmares depicted my worst fears, and Jay couldn't control my dreams.

"In my dreams, I am a child with uncontrolled emotions, a defenseless puppy exposed to danger, or the object of sexual manipulation. The irony, as I recall, was that the only person I ever shared my dreams with was Jay. And he interpreted my helplessness as uncontrolled, dangerous sexuality that would ruin me without his guidance. Since I wasn't communicating with anyone else about my inner thoughts and fears, I had no check for Jay's interpretations, and I was too weak to stand up to him."

Jennifer looked completely spent, thought Rachel. "That's enough for now. Let's go get some frozen yogurt. You up for a walk?"

Jennifer wanted to tell her mother about *her* dreams. She sensed that her mother was right: her dreams were expressing fears and feelings she was not dealing with directly. But she couldn't speak of them. Not now. Not yet.

CHAPTER FIFTEEN
RATIONALIZING

Rachel and Jennifer returned to the carriage house with their half-eaten containers of frozen yogurt. The walk had settled them both. Though the heaviness of the subject matter of their talks hung over them, they chatted, while out of the house, about the new line of winter clothing at Macy's, and upcoming family activities. Rachel asked Jennifer if she had Halloween plans. She said she didn't.

Jennifer had found herself in a Halloween store the day before, wandering the aisles, looking at cheaply made costumes of superheroes, famous artists, political figures, and the like. Last year, she and Chris had gone to a fraternity Halloween party dressed as a nurse and doctor. It was quick and easy to find the pieces for the costumes because of Chris's internship at the hospital. At the time, Jennifer had thought only, "Everyone will know we are together." But now she considered the relative authority of a doctor versus a nurse. Chris was in charge. It seemed to her now that Chris had *always* been in charge.

She didn't have anywhere to go this Halloween. But if she did, she would go as Wonder Woman or some other female character with power and authority.

As Rachel and Jennifer reentered the carriage house and settled back into their chairs, neither woman flinched as Rachel refocused them on the task at hand.

"The summer of 1983 brought some unexpected changes. Mary accused Jay of adultery, and Jay told me we couldn't see each other – *indefinitely*. I don't remember that he provided any details about how we'd been caught. I do remember that I promised him I would keep our secret and deny any involvement if asked.

"This change in circumstances opened the door for me to take charge of my own life. During that second semester of my second year in theology school, I had decided not to pursue

144

ordination in the United Methodist Church." Rachel paused to ask, "Do you understand what 'ordination' means?"

"Sort of," said Jennifer. "It's the process of becoming a minister, right?"

"Yes. The truth is, because I decided not to pursue it, I never learned about all the requirements. In general, to be ordained – that is, to become an officially recognized and licensed member of the clergy – you have to get a certain amount of education in different subjects pertaining to theology, the Bible, church administration, pastoral care, preaching, and so forth. Most people who want to be ordained – at least I *think* this is true – get a Master of Divinity degree, a three-year course of study. That was the program I was in initially. But the degree doesn't transform you into an ordained minister. The professional licensing is a different - but often simultaneous – process. It requires essays, interviews, vows and… well, I'm not sure what else.

"It's similar to becoming an attorney. You need the J.D. or Juris Doctor degree, but to practice law, you have to apply to a State Bar Association – the professional organization in the state where you want to practice – and pass a rigorous test. Make sense?"

"Uh-huh. So, why did you stop?" asked Jennifer.

"Perhaps I would have come to that conclusion anyway. But, given the secret life I was leading with a *theology school* professor and the anti-church authority position that Jay and I collaborated in pursuing, I could not honestly profess belief in many of the creeds of the church," said Rachel. "However, because I was a good writer and student, I had been asked, in my second year, to lead a colloquium – a subset of first year students from one of the large lecture courses. I led discussions of the students' readings and they wrote papers that I graded. I discovered that I liked teaching. So, as I was closing the door on ordained ministry, I was opening the door to a new career in teaching."

"I knew you had been a teacher at some point, but I didn't know how you came to that decision," said Jennifer.

"Theology school led me to teaching. Still, not one to quit when it came to school…"

Jennifer laughed and interrupted, "I know, Mom. You are *big* on education."

"Don't knock it until you've tried it," smiled Rachel. "Anyway, I decided to complete a Masters of Theological Studies instead. That degree is more academic than practical, and it required a thesis. I decided I would complete the degree while also taking education courses to become certified to teach high school social studies. My undergraduate degree in history and philosophy was going to pay off after all!" Rachel smiled again.

Jennifer rolled her eyes. "You are not going to convince me *now* that I need to go to become a minister to get mileage out of my religion major."

Rachel had to laugh. "Not on your life! You will be wiser than I was," she grinned.

"I planned to take the 15 hours of curriculum courses I needed during the summer, and then do my ten hours of student teaching during the academic year. The problem was that I couldn't afford the courses if I paid rent too. So, I came up with the brilliant plan of leaving my apartment, putting my stuff in storage, and buying an inexpensive camper that I could both live in and use to deliver papers – which was my paid work. My parents would have let me live with them. But what about my secret? Even though Jay pushed me away that summer, I held on to the fantasy of our future together. I did not really believe we were over. And if we were not over, we needed a place to meet."

"Did you do it?" asked Jennifer, genuinely curious.

"I did. I bought a 1968 VW Camper. My plan was to go to work at 3 a.m., shower at the athletic club where Sarah worked, and then go to school."

"*Really*?" asked Jennifer. "Where did you park the camper when you slept? Weren't you scared?"

"That was one of the tricky parts I hadn't really thought through well. After trial and error, I discovered I could park in apartment complexes – ones that didn't have designated parking spaces, and no one would know I didn't belong.

"Was I *scared*? This is another example of how I'd lost my grounding. I was unable to determine for myself what was safe and what wasn't. Jay didn't discourage me from my plan, probably because he knew he would still have access to me if I didn't live with my parents," said Rachel.

"As the days passed and I had no contact with Jay, his hold over me started to diminish. I hadn't changed my mind about loving him, but I was so lonely that I needed to tell someone about my heartache. I told Sarah, Tom, and Deborah about Jay because they were not connected to the theology school in any way. I only told them about being in love and in a relationship. I didn't tell them about any of the more unconventional behavior. But breaking my silence meant others could influence me, which led to my willingness to go to parties with Sarah. I remember how good it felt to stand up for myself, to make my own decisions about how to interact with men.

"But the separation from Jay didn't last for long…"

June 23, 1983

Jay contacted me yesterday. He said he wanted to see me. We would have to be very careful, but he needed me and to feel my touch. I can't resist him. But now that I am living in my camper, finding a place to make love poses some problems. Last night, we parked close to some bushes in a park. We were in the middle of the act when a police spotlight caught Jay's rear end. We grabbed clothes and rushed to put them on, just like two teenagers. I thought it was kind of funny. When the cop approached, I could see that Jay was panicked. The officer looked from me to Jay. He wanted ID -- probably to check my age. He left us with a sharp warning. When I tried to laugh about it, Jay was not amused. I realized that he felt a lot more vulnerable than did I because of his marriage and job.

"That is pretty funny," chuckled Jennifer.

"Jay was really worried about being caught, so I kept searching for new locations, like this one…"

June 26, 1983

Tonight we parked behind my old elementary school. In the middle of sexual intercourse Jay tells me that he had an affair with his assistant, Elizabeth Nash, before he met me. He followed this admission with the affirmation that I was a better lover. I had done wonderful things with and for him that a good Catholic girl like Elizabeth would never do. I was special, he said.

As I listened, I felt nauseous and dizzy. Why had he not told me this before? He had pressed and pressed me to talk about every sexual experience I had ever had, and all that time he never told me about Elizabeth! She was with him at New Testament Revisited while I stayed at home with his son! I didn't know how to react. Jay says he was trying to protect me. He did what he thought he had to do -- misguided or not -- because he loved me so very much. He wanted me to feel safe. He says this disclosure will bring us closer. No secrets.

"I bet you were really mad. I hate it when guys lie," Jennifer said. She had wondered about Chris when he stayed out late and didn't look directly at her while providing an explanation for whereabouts.

"Mad? Yes, but hurt more than anything," said Rachel. "Still, I forgave him. But he kept making it harder for me…"

July 15, 1983

Damn him! Jay says he went to Elizabeth's apartment to work on some scholarly project. Then Mary arrived unexpectedly at the door. Jay happened to be getting out of the shower at the time. According to Jay, Elizabeth had no air conditioning and he had "worked up a sweat." Mary was outraged. Jay told me there was nothing to it, that it was bad timing on Mary's part. I believe him. I have to. He says I am the only one who understands him, and I need to believe that.

"You didn't really believe him, did you?" asked Jennifer.

"Not at first," said Rachel. "But I didn't say that to him. I wrote a poem for *myself* the next day that captures my feelings. I read it again yesterday. It's a little embarrassing to read because it is so self-pitying. But I want you to really understand what I was feeling, so here goes…"

July 16, 1983

Screaming at the top of my lungs and nobody hears me.
Disembodied soul but a good fuck nevertheless.
Can I care about a world that doesn't care about me?
All alone again.
Who does he drink with? Who does he talk to?
Who does he write for? Who was there when I called?
I hate Elizabeth!
What do I matter when she can supply everything he needs?
I hate you for making me love you, for setting me up, and for not loving me back.
I will not do this to myself again.
I will not become a victim of my own passion.

If it means becoming someone else's playmate, so be it.
Romance is dead. God is dead. Love exists only for poets
and dreamers.
I hate you Jay!
I hate you for being the best, the brightest, the most
wonderful human being I've ever met!
Retreat! Withdraw! I will not kill myself this way. I will not.

As Rachel read, Jennifer felt her skin grow hot. She moved
in her chair and flipped her hair to partially cover her face.
Fortunately, he mother's head was bowed to the paper she was
reading. These feelings were far too familiar.

"I was tearing apart inside," said Rachel. "I hated Jay and I
loved him. But neither emotion was strong enough to defeat the
other. Perhaps hate would have won, but the circumstances
changed again…"

July 22, 1983

Ironically, the "shower incident," as Jay calls it, is
working in my favor. Jay and Mary are in marriage therapy,
and the incident has become a topic of discussion. Mary is
beginning to see me as less threatening. Now she believes
that her suspicions about Jay's infidelity were misplaced. It
was Elizabeth all along. I will be able to see Ben again.

"I had been cleared of any misdoing, and I was happy
again. It's astounding to me how quickly I could go from furious
at Jay to rationalizing Jay's hurtful behavior." Rachel shook her
head. "When I was with him, it was as if all the good sense I had
completely disappeared!"

This, too, felt familiar, thought Jennifer.

"I finished summer school, moved back into an apartment,
and started theology school for my last semester of coursework,"
continued Rachel. "Jay and Mary separated. He moved out of his

house and into a carriage house apartment near the university. Jay continued to warn me to keep our relationship a secret. If Mary knew, he said, it would affect the divorce and custody arrangements. It would affect the school's decision about giving him tenure. I was highly motivated for both the divorce and tenure to occur.

"Meanwhile, I continued to have vivid dreams, like this one…"

August 31, 1983

I dreamed that I was on a familiar street on a Sunday morning delivering newspapers. The sun was just coming up. The next thing I knew I was being grabbed from behind, blindfolded, and, in a violent blur, raped repeatedly and forcefully until I passed out. When I came to, I noticed a young, well-dressed, black couple staggering and stumbling toward my parked car. As they drew closer, I observed their battered and swollen faces and bodies. I thought, "The rapist must have beaten them too." I said, "I've been raped by the same man." The police came, and I went to the hospital. The Rape Crisis staff met me at the emergency clinic with anxious faces. But when they saw it was me, their anxiety faded. They knew I could "handle it." It bothered me that they didn't worry. I was alone again, and I despaired when I realized what I had yet to do.

Then I was delivering the same paper route again. Suddenly, I was grabbed, but this time I faced my attacker. It was my old boyfriend Jason and he was drunk. "Why Jason? Why?" He raped me again. No words. All power. He stopped to take a drink from an enormous bottle of gold-colored liquor. "Jason, I loved you." He responded, "You hurt me." And I knew I would not turn him into the police.

"As you can hear, I was still very much traumatized by rape. My dream demonstrates how far I had to go before I could call myself a *survivor* and believe it," said Rachel.

"Did you ever think that 'Jason' might be 'Jay'? He was hurting you, but you protected him because he kept saying you were the one doing the hurting," said Jennifer.

"That's very insightful, Jen. You know, I don't think I ever made that connection," replied Rachel. Jennifer is so smart, thought Rachel. I wonder if she realizes she has a gift in being able to make these kinds of associations.

"I'll tell you what I did think though," said Rachel. "Alcohol had been Jason's Achilles heel, his weakness. I knew that about him because we had been intimately involved. And, on principle, I didn't think it was right to use my special knowledge against him. I guess that's the same way I acted with Jay."

Jennifer immediately thought about the different standards her parents used in relations to her and her brothers. Henry got away with so much more when he made bad decisions, while she and Sam would be punished for the same behavior. Cs were acceptable grades for Henry. Bs were fine for her in math and science, but As were expected in English and the social sciences. Sam was required to make *all* As. Her parents knew what each of them was capable of and modified their expectations accordingly.

Jennifer said, "But that leniency you are talking about has a breaking point, doesn't it? I mean, how far do you go? When is bad behavior that corresponds to someone's weakness *too much*? When do you start fighting back?"

"Those are very good questions. I hate to sound like a broken record – or broken CD or broken digital file," Rachel smiled. "But I will remind you again that I was impaired when it came to making decisions that protected me from harm." She paused. "I hope *you* will keep those questions in mind *always* when it comes to your relationships," she said.

Jennifer nodded.

"To continue the story," Rachel said. "Once Jay moved out of his house, he could no longer leave Ben with Mary when he wanted to see me on the nights when Ben was in his care. But his need – or whatever you want to call it – for me was so strong that he would wait until Ben was soundly sleeping and then leave him to come to my apartment."

"That is so *wrong*!" declared Jennifer, who had been a babysitter for her younger brothers and many of the neighbor children. She knew how quickly a safe situation could become a dangerous one with children.

"Yes. And it scared me. But I was so accepting of Jay's judgment that Ben would be fine, I made very little protest."

Rachel knew the next part of her story would be hard for Jennifer to hear, and they'd already covered so much that she would have to process. "Let's stop for today," she said.

CHAPTER SIXTEEN
THE LAW LIBRARY

On Tuesday, Jennifer got off work at 2:00 p.m. Driving home, as she was passing the AU campus, she impulsively turned to the right and onto the road that would take her to the law school. Parking was abysmal on campus unless you had a permit, so she drove beyond the law school and into a neighborhood where she found a spot in front of a house without parking prohibition signs. She walked the two blocks back to the law school. As she approached the building, she stopped. Did she really want the information she could obtain here? Maybe not. But she could get it and hold onto it until she decided what to do, if anything. She stepped forward and pulled the door open, looking left and right for signs to a library.

At the library, Jennifer surveyed the scene. It was a busy one. There were several groups of people, probably students, huddled in hushed conversations. A dozen or more individual students stared at computer screens, books and papers strewn around them on large desks or tables. A few people stood in the aisles of books, pulling them out and flipping through pages. Jennifer finally spotted what looked to be a reference desk, behind which stood a tall, skinny young man, wearing pants too large for his slender frame. He too was staring at a computer screen and running his fingers through his curly locks of hair. She approached him.

"Excuse me," said Jennifer. The man looked up.

"I'm looking for some information for a friend. She may have been..." she paused, "sexually assaulted." There was almost a question mark at the end of Jennifer's sentence.

The man's expression turned to one of concern. He was about to speak. But Jennifer suspected he would offer a kind of help she didn't want, so she cut him off.

"She's seeing a counselor. My friend is," said Jennifer. This announcement seemed to reassure the man and halt him from saying whatever he had on his mind to say.

"I was wondering," Jennifer continued, "if I could find out what the law says about her... situation, you know?"

The young man nodded, still looking concerned. "Are you a student here?" he asked.

"No. I live nearby and I thought this would be the best place to do my research," Jennifer said. She smiled, more aware now than she had ever been before that she was flirting to gain his assistance. "I don't know how to look up these laws." Jennifer batted her eyes. It was working, she thought.

The young man agreed to help. He walked her to a row of computers and logged her into a legal database using his own password. He clicked through several screens before he said, "You should find what you're looking for here, but if you need any more help, let me know." Jennifer smiled at him again and said, "You've been very kind. Thank you."

There was a slight blush to his face when he responded, "You're welcome. I'll be right over there." He gestured to the reference desk.

Jennifer turned to the statutes on the screen in front of her. She was in the Penal Code of the State of Texas. Title Five. Offenses Against the Person. Chapter 21. Sexual Offenses. She began reading the difficult language, pausing to reflect and going back to reread for comprehension. How had her mother done this for three years of law school?

It appeared that the age of "consent" was 16, maybe 14 for some offenses. That ruled out many of laws in her case. She had been 17 at the time. This was not 'sexual abuse of a child,' or 'trafficking' or 'prostitution.' There had been no 'homosexual conduct.' Texas was so backward in some ways, thought Jennifer. Not 'public lewdness,' not 'indecent exposure,' not 'indecency with a child.' Who knew there were so many illegal sexual acts?

Jennifer's breath caught. Here it was. Section 21.12. 'Improper Relationship Between Educator And Student.' She read in a whisper: "(a) an employee of a public or private primary or secondary school commits an offense if the employee (1) engages in sexual contact, sexual intercourse, or deviate sexual intercourse with a person who is enrolled in a public or private primary or secondary school at which the employee works." She didn't need to look any further, but she scanned down the page to find the penalty: "felony of the second degree." Jennifer gasped and looked around, hoping no one had noticed. She stood up and walked to the reference desk again.

"I'm done. Thank you for your help," she said to the young man who had watched her walk toward him. Jennifer gave a tentative smile and headed for the door.

Outside again, she felt her heart beating faster. What was she going to do? What was she going to do?

It was a beautiful day, not a cloud in the sky, she thought. She didn't have to do anything. Why would she? Look what her mother had been through. Jennifer took some deep breaths. If Mom wasn't running errands, she would be home thinking about what to make for dinner. She would go home and help her. She didn't do that often enough. She would go home and do something 'normal' and think about this later.

SUNDAY
OCTOBER 26, 2014

Chapter Seventeen
The Second Rape

Rachel took a deep breath. "Okay. We are about to get into another really intense episode. I don't know how to prepare you for it except to say that Jay was always looking for the next big thrill, and I was his go-to girl. I, of course, didn't comprehend this at the time. I took him at his word. And what he *said* was that he was helping me therapeutically to recover my sexual self from the trauma of rape."

"I'm sure that whatever you read is going to surprise me, since everything else has," said Jennifer, raising her eyebrows. "Just go ahead."

September 26, 1983

Jay's birthday is coming up in October. When I ask him what he wants, he says he really wants for me to arrange to have a couple come over to my apartment so that we can exchange sexual partners. He says it would be good for both of us.

I have told Jay about my sexual relationships with other men, but only because he requested that I do so. I feel like this has backfired on me because now Jay says that couple swapping or "swinging" is the next logical step in my progression toward recovery from rape. Jay also thinks that whatever we learn will benefit us as a couple. He says that someday we will be monogamous. However, during this very unstable period when we cannot date publicly, we have the opportunity to do things that are unconventional.

The idea frightens me. Where am I supposed to find a couple willing to engage in this activity? Even if I could find the couple, I don't want to be with anyone but Jay. I know

Jay enjoys living vicariously through my sexual experiences. I know Jay is insecure about his ability to pick up women. Most of his sexual relationships have somehow been tied to his intellectual prowess. In the arrangement he proposes now, I take responsibility for securing the woman's participation and I can't complain when he has sex with her!

October 5, 1983

Jay continues to plead with me to arrange a couple swap. He has worn me down. I told him I would try to find a couple, but the truth is that I don't have friends who do this sort of thing, and I don't know how to contact anyone else.

October 8, 1983

I did it! I made the arrangements for Jay's birthday party. I got up the nerve to talk with Devon, one of the district managers at the newspaper branch office who I have known for a long time. I have heard Devon talk about his sexual exploits at work. He even made comments, which I ignored at the time, about wanting to have sex with me. Through some of the things he and others said, I got the impression he might be open to the suggestion of a couple swap.

Yesterday, after I finished delivering my route, I went back to the warehouse and asked Devon to come out to my car to talk. I was sweating and my heart was racing. I slowly and carefully explained the proposal to him: He was being asked to come to a birthday party for Jay with a date. Jay's birthday present was to be an exchange of sexual partners for the evening. We would do this in the same room so that we could watch each other. Devon readily agreed to the proposal. The knot in my stomach loosened, and I asked him who he would bring. He said he didn't know yet. We agreed to discuss this in more detail at a later time... It's crazy, but I feel delighted just like I did the night I picked-up a stranger in a single's bar because I have fulfilled Jay's request.

When Jay visited me tonight, I presented him with an "coupon" to his party: "Good for one free "group sex experience" with an agreeable -dare I say "titillated" - black couple on Wed. night, November 2nd. Be there!"

Jay was ecstatic!

October 16, 1983

Somebody please believe me. This is the truth. I swear it's the truth: Devon insisted he had to come over to my apartment to see how I planned to arrange things. He arrived after work this morning. I offered coffee to him and he offered cocaine to me. I have never seen cocaine, much less used it, so I declined, but Devon snorted it. We talked for a while and I walked him to the door to say goodbye. As we approached the door, he lurched ahead, locked the door, and stood facing me with his back to the door. He unbuttoned his pants. Devon said he wanted to "sample my services" to see if he wanted to go through with the birthday party. I thought maybe he was bluffing, but I started to panic. I told myself he was just harassing me the way he often did. Lately he has been so nice. I said, "Not fair. This is Jay's birthday party and he doesn't get the chance to sample in advance."

Devon didn't care. I felt very angry because this bastard knew what I had been through with the rape and trial this past year. He was one of the men who came to the Midtown Retirement Towers to get the undelivered newspapers from me on the morning I was raped. He also knew how hard it was for me to ask this favor. Damn him! But I was torn. I felt guilty for not wanting to appease Devon to make sure that Jay would get his present.

I bargained and pleaded with Devon. I kept saying it wasn't fair to Jay, but Devon wasn't listening. He put his hand on my shoulders and shoved me to my knees. He pulled his erect penis out of his pants and forced my head down on it. I mumbled some sort of agreement -- "but only this..." Devon wanted more.

Suddenly, my rage kicked in. I remembered the trial and the way I had been accused by the defense of not fighting harder to escape -- from my own car, in a neighborhood I didn't know, from a strange man who had bruised and pinched and raped me, and who claimed to have a knife! I told Devon: "No! Not now. You have to wait for the birthday party." He still didn't seem to be listening. I tried to run, but he had hold of me. I crawled and dragged myself, but he was holding on. I got through two rooms. He caught me at the bedroom door. I was on hands and knees and he was behind me. I was exhausted. He grabbed me and threw me on my bed. No way! Not on my bed -- Jay's and my bed. I struggled and slipped through his grasp. I was headed for the locked door with Devon behind me now. He caught me at the bedroom door again and forced me to the floor. I could feel him trying to enter me. "No. Don't do this!" He wasn't stopping. Then I remembered the tampon. I yelled, "Please let me take the tampon out first before you stick it in." He jerked the tampon out, entered me, and my mind disappeared into the clouds.

"Oh my God!" gasped Jennifer. Rachel glanced up at her daughter and suddenly became aware of the tension in her own muscles. She had to finish the story now before she lost her nerve.

Devon thanked me and said something about how he would enjoy the birthday party. I was stunned and numb. This was crazy. Then I thought of two things: call the Director at Rape Crisis and call Jay. The ironic circumstance was that this was the day I was supposed to resume volunteer work at the Rape Crisis Center. I knew I couldn't do it now. I called the Director and told her I had just been raped again and wouldn't be able to come to work. She asked me to come to the hospital. I said, "No."

Maybe my recent dream was a foreshadowing of things to come. What would I say to the police? I brought this on myself, didn't I? Why did I let Devon come over in the first place? I couldn't face the medical and legal ordeal again. I told the Director I would be in touch.

When I told Jay what happened over the phone, he was angry. He said Devon was a son-of-a-bitch. I could tell that Jay wasn't mad because of what had happened to me. He was mad for the same reason I had given Devon: it wasn't fair that Jay didn't get to sample too. I told Jay that it felt like rape. Jay assured me that it wasn't. His big concern now is finding out what kind of woman Devon is bringing to the party. He feels that Devon has taken unfair advantage of him. I feel sick. Jay said he couldn't come over, but that I will see him soon.

I have been sitting here for a long time in my room, knowing I was raped. Jay just can't see it. But I understand where Jay is coming from. I have to accept this. I need to go about my business, knowing I have the birthday party ahead of me, knowing I can't back out.

Rachel thought about the next journal entry, and looked up. "I think we need to take a break, stretch, get a drink, or something," she said.

Jennifer's heart was beating fast. She could almost hear it. Her mother had been raped *again*. And it was worse this time than the last. Mom couldn't tell a soul. Jennifer understood that. Could she have prevented it? It was Jay's fault really. He had trapped her in an impossible situation. Mom *had* to get away from him. When would she figure that out? But she loved him. Jennifer knew that feeling, and she knew how hard it was to let go of someone you loved.

Jennifer took a deep breath and stood up, feeling a little light-headed. She steadied herself and followed her mother out of the carriage house and to the kitchen. Mom had made a pitcher of lemonade earlier. Now she poured two large glasses. Without thinking, Jennifer drank her entire glass without stopping.

"You were thirsty," Rachel said with surprise.

"I must have been," Jennifer replied, wiping her hand across her mouth. She was acutely aware that neither of them was talking about the rape – the elephant in the room.

Just then, Sam and Henry burst through the door and into the kitchen. "You are not going to believe the picture Meredith just posted on Facebook of her and Jake," exclaimed Henry, slapping Sam on the back and turning to Jennifer and their mother.

Jake was a star pitcher on the school's highly ranked baseball team. He had recently started dating the very scholarly senior class president. Meredith, Sam had informed the family, was applying to almost every Ivy League school, and no one doubted she would get into at least one of them. Jake, on the other hand, was a mediocre student, but as a talented athlete would likely attend college on a baseball scholarship. They were an unlikely couple.

Although Henry was now at a private school, Sam kept Henry apprised of the gossip at their local high school, particularly related to the senior class members who had once been Henry's classmates.

"You tell them, Sam," said Henry, grinning from ear to ear.

"Well, Meredith. You know Meredith. She's taken every AP class and aced them. So now she's filling her schedule with electives." Sam smiled in his knowing way. "This semester she's taking sewing. *Sewing!* So, anyway, she made these Salt and Pepper Shaker costumes for her and Jake to wear to the Halloween party at the country club."

Henry burst out laughing again. "Oh, my God! You should see the picture of them that's posted. The costumes have these little holes for their faces and they're crooked! They look ridiculous like… Sam, what's the name of that TV show we used to watch as kids?" Henry said, turning to Sam.

"Teletubbies," grinned Sam.

"Right! They look like lumpy gray and white Teletubbies!" laughed Henry.

Sam turned to Henry and said, "Did you notice the look on Jake's face? It's like 'I'm regretting this already'!" Henry put his arm around Sam's shoulder and the boys turned back toward the office and computers without waiting for a response from Jennifer and Mom.

The boys had broken the tension, Jennifer thought. They were crazy, those two. And it wasn't often that they got along. But Jennifer was remembering a time at Costco. Her mother had taken them there to get some pictures developed, back when printing pictures required developing film first. She must have been around eleven and her brothers were seven and five. They fought over everything: who got to sit in what seat in the car, who got to pick the music in the car, who got the last brownie, and so on. They routinely talked about how much they *hated* each other. "He *always* steals my things," Henry would say. "He hits and pinches me," Sam would say.

On that day at Costco, while Mom was trying to place an order for photos, Henry and Sam were wrestling in the DVD aisle, pulling each other's shirts, yelling and screeching, as

DVDs flew off the shelves. Mom was flustered and Jennifer, well, she wasn't getting involved in another dispute between the boys. Inevitably, she would be blamed for making the situation worse.

After apologies to the nice employee who had started picking up the mess they made, the family was off to make their purchases. At first, the battles continued. But then, the boys' common consumerism emerged. They joined forces to select a certain sour candy, enormous bags of chips, the proper size shrimp, the preferred juice. Pretty soon, they were arm in arm. Jennifer could hear them chanting in the meat section: "We want chicken!! We want chicken!!" They giggled and ran. They took each other to the bathroom and came back reporting that each had washed and dried their hands – a real accomplishment.

As they were checking out, Jennifer had turned to her mother and their very full basket and said, "I thought we just came here for one thing."

Her mom said, "Yep. That was the plan. But after we survived the DVD crisis and the boys moved on to making the most of their shopping experience *without* nagging me about buying toys or claiming that I was treating one of them better than the other, I got caught up in just *being* with them in their enthusiasm. When Henry demonstrates that he remembers how much Sam loves shrimp and goes to find it for him, how can I refuse to buy the shrimp? When Henry and Sam collaborate on selecting a desired dessert, how can I say 'no'? I really am a sucker for brotherly love."

Jennifer looked at her mother now and saw her beaming. She still loved it when her brothers got along. But in light of everything else Jennifer had learned about her mother recently, this love of compromise and reconciliation took on new meaning. Mom had sacrificed herself to keep the peace with Jay and to keep Devon around for the birthday party.

Rachel was remembering many of the times her boys had quarreled and her helplessness in the face of it. It seemed she either lost her temper or folded in weakness. She was always trying to find the right balance. They were so *different* from each other. Henry needed a firm hand, but Sam wilted if spoken to in harsh tones.

She remembered the time Henry stayed with the neighbors across the street for a night when the rest of the family was out of town. He had been given strict instruction to come into the house only to feed the dog. Instead, he had a ten-year-old's equivalent of an unauthorized keg party while they were gone. When they returned home, they found a case of partially drunk root beer cans distributed in several rooms. The furniture had been rearranged to accommodate movie watching in the family room. The pantry had been ransacked, and open bags of chips, pop tart wrappers, and cereal bowls with souring milk were on counters and floors. There was trash in the backyard, broken glass in the basement, and a large snapping turtle retrieved from the creek. Oh, my...

By way of contrast, Sam had such a gentle spirit. Rachel remembered Sam's second grade honors program. He made Principal's honor roll and received the "caring heart" award for the child who is the first to respond when someone has an accident, needs help, or is being teased. Rachel remembered thinking how grateful she was that Sam could be so kind when Henry wasn't around.

On Sam's eighth birthday that year, he had said to her, "I love the gifts, but the best gifts of all are hugs and kisses... Actually, the best gift I could receive would be for Henry to treat me better." All Rachel could do was tell him that she thought that would be the best gift too. So, moments like this, moments when Henry and Sam enjoyed each other's company, always warmed her heart.

Rachel and Jennifer looked at each other. Jennifer was the first to speak. "That was... random," and raised her hands in a questioning gesture. Rachel chuckled. "Yes. But it's good to see them having fun."

"You ready?" Rachel asked. And Jennifer knew she meant "to go back for more of the story."

166

"I am if you are," she replied.

CHAPTER EIGHTEEN
BIRTHDAY PARTY

*B*ack in the carriage house, Rachel said to Jennifer, "I know we haven't talked about me being raped again. We will. But I want you to hear the rest of this part about Devon first, okay?"

"What more could there be?" thought Jennifer. But she said, "Sure. Go ahead."

November 2, 1983

The party was tonight. Jay arrived in advance. He was noticeably nervous. Neither of us had ever done something like this. Jay said I had an advantage because I had had sex with strangers before and I had had "sex" with Devon before. He said I would know what to do. I was a "natural." I was just glad that Jay would be with me. I thought he could protect me. I had seen Devon out of control.

Devon arrived with an attractive, very young-looking, plump black woman. I wondered if she knew what was going on. She seemed hesitant to be here. Everyone seemed nervous except Devon, who must have been high as a kite. We had some drinks and casual conversation. The other woman didn't say much. Jay was looking her over. At some point, the decision was made that we should get on with the task at hand. We moved toward our respective partners and began kissing and touching. Devon was ready. In a matter of minutes, he was fucking me hard and moaning. We were all in the same room. I knew Jay was with the other woman. I didn't want to watch, but I had to see how he was doing. I was nervous for him. From the corner of my eye I could see Jay. He was having trouble staying erect. He seemed frantic. He seemed to be motioning for me to come over to him, to get him started.

I didn't want to care what happened to him. I hated him and didn't hate him all at once. I felt sorry for him, but I didn't want to take responsibility for him. He had gotten us into this. I was going to do all that I had agreed to and nothing more.

My pity overtook me. I knew he wasn't skilled at this. And I didn't want him to feel bad afterwards. I got loose from Devon and went over to Jay. We briefly exchanged partners. Devon's date seemed much happier and I knew how to touch Jay to excite him. Then we exchanged back. Jay was still having problems, but I wasn't going to care anymore. I acted my part to the maximum. I moaned and groaned and played right along. When it was finally over, I was tired and I could see that Jay was frustrated and jealous.

Devon and his date left. Jay wanted me to talk about what it was like to have "that big cock thrusting and grinding inside of me." I just wanted to be left alone. But I knew that Jay wouldn't back off until I told him all about it, and then told him he was a better lover. I was sore and bruised, but Jay, who had not really been able to do much with the other woman, wanted to fuck me again. I let him, though it hurt.

Jay confessed he felt like he had failed, but that it was the girl's fault. She hadn't gotten into it. She seemed to want only Devon. Then he said I should try to arrange another visit from Devon and a different lover! Jay was sure he would be better prepared the second time around.

The last thing I want is to have Devon's cock inside of me again. I will tell Jay that it can't be done. There isn't another girl. Jay says he wants to talk with Devon directly to demand a better sex partner, but I doubt he will do it.

Rachel slowly put the journal down, afraid to look at Jennifer.

Jennifer leaped from her seat and exclaimed, "I am so freakin' angry at Jay! And I don't know whether I'm angry at you or just so, so sorry and hurt for you."

Rachel shook her head slowly. "I know. I have similar feelings. It happened so long ago that my distance prompts me to judge – You fool! But there is another part of me that can't forget how small my world was then. Jay was 'God' and I was his servant.

"I remember what my hopes had been: A night of couple swapping with Devon and his girlfriend would put an end to these uncomfortable sexual experiences with strangers. Jay and I could settle down to a more ordinary life. Instead, the whole thing backfired. Jay said, in his charming manner, 'You are obviously a person who needs a lot of good, hard fucking. You are not ready to settle down.' It was outrageous! And it was a 'Catch 22.' I knew that if I didn't participate fully, Jay would accuse me of not being my true self. He would say I was holding back. He would ask for a repeat performance. There was no way to win the argument."

"But Devon *raped* you," said Jennifer.

"Jay never, *ever* mentioned the day Devon raped me. I had proven, after the fact, that – quote: 'You got off on his big cock.' There certainly wasn't a legal remedy. No police officer, lawyer, judge, or jury would believe that I had not asked for what I got. I let Devon back into my house to fuck me 'consensually' just a few days later. My only recourse was to try to put it out of my mind. I thought I could, at the time. But a person doesn't forget when she's been raped and not believed."

"Oh, Mom," sighed Jennifer.

"I was boxed in," said Rachel. "Jay could be so understanding and empathic. I had put all my trust in him. But then he would torment me with demands for sexual performance that prevented me from healing the division between mind and body when it came to sex. I wasn't a whole person. I had no defense. I should have run to others, but my behavior seemed unforgivable to me. There seemed to be no place for me in the legal system, in church, at school, or in my family. I was caught in a vicious cycle and couldn't see my way out."

Jennifer thought about her mother's allegiance to Jay. Outrageous! But then her thoughts turned to Henry. Hadn't her mother been similarly protective and loyal to her brother?

When Henry was little, he never did as he was told. When it was time to cleanup, Henry would dump another box of toys in defiance. When Mom put him to bed, he never stayed put. Mom often looked exhausted in the morning while Henry slept peacefully when he should have been getting ready for preschool.

In elementary school, it was his ADHD. Henry was always in trouble for being disruptive and not doing his work. He got into fights with other kids. He was rude to teachers. But Mom insisted he be tested for learning differences. She found another school for Henry that catered to kids with ADHD, and hired tutors who were patient with him. She took him to see a play therapist. She kept him busy with sports to burn off some of his energy. And she apologized for his behavior all the time. It seemed to Jennifer now that Mom had made apologies in her own mind for Jay's "differences" too.

Then Jennifer remembered a morning that Dad was out of town and Mom was getting everyone ready for school. The bus that stopped in front of their driveway was coming, and Henry had not eaten or put on his socks and shoes. He kept wandering off to get his hamster out of its cage. When the bus arrived, Mom grabbed Henry, his shoes, and his backpack and carried them out the door while Henry wailed. Jennifer was already on the bus and saw her mother shove the shoes and backpack into Henry's hands as she dropped him on the bus steps. Henry was crying and stuck his tongue out at Mom as the bus roared away.

Right after lunch, Jennifer was in the front office delivering some papers for her teacher when Mom arrived and asked permission to speak with Henry. Jennifer dawdled in the hall, watching, as her mother took Henry from his first grade class and walked him to the cafeteria. Jennifer couldn't hear what her mother was saying, but she saw Henry rolling around on the floor. She remembered thinking, "Mom tries too hard. Henry is not worth the effort."

After school, Mom sat with Henry to try to get him to focus on doing his homework so that the family could all go to the neighborhood pool. Henry refused to cooperate. He kept leaving to play with his hamster. But, when she and Sam, who was in Pre-K, had finished their homework, Mom packed them into the van and headed for the pool. She told Henry that he could not swim until his work was done. When he saw the others swimming, he quickly finished his homework and joined them.

As they climbed in the van to return home, Henry handed Mom a scrap of cardboard. He said, "I did this at school." As Mom read it, Jennifer remembered that she looked like she was about to cry. Jennifer asked to see the cardboard. It said, "I Luv Mom."

Yes, Mom had patience. And that wasn't always a bad thing, thought Jennifer. She was patient with Henry, and her loyalty and assistance paid off. Even though he rarely acknowledged her advocacy as a good thing, she didn't doubt that Henry knew he benefitted from Mom's faith in him.

Jennifer wondered if Jay had felt the same way. She wondered if Jay knew how patient, loyal, faithful, and trustworthy her mother could be. He didn't deserve her. But Jennifer suspected he knew he had someone special in Mom.

Rachel's voice interrupted Jennifer's thoughts. "I won't put you through hearing about most of the other sexual episodes – of which there were many. But let me explain the basic set-up. After the night with Devon and the girl, Jay told me that our future together would be exclusive, but that *this* was the time for us to explore our sexual desires so that when we did become exclusive, we would have a better understanding of what we wanted from each other. My assigned mission was to meet men, have sex with them, and report back to Jay. I went out dressed very seductively each time, accepted drinks from strangers, played pool or darts, and flirted to gain attention until I could score. When I returned to Jay, he wanted to hear all the details of these sexual encounters: penis size, acrobatic ability, stamina, pleasure noises, and so forth."

Had she said too much? Rachel wondered again. Could Jen handle this? Rachel remembered the time she had shown a scary Halloween email to Jennifer when her daughter was five or six. The email instructed the reader to look for something in the picture and then, suddenly, a ghoulish face appeared and made a hideous scream. Jennifer had responded by screaming herself, crying, shaking, and clinging to Rachel's legs. Jennifer was unable to go to bed alone for many nights after. She would not even go in her room when it was time for bed, but slept with Rachel and Kevin. When Kevin carried her back to her own bed, if she woke, Rachel had to take a pillow and blanket into Jennifer's room and stay with her until she fell asleep again. It was an unsustainable situation.

One night, as Kevin carried Jennifer back to bed, Jennifer wailed, "Monsters!"

Rachel asked, "Where are they?"

"Under the bed," Jennifer replied.

"Let's look," Rachel suggested. She peered under the bed and said, "There were no monsters."

"They come later," Jennifer protested.

"Well, then. We must make monster poison."

Off they trouped to the kitchen. Rachel got out a pan, put a little water in it, and opened the spice drawer. To the water they added Tabasco sauce, red pepper flakes, garlic, bay leaves, black pepper, and everything else they could think of to make a distasteful "poison" that would kill the monsters and send them away *forever*. Then Rachel carried the pan to Jennifer's bedroom and placed it under her bed.

Jennifer still wanted Rachel to stay in her room, though she was markedly less stressed. From a different room, Henry called for "Mommy." Rachel told Jennifer she had to see what Henry wanted, but that she'd be back. After Rachel comforted and settled Henry, she listened. No cries. Jennifer had gone to sleep. In the morning, thanks to some help from Kevin in the middle of the night, some of the liquid had been "drunk" – a sure sign that the monsters had been poisoned. After that, Jennifer could sleep alone again.

Did Jennifer need "monster poison" now? If so, what would it be? Rachel had already gone so far into the darkness of her journey, she couldn't simply stop. She was going to find the light again. But she needed to show Jennifer the *way* to it. And that required going through more darkness first. Rachel sighed...

CHAPTER NINETEEN
KEEPING TRACK

At her mother's mention of "penis size" and other descriptors, Jennifer felt herself blushing again. Would she ever get used to Mom's graphic language? She gulped, "I hesitate to ask… Did you enjoy it at *all*?"

"Truth?" asked Rachel. "I'd like to tell you that my body did not respond to the touch of other men, but that would not be true. Those subsequent sexual events were not like rape – the forced entry of a penis into my dry vagina. But my physiological response to the sexual touch of strange men was just that: a *physiological* response. I learned this from adult survivors of child sexual abuse years later. Many survivors carry the heavy weight of guilt for what happened to them because their young bodies responded to touches that were forbidden, touches that emotionally hurt and scarred them. But a child's physiological response does not make him or her culpable. Their bodies – all our bodies – are designed to respond to sexual touch. I, too, felt guilty and culpable because my body did what Jay asked it to do. My physical response to touch seemed to confirm Jay's suspicion that sex is what I desired."

Jennifer thought about this. She thought of David. What her mother said resonated with her. She wasn't "bad" because she responded to him.

"There is one thing I wrote about this time that I want to read to you," Rachel said. "I didn't write this in 1984. I wrote it years later when I was working with a therapist to recover memories of what I'd been through."

All of my dealings with men as sexual partners prior to June 1982 were with men who were "whole people" to me. They had jobs or school. They had parents, siblings, and friends. They had endearing or annoying characteristics or habits. Before I was raped, the men I had sex with had first and last names. I had heard jokes about men with little black books filled with names of women and their phone numbers, or jokes about notches on a bed post to indicate sexual scoring, but I never imagined I might one day carry my own book or keep score. Still, I started to wonder if I would remember them all. I didn't want to forget them. Remembering seemed like a way of holding on to my sanity. This was happening. It was not a dream.

I saw an advertisement in a magazine for a "sperm bank." It was a white ceramic bank shaped like a sperm with a large head and squiggly tail. There was a slot in the head of the sperm to insert coins. I ordered it. When it arrived, I cut small squares of paper and on each square I wrote the name of a man with whom I had had sex. I wrote last names if I knew them. I put each piece of paper in my sperm bank. I added new squares of paper to the bank over time. I could open the bank and spread the bits of paper out in front of me. I could pick up each one and try to recall the time and place, his face and some of our conversation.

Rachel reached in the cardboard box and felt the cool, hard shape of the sperm bank. It was still there. She did not need to open the bank or read the names. It was enough to know the bank and men were real – evidence of where she'd been, physically and emotionally, at that point in her life. She lifted the sperm bank to show it to Jennifer.

Jennifer was both intrigued and repulsed by the sperm bank. "I'm not sure I get it," she said. "Why was it important to you to keep the names?"

"I wasn't proud of what I was doing. I had this perfectly normal student-worker persona in the light of day. But I also led a secret life at night, a life that made me feel ashamed except when I was with Jay. You've probably heard of people having amnesia about really tragic events. Their minds forget to protect them from being re-traumatized. For me, it was like that too. My nightlife was becoming a blur. But I still had a rebellious part of me that was angry enough at Jay to say: 'Through this act of keeping the sperm bank, I've got evidence that I let real men put their body parts in mine because you told me to. It's not something I am going to forget when you decide it's time for me to forget.'

"I've always tried to be a truthful person, Jen, even when I was being *untruthful*. I knew, at some level, *this* truth about what I was doing was important. I needed a way to hold it or capture it until the day I would be able to bring it into the light."

"And that day is today... with me," said Jennifer.

"It is. But there was a time before today when this truth came to light in therapy. It was part of my healing process. Today, I'm sharing it with you because you deserve to know who I really am. We are part of each other – the good and the bad. What each of us has been through and will go through affects the other because we love each other."

Rachel's words warmed Jennifer. Yet, she was frustrated because she couldn't put all the pieces together. She wanted to get to the end of the story so that her mother's message would be clear. But she'd seen the cardboard box. There were more notebooks. She would have to continue to be patient.

"I want to share this next journal entry with you because I think that after hearing about Devon and more sex with strange men, it's easy to lose sight of how I felt about Jay," said Rachel. "Here's what I wrote..."

January 15, 1984

Oh, Jay. I fantasize about going to sleep with you by my side and awakening to find you there still nestled close to me in the warmth and peacefulness of sleep. To walk hand-in-hand down a wooded trail with the afternoon's sun breaking through the tree-tops and the crunch, crunch of autumn's fallen leaves under our feet. Lying face-up on an old wooden dock at night making wishes, identifying constellations, telling ghost stories. Setting out at 4:00 a.m. through the silence and whiteness of a snow-covered world to trudge in unison to that special clearing where the moon's reflected light reveals our weary but happy faces after a long night's work pouring over books and letters in stuffy libraries and studies. Running into the surf, tumbling into each other's arms, laughing, licking and kissing away the salty stickiness on nose, ears, eyes, and neck. Bundled in winter's trappings, fighting through Christmas crowds, noises, and colored lights, caught up in its whir of excitement, we sit still for a bit to share a steamy hot cup of coffee and I gasp when I am caught by the sudden fire in your eyes.

"You were such a romantic!" said Jennifer. Her thoughts immediately turned to David and their romantic beginning. After those first kisses in David's coaching office, he had offered to drive her home. She watched him as he drove and took in his beauty. He was so sexy! She couldn't believe her good fortune. He had chosen *her*.

When he stopped his truck a block from her house, beside a wooded area where no houses had been built, he slid over the bench seat and pulled her to him. They were hot and sticky. Their arms and legs wrapped around each other. His hand slipped under her bra and he cradled her breast. His hand moved between her legs and she moaned. She could feel his hardness pressed against her and she stroked him through his clothes until he, too, was moaning. He whispered, "Oh my God, I want you so much."

Then he pulled back and looked her in the eyes. "Do you want this as badly as I do?" he asked. She nodded.

He looked around at the neighborhood. "Not here," he said. He looked deep in thought as his breathing slowed.

He looked back at her and gently smoothed her damp hair away from her face with one hand, while he held her hand tightly with his other hand. "I checked the schedule," he said. "You have a soccer game tomorrow and I have a track meet. We should both be back at school by 7 o'clock. Can you meet me after? I'll take you out to dinner."

Jennifer nodded. She thought, Henry has a soccer game out of town and Mom will be with him. Dad will be driving Sam to dance class and then taking him to dinner. She had overheard their conversation yesterday.

The next day, she could barely focus on anything but her upcoming date. It was hard to pay attention in class or to listen attentively when friends spoke to her. It was only during the soccer game that she forgot about David and, surprisingly, played one of the best games of her life. Afterward, she silently attributed her success to his influence.

For the first time ever, she took advantage of the showers in the locker room, foregoing her usual modesty. She couldn't go out dirty and smelling of sweat. Though her hair was still wet, she was clean, dressed, and waiting for her date fifteen minutes before the scheduled time. At five minutes before seven, Coach Reese arrived back at school with two team members. Jennifer pretended to be reading one of her assigned novels for British Literature as he said "goodbye" to the students, watched them get in their own cars, and drive away. She noticed that David looked around before walking toward the gym where she was standing. The school was deserted.

"Let's go," David said, and Jennifer followed him to his truck. Once seated, he patted her leg, smiled, and began a thirty-minute drive out of town to a small Italian restaurant that Jennifer had never seen before. As they drove, David told her about the track meet and she reported on their winning soccer game.

The restaurant was dimly lit with candles on the tables. Once they were seated, David told her how beautiful she looked in the candlelight. He was quick to add that any contact between them outside of school needed to be their secret. He gently admonished her to never speak of their relationship to her friends. She was so flattered by his interest, Jennifer thought now, she would have agreed to anything he asked of her.

David took control. He seemed to know the menu, and he ordered for them. Though she had been hungry before, Jennifer could barely eat. She forced a few mouthfuls so as not to appear impolite in the face of this generosity. When he reached across the table to take her hand, his touch made her shiver. He smiled. "Let's get outta here," he said.

David paid the bill, and then motioned for her to get up, wrapped his arm around her waist, and ushered her out the door and back into his truck. He drew her across the bench seat to him and kissed her deeply on the mouth. "I know a place," he said. Jennifer nodded.

While David entered the office of the Sleep-Inn to purchase a room, Jennifer sat in the truck. There were only three other cars in the parking lot. She couldn't turn back now, she thought. She didn't want to. This felt like a dream, and she pinched herself to make sure she was really here, really with HIM.

David approached her side of the truck, holding out a keycard in his hand, and smiling broadly. He opened her door and whisked her into his arms. His excitement was a complete turn-on. She felt electrified.

They found the room and entered. He pulled her close, moving his hands up and down her sides, and then cupping her face as he kissed her. Suddenly, he stopped and straightened. "I don't want to move too fast. I want to see everything. I want to experience all of your beauty," David said. Jennifer felt a surge of pure elation. David found the light switch and turned it on.

What happened next was poetry in motion. They took their time, removing items of clothing and exploring each other's bodies. David's tongue and fingers were everywhere. He asked what pleasured her and, when she found it difficult to respond, he experimented with all of her parts, from toes to earlobes, enjoying the sounds and movements she made. When he finally entered her, she exploded in a kind of ecstasy she had never known before

"You look lost in thought," said Rachel, breaking Jennifer's trance. Her mother's head was tilted to the side as if waiting for the answer to a question.

"Oh. It's nothing. I was… I was just remembering…" Jennifer didn't know how to complete her sentence.

"Chris?" Rachel asked.

Jennifer nodded, hoping she appeared sincere. She had regained her composure and said, "After all that you'd been through. I don't know how you could still feel this way about Jay."

"He was an amazing man – at least to me. He was the *wrong* man. He was working out his own demons through me. And because of all I'd been through, it took me a long time to figure that out. But part of the reason I put up with all I put up with was because I loved him for a long time," said Rachel.

"Let me stop reading for a few minutes and add some analysis to my relationship with Jay, okay?" said Rachel.

Jennifer nodded.

"I remember that Jay believed firmly in the idea that one could alter contexts and produce 'pure' or 'fundamental' behaviors. One could obtain 'real sex' absent the moral context in which it had first appeared in our histories. He believed utter disorientation was the goal to be sought because in that state new meanings would emerge," said Rachel.

"The difficulty, of course, is that utter disorientation deprives everyone - except the creator of the new situation - of self-protective defenses that insure survival. I understood challenging limits, but I never understood abandoning them altogether. My relationship with Jay was one in which he - more frightened than I - called the shots. Owing to my vulnerability and dependence on his judgments, I initiated the prohibited activity to facilitate achievement of goals he would not have been brave enough to attempt without me. He brought the ideas. I brought the backbone. He clarified his needs and values through this dependent relation on me, whereas I lived the sensual life he longed for and became more and more divided between body and soul.

"I do not believe it is an overstatement to say that Jay, at that time, wanted me to embody or to *be sex*. And the exercises he assigned to me or to us both were supposed to bring me closer to that ideal. However, the more sexual I became, the less likely Jay would take me into the public world because I represented the opposite of academia. At the same time, I allowed Jay a sensual self and, therefore, he could not give me up. My self-definition increasingly became: a sexual being to be used for sexual purposes."

"That makes sense in a bizarre kind of way. So, how long did this go on? I mean, the time you spent picking up strangers for sex," Jennifer asked.

"Devon happened in October and November 1983, and then the pick-ups for four or five months. By March 1984, I'd had enough. I needed a break, and I told him so," said Rachel. "It was self-preservation. I had been doing all the risk taking. I used Jay's logic against him. I said we needed to experience what it felt like to be single so that we could freely choose each other. Also, I hoped some distance would help him appreciate all of my efforts. It was risky – letting him loose – but I was exhausted by the pattern we had set.

"Initially, I breathed a sigh of relief. But it didn't take long for me to feel lonely. The problem was, by this point, I had forgotten how to have a *normal* relationship – a relationship where you meet and get to know each other by spending time together eating, playing, and doing activities you both enjoy. I had learned the habit of responding first to men's sexual desires. Indeed, I was attracted like a magnet to men who wished to control me. One such man was an old college professor. I struck up a conversation with him, and by that night, we were in bed."

"A *professor*?" asked Jennifer.

"Another old habit… I'm not sure how, but Jay discovered that I was involved in this new relationship and came storming over to my apartment. Listen to this…"

March 21, 1984

Jay showed up at my apartment unannounced, drunk and angry. He was so angry that he started throwing glasses and shattering them. I was scared.

Then Jay calmed down and told me that he had been to see his father. His father verbally abused him and kept the liquor coming. Jay said his father "tried to kill him" by putting him into his car when he knew Jay was in no condition to drive.

I knew that Jay's anger with his father had intensified his anger with me. My lover and best friend was in extreme pain. He asked me to make love to him -- actually, to "fuck him." It was the last thing I wanted to do. He needed to be held and comforted, but he couldn't see it. He also couldn't get an erection. He pushed my head down on his penis and told me to get him hard. He reeked of alcohol and sweat. I thought I was going to vomit, but I did what I was told. For what seemed like hours, I sucked and stroked him until he finally had an erection. Then we had sexual intercourse. I left my body while Jay was with me. I couldn't stand him that way.

"Gross," grimaced Jennifer. "It was almost like when you were raped."

"Yes. But this was new with Jay. This was unwanted sex *with Jay*. I made excuses for him – and for myself," said Rachel.

Jennifer didn't want to think about undesired sexual activities. "What happened with the college professor?" Jennifer asked.

"I told him I couldn't see him anymore," said Rachel. "Jay needed me. And we had so much history together that I felt like I was the only one who understood his pain. But it wasn't long before Jay confessed that he had been with Elizabeth again. That hurt. But what right did I have to criticize?

"In therapy, years after these events, I learned that men like Jay who have been deeply hurt by childhood experiences may use destructive aggression and sexualized fantasies as a substitute for connection with others. Taking control of another's sexuality -- with the extreme form being rape -- is a more comfortable way of being physically close for someone who is incapable of intimacy. The need for touch is met without the frightening possibility of vulnerability to another. But in 1984, all I knew was that I *identified* with Jay's pain, and my heart went out to him. I was treading water, moving no closer to healing after all this time."

Jennifer wondered how her mother was ever going to leave Jay. She knew she did. Jennifer was living proof of that. How would the cycle – and insanity – be broken?

Chapter Twenty
STD and Cocaine

"*Moving* on," said Rachel. "It wasn't until the spring of 1984 that I did my ten weeks of student teaching in high school social studies to complete the requirements to be certified as a teacher by the state. I was ready to start job-hunting that summer.

"Finding a job was difficult. The counties in which I wanted to work were trying to hire more minority candidates. I supported the idea – much as I supported affirmative action. But the policy disadvantaged me. My willingness to coach basketball, volleyball, or soccer didn't compensate for my majority status -- white female -- or my lack of experience. But I kept looking and interviewing.

"Then came some shocking news in mid-June. I found out I had herpes," said Rachel.

"A sexually transmitted disease," interrupted Jennifer. "Maybe that was inevitable. I'm sorry, Mom. Did you know where you got it?" Jennifer knew herpes was a virus for which there was no cure. It stayed in your body permanently. It was hard to imagine her mother having a STD.

"No. My doctor said it could lie dormant for several months and, as you know, I had been with many men in several months," replied Rachel.

"Hearing you speak so calmly about STDs reminds me that I ought to tell you, I was living in a different era than you are now. Your generation is educated about HIV and AIDS, and about using condoms – not only for pregnancy prevention, but also for prevention of STDs.

"The 1980s was a period of freedom and of ignorance. We were 'free' to have sex with anyone and everyone because of the availability of the birth control pill. But we were also 'ignorant' because the first AIDS cases were not identified and publicized until the 1980s. And it took time for word of the disease to spread. Also, at that time, AIDS was primarily believed to be transmitted through gay sex or intravenous drug use. The rest of us, myself included, were not insisting on the use of condoms and we weren't afraid. It was a big shock to find out that I had contracted herpes.

"When your dad and I married in early 1991, we knew we wanted children right away. I was 33, and my biological clock was ticking. One of the things I didn't talk to your dad about was how much I worried that I had somehow screwed-up my reproductive organs during the years before I met him. I had law school, the Bar Exam, and work at the Women's Center to distract me. But it wasn't enough to prevent me from being aware as the months ticked by with no pregnancy. In October 1991, when I discovered I was pregnant with you, it felt like a *miracle*." Rachel smiled broadly. "Being pregnant with you was pure joy."

Jennifer never tired of hearing how 'wanted' and loved she had been. "I'm glad I could be of assistance," she grinned.

"Getting back to the story," said Rachel, redirecting them, because she did not want to lose momentum, "When I told Jay about the herpes, he was very upset and said he needed 'time to think.' That made me furious! How dare he pull away under the circumstances that he had helped to created?!"

"No kidding! So, what did you do?" asked Jennifer.

"I did the only thing an angry, heartsick woman who identified as a sexual object could do. I had sex with another crazy person," Rachel smiled again.

Jennifer raised her eyebrows. What her mother said wasn't funny, but... She said, "Go on."

June 19, 1984

Don, the head basketball coach at the school where I did my student teaching, called me today and wanted to come over to my apartment. He didn't give any details. He arrived with a six-pack of beer and some cocaine. He spread the cocaine out on the table and began drawing lines with a razor blade. I told him I didn't know anything about cocaine. He said it would make me feel good and couldn't hurt me. I agreed to give it a try.

It was a strange evening. The cocaine only kept me wide-awake all night, but it made Don horny. He said that what is great about cocaine is that a guy can stay hard longer without coming. That must be true because I wanted the sex to be over long before Don was done with me.

"You, Rachel Adamo, snorted cocaine?" Jennifer was shocked. "I never knew that about you either. It's kind of hard to believe. Did you really believe cocaine couldn't hurt you like the guy said?" What Jennifer *didn't* say aloud was how disturbed she was to hear that her mother had been sexually involved with a high school teacher and coach. She reminded herself that Mom was an adult then, not a student.

"I'm ashamed to admit it, but I did believe him. I was so naïve. While many of my high school and college classmates were experimenting with drugs, learning the effects, getting caught sometimes, and paying the price for their decisions. I was playing sports, going to church, and pursuing my studies. It's not that I wish I had been experimenting in those days. But, as a result of my naivety, I wandered, like an innocent child, into a danger zone with no knowledge of what I was getting into," replied Rachel.

"I was back with Jay, but we had this 'open' relationship again that I hated. He wasn't ready to commit, but he always demonstrated mixed emotions about me being with other men. I probably could have kept my mouth shut about Don because it was a one-time thing. But, as I've said before, I was also angry about the way Jay had responded to my diagnosis. I wanted him to know that herpes had not put end to my sex life. So, I told Jay about the night. He was upset because I hadn't asked him first and because he thought I was being careless. I repeated what my doctor had told me: a person can have sex without transferring the virus when the herpes isn't active, or when there is no blister. God, the last thing I wanted to do was to give it to anyone else."

Rachel was flipping through her journal to the next part she wanted to read.

"Using cocaine had not been a great experience for me. I guess that was why it didn't occur to me that Jay would insist we try it together. He did. Of course, I didn't know anything about buying illegal drugs. But it was clear that this was going to fall on my list of risks and responsibilities," said Rachel.

June 22, 1984

After cautious investigation, I have found someone who can set me up with a dealer to buy cocaine. It is very expensive. I told Jay I could not afford to buy it. He said we could split the cost.

June 24, 1984

It is the second anniversary of the day I was raped by Isaiah Barry. Jay says it is time to stop "celebrating." He says I should be over wanting to remember it by now. Something must be wrong with me because I can't forget.

"Did you really think something was 'wrong' with you?" asked Jennifer.

"I must have. Everyone around me had moved on, but I was stuck," replied Rachel. "Now let me tell you more about cocaine."

June 29, 1984

What an incredible evening! Tonight, we used cocaine together for the first time. Before we began, Jay said I was the woman he trusted most in the world to keep secret these unconventional adventures. How else would something like this be possible for a university professor? Our experience with cocaine was fantastic. We felt vibrant and alive, and our sex was magnificent. We have promised each other that we will do this again whenever we can afford it.

"I was hooked. Not literally. Not in the addiction sense..."

"But you associated the good feelings with Jay," interrupted Jennifer.

Jennifer's mind drifted briefly to David. They had gotten high together a few times smoking pot. Outside of that relationship, she had never used drugs – unless you counted alcohol as 'drugs.' She understood how drug use could be associated with a *person.*

"Creating yet another secretive link between us," continued Rachel. "And this new link seemed to increase Jay's power over me again because this is what happened next..."

July 7, 1984

Jay told me to find another lover. Daniel came to mind because he seemed like a sure thing. Daniel is a student I met at a Austin University hangout. We talked about our families and values, shared drinks, a few laughs, and our dreams for the future. I met Daniel a few more times at the same bar, and I really like him. Though I felt torn, Jay persuaded me to seduce him.

Tonight, I took Daniel in my camper from the bar to a dark, deserted dirt road behind a church. The sex went on and on. He said he reached orgasm five times and that this had never happened to him before. He said I was an amazing, powerful, sensual lover. I didn't want to hear that. I don't want him to want me this way. I feel guilty and confused. Daniel is acting like this is the beginning of something. Why can't Jay understand that this is one of the risks I take?

I could have predicted that Jay would be more impressed by Daniel's ability to reach orgasm five times than he was by my insistence that there is something fundamentally wrong with what I just did. *Jay* wanted to reach orgasm five times. He wanted to stay with me until he achieved this feat. But it wasn't the same with Jay. After the second or third time, I was in pain. Jay accused me of doing something different with Daniel. I don't know what I did or didn't do. Jay says I must have sex with Daniel one more time and then break it off. I know that what Jay really wants to know is whether Daniel can repeat his sexual performance.

July 9, 1984

My heart just wasn't in it and Daniel sensed that something was wrong. After we had sexual intercourse, I told him that there is "someone else." Jay was pleased that Daniel had failed to repeat his previous performance, but multiple orgasms has been added to the list of accomplishments Jay must someday achieve.

Rachel paused. "I'm not sure if Daniel's previous performance caused Jay to want to look elsewhere for our next experience, but he did change gears. Listen," she said.

July 14, 1984

Jay wants to make love to two women at the same time before the summer ends. I warned Jay that since I am the sole arranger of unorthodox sexual experiences, and as

I only know men as sexual partners, making the arrangements might be impossible. Thank God!

July 17, 1984

I can't believe it: Jay thinks my sister and I should have sex with him at the same time. The idea is repulsive to me, but Jay insists that we cannot move on to the deeper level we were striving for if we don't share this experience. I finally gave in. I told him I could not ask her, but if he is willing to, I won't stop him.

"Aunt Sarah?!" exclaimed Jennifer.

"Sarah," confirmed Rachel. "You know, of all the things that happened to me – against my will or because I allowed them to happen - involving Sarah is the one that still troubles me the most."

"Did anything really happen?" asked Jennifer with concern.

Rachel read again from her journal.

August 10, 1984

This is what I know about tonight. Two days ago, I invited Sarah over to my apartment so she and Jay could talk about some problems Sarah is having at work. When she arrived, Jay suggested that they go out for a drink or coffee sometime to discuss the matter. Thinking that I would come along, Sarah looked to me for approval, received no discouragement, and agreed to the date. Then Jay told her I would not be able to make it, but Sarah was trapped because she had already agreed to the date.

Tonight, Sarah met Jay at a bar. Jay ordered drinks for her until she was tipsy and then convinced her to come back to his apartment for yet another drink. Once they were there, he started to touch and kiss her. Jay told her that I would approve if they had sex now and then he had sex with me later. He also told her of his fantasy about having sex with both sisters together. I can only imagine how she must have felt. Ultimately, Jay says she did not have sex with him, but agreed to consider his proposal for the future.

I was at home trying not to think about what might be happening, hoping Sarah would be stronger than I am. She is my flesh and blood. It seems out of my control. I hope enough time passes that Jay will forget about this whole plan.

"Oh, Mom! This is mind-blowing. I don't know how you... Well, at least there was no sex," sighed Jennifer.

"Right. There is that. But I have no excuse for my complicity. Sarah and I talked about that night after the fact and in later years. She never blamed me. In some ways, Sarah was a prisoner of Jay's logic and persuasion as well. But I blame myself... and I always will.

Jennifer observed that her mother was in obvious emotional pain. Had she ever thrown her brothers under the bus this way? Certainly not in any sexual sense. But had she been insensitive and uncaring? She was short-tempered with Henry. But she excused herself because everyone else was. That didn't make it right, of course.

But what about Sam? Jennifer knew he was a different kind of boy from the time he was in preschool. She remembered that he always wanted to get to school early so that he could claim the blue gown in the dress-up box before any of the girls got there. Girls were his best friends until around third grade. When they rejected him, and he didn't 'fit' with the ball-kicking boys, Sam was sad and alone much of the time. But Jennifer hadn't come to his aid. She hadn't really paid much attention until the bullying started a year or so later. By then, Sam had a chip on his shoulder. He was angry at the world and she had tended to steer clear of him. Maybe it wasn't her job to help, but she could at least have been empathetic.

She remembered that it was around this time in Sam's life, and she was in high school, when Mom took them shopping and Sam found a large woman's purse with the letter "S" embroidered on it. He insisted to Mom that he *had* to have it. Jennifer had started to say, "Boys don't have purses," but Mom had cut her off. Instead, she asked Sam if he was at all worried that the other kids would laugh at him if he wore a purse. Sam said, "I don't care." Mom then tried to convince him to look at men's bags and backpacks with his initial or name on them, but Sam refused. Finally, Mom looked at the price tag on the purse Sam wanted and declared that it was "too expensive." He was downcast, but she promised to take him to the Thrift Store to look for purses.

A few days later, Mom took all the kids to the Thrift Store. The boys ran for the toy section while Mom began examining the purses. She found a small, square bag with a handle and a strap that had lots of compartments, zippers, and snaps. She called Sam over to look at the bag. He was thrilled. Then he ran off to the toy section again.

When they got home, Sam left the bag lying on the kitchen table, and Mom had to remind him several times to put it away. She asked him if he was planning to wear it to school the next day. He said, "No. We are only allowed to bring our backpacks." Mom asked when he intended to use the bag. Sam said, "Maybe when I go shopping with you."

As Jennifer thought about this now, she realized that the important thing Mom had done was to accept Sam the way he was – and is. He had the tools to figure out when and how to express himself, with a little guidance. What he needed from the rest of his family was the acceptance and support of his differences. Mom was beating herself up because she knew her sister, Sarah, was fragile, but she allowed her to go into a dangerous situation anyway. She let the bully have his way.

Jennifer knew she could be a better sister to Sam. Instead of simply tolerating his presence, she could listen more. She could go to his shows. She could express more interest. And she could stand up to the bullies when she encountered them.

Chapter Twenty-One
Narcissism and Alternatives

"*The* summer ended and Jay decided to take the fall semester to do some writing on a ranch in Montana," said Rachel. "He said this would be an important time to shift the balance of our relationship. I would be teaching – hopefully - and establishing myself as a professional, and he would be legally divorced by autumn's end. He wanted the time away to prepare to reemerge at the university with a new sense of himself as a single man. His rationale to me was that as two single professionals we would be better situated to make a reasoned decision about a commitment to one another."

"More delay," opined Jennifer.

"Yes. But it made sense too. I held onto the belief that we were still moving in the direction of marriage.

"A social studies teaching job did come through in mid-October at Pine Tree High School when the first teacher hired for that position abruptly quit," said Rachel. "Meanwhile, I received a letter from Jay and wrote about it…"

November 2, 1984

Jay wrote about how emotionally draining the last years of his marriage have been. He reaffirmed the need for our separation, that only with such a break would it be possible for us to establish new ground for a relationship. No more professor-student imbalances, no more professional-occasional employment opportunity imbalances. He acknowledged my frustration with this separation and reminded me that I was still invited to visit him and know him under different circumstances than those that prevailed for the duration of "our friendship" before now. He acknowledged that it was his responsibility to get his own house in order, to avoid implicating others in his own sink traps, and to come to terms with the ways in which he remains captive of his own self-deceptions.

Rachel paused and noted, "I must have copied these words straight from his letter because it sounds so much like Jay." She continued reading.

Jay has been reading about narcissism. He offered an apology for the times he has mistreated or misunderstood me. I think he finally understands something about how his demands regarding my sexual behavior these past months have made me feel.

Some folded papers slipped from the journal to the floor. Rachel picked them up. "Oh, here's the letter. Listen to this so you can hear how he sounds…"

You expressed concern on more than one occasion about what would happen to me when I delved into the whole matter of narcissism. I, as I recall, down-played that concern, but I think now that you were right in sensing that I would go to the mats with the issue; it would be my version of wrestling with the angels. For too long, I have been afraid of the experience of passion; despite my pleas for immediacy, I have related to it only as I have remade it -- following out some scenario where I understand the ordering. Where I have violated you, and I have, is in remaking you into what I needed you to be. This, of course, is self-deception. You are not what I make you into. You are who you are, and much of me feared meeting you on these terms. I am both sufficiently complex and sophisticated to have set up a fairly good smoke screen. But in the end, the plain and simple truth is that I feared meeting you as you, however much I may have 'understood' you, and thereby seduced you into a kind of submission.

I do think that I erected barriers to engaging you directly. This, of course, led to constant disappointment, because what I was searching for was an ordering of my own devising; I could scarcely revel in what you offered unless it touched what I wanted it to be.

That, of course, is a horrible admission; I shudder even as I write these words. But it commends something of the spirit with which I have entered into this pilgrimage. It is not you, but I who have fallen short. It is not you who did not bring everything to the relation, it was I who was unable to tarry and delight in what was afforded me. I remember how, by way of example, I was hurt and angered when I came to you the night you had been with Daniel, wanting so much to feel you in your fullness, and being mystified by your silence, your dizziness, and your reticence at showering me with what I wanted. WITH WHAT I WANTED -- my God, I can hardly believe the crassness of my soul.

Rachel looked up expectantly.

"Wow. I mean... Wow. You don't know how much that helps me understand why you stayed. He sounds brilliant and articulate. He even seems to understand what he's done to you and how it's hurt you," said Jennifer.

"I'm experiencing a similar 'wow' moment," said Rachel. "I got up this morning depressed and thinking: How can I continue to put Jennifer through this? I was foolish and weak. I was almost ready to burn the journals as the only evidence of an embarrassing and humiliating past life. But this letter reminds me of why I played along. I wish I could recreate our conversations for you. But at least this letter gives you an idea of how he sounds.

"I may be getting ahead of myself, but I think this is a good place to talk a little about narcissism." Rachel dug through the cardboard box and found her copy of *The Abuse of Power: A Theological Problem* by James Newton Poling. She held it up for Jennifer to see. "I read this book and wrote some notes a few years later, in the course of therapy and recovery."

Rachel extracted the pages of notes from the book and read aloud.

In relation to sexual abuse, a person with a narcissistic disorder may know that a behavior is "wrong" because of social taboo, but truly believe he (or she) has done no harm. The narcissist's ability to accurately evaluate self, other, and the relationship between the two is damaged in some way. One result may be what is referred to as a "grandiose self." The "grandiose self" is never wrong and is entitled to whatever privilege and pleasure is available in an interaction. A "grandiose self" that is not satisfied can become enraged and harm the other person.

Although I did not recognize it at the time, Jay's behavior with me may have reflected this kind of disorder of perception. He perceived and believed his needs or desires were mine as well as his.

"And he didn't know he was harming you," interjected Jennifer.

"Right – or, at least, not the same way that you or I might recognize 'harm.'" Rachel continued reading from her notes.

Poling also writes that persons who suffer narcissistic disorders may perceive another person as an "omnipotent object." An "omnipotent object" is a demanding, all-powerful "other" against whom there is no defense. An abuser may organize his or her life around fear of the "omnipotent object."

From Jay's perspective, my passion was beyond his control, and in monitoring all of my interactions with men, he demonstrated a real fear of that imagined passion. He mistook my ability to perform sexual acts with others for strength, when in reality it was a sign of my weakness. Yet despite our differences in perception, I dared not challenge him. Since 1982, I had trusted Jay to guide me through my upheaval of emotions. Because he, consciously or unconsciously, saw the first rape as more about sex than violence, he defined the experience for me as demonstrative of the power of my sexual nature. The events that followed reinforced that paradigm. It became harder and harder for me to think of myself as anything other than "body" and "instinct."

"Very insightful, Mom," said Jennifer. "But you didn't learn about narcissism or figure out how it applied to you and Jay until years later. Right?"

"Much later," responded Rachel. "Meanwhile, I planned to visit Jay in Montana around Thanksgiving. We agreed that I would purchase cocaine for the occasion. I was worried about taking an illegal drug on the plane. This was long before the increased security measures that came after 9-11. But I was not an experienced traveler, and I didn't know for sure that my bags or person would not be searched. On November 17, 1984, I wrote…"

Breaking the law and getting caught would change my life. I resent the fact that I always bear the risk. The coded language used over the phone to a dealer, the secret meetings to make a purchase – it all makes me feel like an actor in a play. When I sit in a room of people who have come to purchase drugs, a veiled desperation and anticipation masks their faces. I don't belong there, but it is the only way I know to get the coke.

199

"I didn't get caught carrying drugs. I visited Jay and, during the cocaine-induced sexual frenzy that followed, Jay told me that he had a sexual affair with a woman at the ranch. Again, he rationalized this affair as part of the process of coming to a new understanding of who we are as individuals so that we might have a chance together at some future time."

"It's hard to be on your side," said Jennifer rather sharply. "Drugs. Jay's unfaithfulness to you."

Rachel felt slightly stung. She wanted so much for Jennifer to understand how weak she had felt at the time, how powerless. But, of course, this wouldn't make much sense to someone who had always been in control.

"I'm ashamed of my inability to stand up to Jay. I'm ashamed of how I let him control me," said Rachel.

"At this point, however, *cocaine* was starting to be a factor. I still remember the splendid feelings associated with the first few times I used cocaine. I was convinced that I had never felt that 'good' in my entire life. It's no surprise, considering the way I was accustomed to feeling. Using cocaine was a way of avoiding my pain, of anesthetizing myself so that I could not be hurt. It was psychologically addictive, if not addictive physiologically. But the secrecy surrounding cocaine use added another barrier to whatever sense I had that I needed to break the silence and get some outside help. Jay, who hurt from wounds of his own, also found relief in cocaine. We were never good for each other when it came to seeing the hazards of drug use."

When Jennifer did not respond, Rachel continued her story. "Back in Austin, away from Jay, I decided that I, too, would start dating."

December 8, 1984

What an evening! Last night, Stan, a guy I met at the newspaper office, invited me to go with another couple to one of my favorite restaurants. The date began in an apartment full of people who all seemed to live in the complex. The thing that immediately struck me was the presence of cocaine, marijuana, and little children. That seems wrong to me. A woman was telling a story about going to the dentist to get teeth pulled. She talked about using cocaine to lessen the pain and about how the cocaine prevented her blood from clotting. Meanwhile, other adults were distributing the drugs. I was asked to partake of the cocaine and did. There was so much of it. I had never seen so much of it, nor had I ever inhaled such enormous quantities. I began to feel hot. I asked Stan if I could step outside to get some fresh air. As I put my hand on the doorknob, everything went blank. When I regained consciousness, I was lying on the couch and Stan was leaning over me, obviously very concerned. Apparently, I had dropped to the floor and been moved to the couch. I have never passed out before. I knew it must be the cocaine, but the group offered me more of the drug before we left for our dinner reservations.

When we arrived at the restaurant, we were escorted into a private room and ordered mountains of food. We were all so high that we barely touched it. We laughed and drank and tried to force a few mouthfuls of food down. Back in the car, the occupants began to pass the cocaine tray again. I was disgusted. We had just wasted all that food; and I had to get to work in just a few hours. What kind of junkies are these people?

Rachel chuckled, "It's funny, in a way, that I didn't stop snorting cocaine after I passed out. What made me *stop* was the food waste. I was able to support myself financially because I was tight-fisted about money. I never bought food, clothes, or any other items unless I was sure I *needed* them."

Jennifer smiled in spite of feeling queasy. Mom was right. She was tight-fisted about money. How many times had she heard her mother say something like: "You will complete these piano lessons because I paid for them!" or "You will wear this dress again because it was so expensive." And yet, the thought that her mother would spend money on drugs or spend time with these sorts of people... well, it was just so unlike her.

Rachel interrupted Jennifer's thoughts. "Life was happening *to me.* Whether it was drugs or sex or anything else, if someone wanted a piece of me, I went along instead of being intentional about *creating* my own opportunities. Stan happened to me. But Andrew also happened to me. I want to tell you about Andrew because he also plays a role in my thinking and recovery later on. This is what I wrote..."

January 1, 1985

I had the best New Year's Eve of my life. I spent it with the brother of one of my dearest childhood friends. Andrew is visiting his parents in Austin. He took me out to a restaurant and some clubs. We discussed our common childhood and diverging paths at adolescence and beyond. It is remarkable how comfortable I feel with him. It is remarkable just to be sitting in a public place with other couples. Andrew treated me like a "lady," as my Nana would say. I can tell he really believes I am unique and beautiful, and he has for a long time. I asked Andrew to come home with me and spend the night. He was a tender and splendid lover. Somehow Andrew was able to love all of me - mind, body, and soul. We spent today together as well.

"Although sex probably came sooner in the relationship because of all I had experienced in the past couple of years, Andrew was the first person I'd been on a 'regular' date with since I met Jay. You know what I mean?" asked Rachel. "It was refreshing."

"What happened with Andrew?" asked Jennifer.

"Well, since he didn't live in Austin, the relationship was not going to progress quickly," said Rachel. "There were no cell phones, texts, emails, or Skype in those days. None of the technology existed that keeps your generation connected 24/7. Our communication would have been by letters aka 'snail mail' or expensive long distance phone calls from home phones plugged into walls. Still, the relationship might have continued if I was not so psychologically bound to Jay. But I was.

"Andrew came back to visit later in March. Let me skip ahead to that part of the journal. It says a lot about how miserable I had become, but how sweet Andrew was."

March 15, 1985

Andrew was in town this week to visit his parents, so we made a date to meet at a local bar. I got extremely drunk and then sick after allowing several male acquaintances who were also present at the bar to buy me different kinds of drinks. I stayed in the bathroom vomiting for a long time. When Andrew sent a waitress in to check on me, I clung to the toilet bowl and told her I was not coming out. I really felt like a fool. I felt like a fool about everything. I can't handle liquor. I can't handle men or relationships. I can't handle my job. I am a total failure. When I finally emerged from the bathroom, the bar was almost empty -- but Andrew remained. He took me home and tucked me gently into bed. It was a crazy night, but Andrew accepts me the way I am. In some ways, it reminds me of the night Jay came over to hold me after I learned that Gustav was very ill.

"Andrew was great," said Rachel, looking up. "And I still consider him a friend. But to answer your question about 'what happened,' I don't think it could have worked out long-term. Andrew was considering becoming a Rabbi and I, as you know,

203

call myself a Christian. Eventually, we decided to go our separate ways. But Andrew's attention and romantic behavior confirmed that I should really expect more from Jay or other men than a sex-only relationship. It was a tiny crack in my wall of self-delusion.

"Now I need to get you caught up with what was happening while Jay was still in Montana. I started teaching high school in October. I received my M.T.S. degree from the theology school in December. And I was asked by the Youth Minister at our church to coach the girls' high school basketball team. He told me that one of my players would be Katherine, a girl who had recently been raped by a stranger. The rapist was caught and pled guilty without going to trial. Katherine and I immediately connected. Despite our ten-year age difference, I felt a kinship with her that I had not felt with anyone before."

"Was it because she was raped by a stranger like you?" asked Jennifer.

"That was part of it. Bonding with Katherine because of our common experience with rape brought feelings to the surface that had been hidden for some time. I had not felt comfortable with the women at the rape crisis support group that I attended in 1982. They had discouraged me from pursuing prosecution of my rapist, and they came from backgrounds that seemed more different than similar to mine. Katherine, on the other hand, went to the same high school that I had attended and lived in the same neighborhood. We 'got' each other. As I identified Katherine's need for better support and understanding, I began to realize *I* was still in need of support. In spite of her youth, Katherine was a role model. She was getting on in her life in a healthier way than I was. I wasn't yet ready to do the work of change. I was too frightened and too ashamed of Devon's rape and other sexual events. Frankly, I still believed Jay would magically transform all the 'bad' into 'good' when we were finally a legitimate couple.

"Then, my positive experience coaching basketball led to my being asked to be a Senior High -11th and 12th grade -

counselor with the church youth group. I accepted. It would require preparing one-hour programs for Sunday nights. I thought it would be a great opportunity to share some of my insights from theology school," said Rachel.

Rachel studied Jennifer. She wondered if Jennifer was tired. She had been talking for a long time. She wondered if they should stop on a positive note. But she didn't want to drag this out Sunday after Sunday for months. She didn't want to still be telling this story when the Christmas holidays rolled around.

"Jen," said Rachel. "There's one more graphic, kind of difficult part of this story that I want to share today before we do other things. Are you still with me?"

Jennifer suddenly felt her exhaustion. She knew it wasn't physical. She'd slept for 10 hours. This was emotional exhaustion. But she didn't want to disappoint her mother who seemed to have an agenda. She'd go for a walk or a run later and burn off the accumulation of 'ick.' "I think I've got enough energy to keep going," she said to Rachel.

"Great," said Rachel. "Okay. So, Jay returned to Austin in mid-January 1985. He offered to pay for cocaine if we could go to X-Rated hotels, watch the movies shown on TV and try to reenact them in the room. We did this a few times. I would get totally wasted on cocaine and alcohol to the point that I didn't really care what we did.

"By March, Jay was planning more new adventures…"

"Wait a minute. You read about being with Andrew in March," said Jennifer, puzzled.

Rachel nodded. "This is more of that insane double life I was leading. Andrew was public. Jay was private."

"But it sounded like Jay had learned how he hurt you at the ranch in Montana," said Jennifer.

"I know, I know," said Rachel, touching the side of her head. "There's 'knowing' in your head, and then there's being able to act on that knowledge. Whatever Jay 'knew,' his actions and desires didn't conform. And me? Well, I was still his psychological prisoner."

Rachel paused. "Should I go on?"

"I guess," said Jennifer, slowly shaking her head.

March 9, 1985

Jay is back to thinking we should have sexual experiences with other couples. I noticed an ad in a community newspaper that gave a number to call if you are a "swinger." I called and learned about a private nightclub in Austin for single persons and married couples to meet "swinging liberal minded young couples." For a fee, you can attend regular weekly socials on Friday and Saturday nights to mingle with others. Jay wants to try it. I still don't like the idea, but, at least, Jay will be with me if any hook-ups are arranged.

March 29, 1985

We went to the swingers club last night. When we first arrived, it was difficult to know what to do, how to approach people, or how to conduct ourselves. We sat at a table with our drinks, waited and watched. Most of the couples were older than us, or at least older than I am. The ones who approached us were repulsive to me. Then, suddenly, Jay perked up. He asked me to take a look at a youngish couple who had just arrived. He said the woman was acceptable and wanted to know what I thought of the man. There was no one else in the room that even came close. I thought that if Jay wanted to risk it, then I would too. We started talking with the couple, Carl and Lucy. We laughed discreetly about the other couples in the room. I was aware that Carl was sizing me up. I felt cheap. When Jay later asked me what I thought about Carl's "ass," I realized that I hadn't even noticed it.

The men got down to business. Did we want to "swing"? Yes. Was there somewhere we could go? Perhaps a motel. Should we go now? I thought, "We'd better go before I lose my nerve." We decided on a place to rendezvous and Jay tried to encourage me on the drive over. We had stashed some cocaine for the occasion. Jay had learned that getting erect could be a problem for him with a stranger, but he had also learned that cocaine was an aphrodisiac.

We managed to arrive at the motel and get into the room before I panicked. What if Jay couldn't get an erection? He had thought of that. He suggested to the group that we start with our own partners and then exchange. He seemed very comfortable giving instructions. I thought to myself, "If they are as good at taking instructions as I am, this will work out fine."

Jennifer laughed. "Sorry for interrupting, but that was funny. You hadn't lost your sense of humor entirely."

Rachel smiled. She wished she thought this was funny, but she was focused on the remembering – how scary, how dangerous, how stupid! Good for Jennifer, she thought. Laughter is a great way to break the tension. She continued reading…

After some initial stimulation by me, Jay gave the go-ahead to switch. I began touching and stroking this stranger, ever cognizant that his wife and Jay lay on the bed beside us. I feigned a few moans and groans, closed my eyes, and pretty soon it was over. We all sat up and agreed that it had been a successful encounter. Someone suggested we try it again. I hope we don't. Maybe since Jay has finally been successful at group sex, this will be the end of it.

Jennifer couldn't think about her mother that way. She just couldn't. In her mind, it was another woman who did these things. "Mom? I'm afraid you are going to tell me this was *not* the end of it."

Rachel sighed, "Nope. It wasn't. But this is enough for today.

"I'm sure you must think I've lost my mind reading all of this sexual stuff to my daughter. It kind of feels like that to me too. But, you see, I know something you don't know. I know that I am not the only one who has had these kinds of experiences. I know others who have felt the kind of shame I felt, who kept the secrets, who lost their power to another person who controlled them. I want you to know about this so you can help others who are in trouble the way I was. As you can see, it's not easy to detect. The only way I know to teach you about the problem is to give you the specifics – to make it personal.

"I know Andrew's romantic gestures, friendship with another rape survivor, and volunteer work at the church stand in sharp contrast with my other journal-worthy activities like group sex enhanced by drug use! Yet, at the time, these disjointed experiences did not seem unusual or abnormal to me. I was accustomed to walking on both sides of the fence at the same time without feeling the fence cut through me. Moreover, at this juncture, I was able to avoid seeing the conflicts by numbing myself with alcohol and cocaine."

"I made a commitment to see this through. Like I said before: I trust you... But you know it's hard for me to think of you this way," said Jennifer.

"I do. And I appreciate your time and attention more than you will ever know," responded Rachel.

SUNDAY
NOVEMBER 2, 2014

Chapter Twenty-Two
The Third Rape

"*B*race yourself" were the first words out of Rachel's mouth on the fifth Sunday morning that she and Jennifer met for their weekly session in the carriage house.

"Oh, no," responded Jennifer. She was bundled in baggy sweatpants and her father's California sweatshirt. She had finally moved Chris's clothes into a box and under her bed.

"Let me remind you where we are. It's spring 1985. Once I got a teaching job and a regular 'grown-up's' salary, I rented an apartment with my cousin John who was working at the hospital at AU. John knew I was dating someone – that someone being Jay, but Jay never came to our apartment. The apartment was in a great location – walking distance from Oxford Village and right across the street from Oxford Park. After work, I would often go to the park to play pick-up basketball games. It was a good way to relieve stress on sunny afternoons. That was a tough year for me because I was preparing all of my curricula from scratch. Plus, in my naiveté, I assigned way too many essays to my students. I was up late at night and again early in the morning, grading a perpetual mound of papers.

"When I played basketball, I was usually the only woman playing. But that never bothered me. On a couple of occasions, one particular young man had asked me to go out after a game. I shrugged him off with the genuine excuse that I had papers to grade and lessons to prepare.

"However, on April 8th, this same guy — whose name I learned was Sean — asked me again to go for a beer after a game. It was a Friday and a beautiful spring day with the weekend ahead. I was feeling great, so I agreed."

Rachel picked up another notebook and said, "I'll let my journal take it from here…"

We walked the mile to a pub in Oxford Village and ordered a pitcher of beer. Sean told me he is nineteen and works as a landscape laborer. We swapped stories about our jobs and families and aspirations. He was pleasant company and seemed to me like a young, harmless boy. After we finished the pitcher, we walked back toward our apartments in the same complex. He asked if I would come to his place for another beer. He said he had to call his father first, and I told him I needed to check-in with my roommate, John. I agreed to meet him at his place in ten or fifteen minutes. I went home and said "hello" to John, told him where I was going, and then walked across the complex to Sean's apartment. He met me at the door with a beer and invited me in.

With my back to Sean, I entered the living room. Suddenly, the room went black and I was grabbed from behind. I knew immediately what he wanted. I wrestled and protested. I said, "No. I don't want to do this! Let go of me!" He had me firmly held and was dragging me somewhere. I couldn't see a thing. As I struggled and fell to my knees, we seemed to be passing a doorway. Then I was hoisted on a bed. He was murmuring dirty sex words like "fuck" and "pussy." Isaiah Barry and Devon flashed in my head. Could I reason with him? No. Barry had not listened. Could I fight him off? No. Like Devon, he was too strong. I continued to protest and struggle, but as my clothes were being torn from my body, I felt a great sense of despair. I cried. I couldn't help it. All I could do was cry in loud sobs. I couldn't see him. I could only feel that this familiar, horrible thing was happening to my body.

"Oh, God. Not again," whispered Jennifer.

When it was over, Sean lay still on top of me. Then he said something I couldn't believe I was hearing. He asked, "Can you spend the night?" I was horrified. What did he think had just happened? I quickly composed myself and began searching for my clothes in the dark. I told him, "No. I can't stay. My roommate will be wondering where I am. I have to get home." He released his grip on me. He asked if I could just tell my roommate where I was and come back. I said, "No. No. I have to get home. There is something I have to do." I gathered my clothes and dressed. He followed me into the living room as I headed for the door, still asking me to come back after I notified my roommate.

I didn't look back. I opened the door and marched out into the cool spring night. I escaped. As I got near the pool between my apartment and his, I halted momentarily to pull myself together. Then REALITY hit me. I had been raped *again*!

My mind raced through images of the aftermath of the first time I was raped. Police. Lawyers. Rape Crisis volunteers looking pitifully at me. I knew too much. No one will believe me. All the wisdom I had gleaned from the trial rushed back to me. Only strangers rape. If you were drinking, you must have asked for it. Wasn't this a date? You went voluntarily to his apartment? You must have known what he wanted. I couldn't face it. I decided, in that moment, to pretend that nothing happened.

I walked up the stairs to my apartment and entered my own living room where John lay on the sofa watching TV. Spontaneously, I said, "I just got jumped."

Rachel remembered being unable to use the word 'rape' – a word that stuck in her throat. But she wanted to test the waters…

212

John remained focused on the TV screen, but responded, "What did you expect?" His words felt like a punch in the stomach. I walked to my room and began to write this down.

Rachel looked up. "That was the third time I had been raped in less than three years. But let me keep reading about what happened next."

Jennifer had been about to open her mouth to say... she wasn't sure what. This was unbelievable.

April 12, 1985

I returned to school Monday, but I was in a lot of pain. The pain seemed to come from my ribs. I had difficulty standing for long without doubling over. I decided I needed medical help for my injury. I don't have a personal physician.

Rachel stopped reading abruptly and turned to Jennifer. "This is true for a lot of young, healthy adults. Once you are no longer in your parents' care, there seems to be no need to pay a doctor with your limited funds for annual visits." Rachel digressed, "And this reminds me that we need to get you set up with a personal physician since you no longer have college health care." She returned to the story.

"The only doctor I had, at this point, was an OBGYN who prescribed my birth control pills. I certainly wasn't going *there* and blow my secret. Instead..."

I knew the quickest way to get help would be a trip to an emergency room. I didn't want to go alone, so I asked my mother to go with me. I told Mom that I had fallen against my ribcage. She agreed to sit with me in the emergency room while I waited.

"Sorry to keep interrupting myself. But it occurs to me that it's odd how I would go into dangerous, sexually charged situations alone, but I was afraid to sit in an emergency room alone," said Rachel.

"Maybe it was your way of seeking comfort from Nanna," said Jennifer.

"I think you're right," nodded Rachel. "I think I was probably also desperate to tell someone, but couldn't admit it to myself."

"And Jay would not have believed you. You knew that because of Devon," Jennifer said assuredly.

Rachel felt proud of her daughter for making the connections. She continued reading.

When I finally reached an examining room, I lost my composure. The doctor didn't believe my fabricated story. She probed further at my inconsistencies and, probably, read my face. I confessed. Yes, there had been forced sexual intercourse and somehow in the struggle I was injured. She told me she was going to call the police. I made it very clear: NO! I do not want to call the police. It's *my* decision. You can't make me. The doctor conceded my right to make that decision. However, I yielded when she insisted I nevertheless have a pelvic exam, some medication, and a pregnancy test. She said it would take a while to get the results of these tests, and I would have to wait.

I walked back to the waiting room, knowing my mother would still be there wondering about my ribs. I told her there didn't seem to be anything broken, just bruises. Then I paused. I had to tell her. I didn't want to, but I needed to because this longer wait required some explanation. Mother had an appointment, so I offered to walk her to her car while I told her what was happening: "Mom, I have to wait longer than expected because I took some other tests... I was raped." I explained the details of my "date" with Sean. Mother hugged me and held me.

I went back to the hospital alone to get my test results. I am not pregnant.

Rachel paused. "You know, I could have avoided telling Nanna."

"You could have," said Jennifer. "But you didn't *want* to. You needed her support. You needed somebody to care and believe you. Who could be better than Nanna?"

Rachel knew her daughter loved her Nanna very much. Nanna had a calming presence that had always settled Jennifer, from the time she was a colicky baby through her high-strung moments as a teenager. Nanna was reassuring. She saw a positive angle to every situation if there was one to be found. She let Jennifer – and Rachel herself – know that everything would be okay. And she always made herself available when there was a need. From sewing costumes for school plays and carpooling when Rachel's schedule got too busy, to consulting about Henry's bad behavior or Sam's differences from his peers, Eleanor Morris was always there. Jennifer knew it, and Rachel knew it.

Rachel also knew that when her mother criticized, it was because she had thought long and hard about what to say. Eleanor never criticized, choosing to believe the best about others most of the time, unless she was sure. Eleanor was smart and wise, so Rachel could not help but take her words to heart even when she didn't want to agree. That had happened this time, with this rape.

"So true," said Rachel. "In fact, Nanna wrote me a letter after our conversation that day. I want you to hear it."

I've thought a lot about some of your attributes which are so very disarming and endearing—your openness, your loving and giving nature, your impulsiveness, your enthusiasm and eagerness, your sense of wonder at life. I can't begin to say or even think how much richer my own life has been because of the things you have helped me see and the things you have encouraged me to do and the wonder and excitement at life (as well as the deep despair!) you have evoked in me. You have amazed me all the more because you've maintained these qualities in spite of growing up exposed to "the ways of the world" to so much greater extent than I ever was—or am!—without the safety of a homogeneous culture where you could count on everybody to be guided by basically the same principles as you were.

My sense of how you have managed to do this—to carry these "child-like" qualities forward into life with you to such a remarkable degree—is that there is another side of you which is smart and tough enough to be able to create and maintain a safe place in the world for that "child" in you to still exist and wonder at life—and to share that sense of wonder and eagerness with people around you. It makes you a very special person.

When things happen to you like the incident which led to our day at the hospital, I find myself with a mix of feelings. Relating those feelings to the above, I hurt with the betrayed child in you and I am furious with the capable adult you also are who has irresponsibly looked the other way while the child wandered into the world unprotected. You are too smart to turn yourself over to your impulsiveness without first making a realistic assessment of the circumstances. And you are far too precious to make yourself vulnerable to needless abuse—physical, verbal, emotional, or any other kind.

As people grow up, it seems to me that they have three choices for dealing with the vulnerability inherent in being a child. They may stay locked into it and live their lives out as victims. More often, I think, they build sturdy walls of defenses around it and bury it so deep within themselves that it is allowed out only in the safest and most intimate situations. I see you as having chosen the third option of trying to use adult "savvy" to control the circumstances of life so that vulnerability can continue to have a positive place in life and relationships.   It may be that the circumstances of your life at this time—both external and internal—call for you to be <u>less</u> free and vulnerable, without its meaning that you leave that option behind forever. This may be a time in your life when you need to protect yourself more closely.

You spoke of feeling helpless in the presence of angry men and of being aware of the broader impact of that experience on your life and work. I encourage you to follow up on your impulse to get help in exploring that feeling and breaking out of its control over you. "Power" has never been a big issue for me, but I know it certainly is for lots of folks. And I wonder if your feeling of powerlessness may be translating itself into a loss of self-respect. That touches on another part of my anger at you, you know: how can you be so careless with the priceless treasure of your life and promise!

"Gosh, Mom. That's a remarkable letter. I could hear Nanna's voice when you read it. I've never heard her mad at you before," said Jennifer.

"Yes. I think that's the first message I heard too," Rachel replied. "When I received the letter, I read it over and over again. Each time I felt something different. I felt my mother's love. I felt my mother's judgment. I felt shame for not having protected myself. I felt angry with *myself* for having brought Mom into this. But I also felt grateful that Mom now knew how scared and helpless I really felt.

"Reading the letter now, I think about what my mother *didn't* know. She didn't know how worn down my defenses were because I didn't get therapy and move on from being a victim. She didn't know about all the years I had allowed Jay to control me. Although Mom recognized that my ability to maintain the balance between vulnerable child and savvy adult was 'off,' she had no way of knowing what prevented me from simply changing my behavior. It wasn't a decision I could just make and do.

"I *hate* thinking of myself as a 'victim.' I have come to despise that word except as used to describe someone in immediate danger or in the middle of a crisis not of her own making. 'Survivor' is a much better word. It acknowledges the violence or abuse, but it also suggests one has made it to the other side. Still, I had to admit that, like it or not, I was acting more like a victim than a survivor. Was I abnormal? I wondered how long it took the 'usual person' to leave victimhood behind and achieve survivor status?"

Jennifer said, "When I was in college, I took an introductory women's studies course. We read a book called *I Never Called It Rape* by Robin Warshaw. I remember that she said the risk of a woman being raped by someone she knows is far greater than her risk of being raped by a stranger. One in four women are victims of rape or attempted rape, and 84% of those women know their attackers."

Her mother looked 'impressed.' Jennifer continued, "I only remember this stuff because I wrote a paper on the book. Not reporting date rape is a pretty typical response.

"Another thing I remember is that victims of acquaintance rape may be overcome with the realization that they fear *all* the men they know after they've been raped. The thinking goes, 'If someone I trusted could do this to me, any man could assault me.'"

"That is so true," said Rachel. "For me, the worst aspect of being raped by Sean was the feeling that I had been betrayed by my own judgment. My mother's letter confirmed that feeling.

She noted that I was 'irresponsible' and not able to make a 'realistic assessment' of situations with men. And she was right.

"The best thing about Nanna's letter, the most helpful thing, was that she *knew* me. She knew my history and temperament and personality. I was so completely focused on the past few years, that I often lost sight of who I was and could be. After that day at the hospital and her concerned letter, Mom persisted in caring for me in the ways she was able, and I began to absorb her helpful messages. Eventually her suggestions that I protect myself more and seek professional help outweighed the blaming messages I heard initially."

"Yay, Nanna!" said Jennifer.

CHAPTER TWENTY-THREE
THE LITTLE VOICE

"So what did Jay say about this third rape?" Jennifer asked.

"He had gone off on another retreat – this time to southern California. I told him about Sean. He wrote it off as foolishness on my part, as I suspected he would do. But the way he communicated that was much more poetic," said Rachel. She pulled out another folded letter from the journal. "This is part of what he wrote..."

May 20, 1985

There is a world of difference between finding yourself in a set of circumstances that seem to dictate responses, and having a sense that whatever the circumstance -- at least for the most part -- you can elect a course of conduct to follow. From that latter course there follows the sense that regardless of what others may think, there is a sense of affirmation of yourself in and through your dealings with others that is constitutive of your identity. Therein, or again, so it seems to me, lies the prospect of experiencing yourself as a unique and full vessel, and not as an empty shard for which you must seek and derive content from others. I have always found the unique vessel that you are stunning, a special gift in the world, whom I cherish and dearly miss.

"But that also sounds very positive," said Jennifer.

"It does. He reprimanded me. But he also told me how wonderful I was."

"He wasn't letting you go," surmised Jennifer.

"Uh-huh. Meanwhile, I was back in Austin. The school year had ended. I had a one-year contract, and the school was letting me go. So, I needed to find full-time work again. I was still a senior high counselor with the Wesley Church Youth Group. And the kids liked me, so they asked me to be a chaperone on their three-week choir tour that summer. There was a tour bus, but I traveled in the equipment van with one of the two youth ministers, Jack Fuller. We traveled throughout the Southwest, staying in the homes of members of the congregations at churches where the youth sing. I was having a great time, though I missed Adagio."

"Sweet Adagio!" interjected Jennifer. Adagio was still her mother's dog when Jennifer was young. There were several pictures on walls around their house featuring various stages of Adagio's life.

"I'm telling you this because there was an incident toward the end of the tour of some significance…"

July 11, 1985

Today was the last day of the tour. Jack and I have become pretty close friends during these three weeks of riding together, and we have talked openly about our past relationships with members of the opposite sex. I am not completely naive. I know that talking about dating and attractions is tantamount to flirting. I knew that Jack was developing a crush on me. As we were driving down the highway, Jack suddenly pulled over and started to kiss me. I didn't resist at first. Jack pushed to see how far I'd go. I stopped him. I don't have an explanation for my flirting. I don't understand it myself.

"The Youth Minister was coming on to you?" asked Jennifer, sounding puzzled.

"Yes. But we've already established that theologians are not exempt from sexual desires, haven't we?" replied Rachel.

Jennifer laughed at her blunder.

"The point is that I was able to put the brakes on when it was something I didn't want to do. Being around people who saw me as having something to offer other than sex had bolstered me," said Rachel.

"So you had made progress... I still want to know when you dumped Jay," said Jennifer.

"Oh, the impatience of youth," smiled Rachel. "Remember, I'm just *beginning* to respond to my own instincts. I haven't even decided Jay is bad for me yet. The support that will enable me to make a run is coming, but it isn't there yet.

"By the way, do you remember learning the statistic – in school or somewhere along the way – that it takes a victim of domestic violence an average of *seven* attempts before she - or he - finally leaves the abuser? Why? She needs a plan that covers all the contingencies – kids, money, safe location, etc. And she needs to resolve to leave someone she has loved deeply, the person with whom she shares a history. He is someone who has said he didn't mean to hurt her, is sorry he hurt her, and will never do it again – on countless occasions! Each apology brings a ray of hope. It's called the cycle of violence.

"I think it was Oprah who talked about each of us having a 'little voice' that senses danger and urges us to be careful. My little voice had been muffled or gagged after I was raped in 1982. But as I received unconditional kindness from my mother, church members, and others, the little voice gathered strength. That I was able to resist Jack had a lot to do with the fact that I had been spending time with the youth choir members in the preceding three weeks. They nourished me. They filled me up with 'soul food.' They unknowingly strengthened my instinct for danger."

"I felt that in Youth Group. I felt that I could be myself and not be judged," said Jennifer. "It's still depressing to know that you didn't leave Jay."

"Take heart. You know this story will end well," and Rachel smiled. Again, she wished, for her daughter's sake, that she could skip to the end and avoid all the intermediate steps.

But she wanted Jennifer to appreciate how difficult recovery could be, and this was the only way to show her.

"After the choir tour, in early August 1985, I interviewed for a teaching position at Spring Lake Hospital. I was hired to be one of two teachers on a locked adolescent psychiatric unit."

Jennifer didn't have to ask what that was. Henry had spent six months when he was fifteen locked away in a different hospital on an adolescent unit. Now that she thought about it, she remembered her mother saying: 'This all feels too familiar' the first time they visited Henry. At the time, Jennifer hadn't thought to ask 'why.'

"Jen?" began Rachel. "Do you remember that Henry went to school in the hospital?"

"Sort of," said Jennifer.

"His set-up was familiar to me because I'd been in that setting as a teacher for kids like Henry. The students on our locked psychiatric unit ranged in age from twelve to eighteen. Each one studied several subjects in different books at a pace that reflected his or her individual abilities. Lily, my co-teacher, and I prepared daily schedules for each of our students. We helped them individually during school hours and graded their work after class. We did initial educational testing, diagnosed learning disabilities, and also participated in group therapy on certain days.

"Our students came to us with a variety of psychiatric problems that included schizophrenia, depression, attempted suicide, and behavior disorders that had led to violent and dangerous incidents."

"Like Henry," said Jennifer.

"Like Henry," confirmed Rachel. "We had to contend with the manifestations of all of these illnesses in the classroom, including outbursts that sometimes resulted in the physical restraint of a student by hospital staff. As frightening as the job could be at times, it also provided me with the opportunity to learn about mental illnesses and approaches for recovery.

"I didn't realize at the time that this information would later help me with my own son. At the time, I was applying what I read and heard to *me*. I considered whether I might be depressed. I thought about 'denial.' I worked with teens who had addiction problems and learned about my drug of choice, cocaine, from a treatment perspective. I started to worry."

"Mom," said Jennifer. "I'm thinking about your cocaine use. Don't be offended, but were you really healthy enough to be working with kids who had drug problems?"

Rachel had suspected her daughter would raise this issue. "Let me reassure you that I was competent," she responded, somewhat defensively, she realized. "I was very much a recreational drug user. I didn't go to work high. I was always very professional while at work in this job.

"Should I have been working with kids with drug problems? From this distance, and as a parent, I would have to say 'no.' Someone who is actively using illegal drugs or abusing prescription drugs should not be working with kids who have drug problems. That person is breaking the law and being a hypocrite as well.

"Still, I think I was such an occasional user that my judgment was only partly clouded – thank God!" Rachel knew her answer wasn't satisfactory. She wished she could tell Jennifer something different about herself. But the truth was, at the time, she *was* using cocaine when she and Jay could afford it. If she thought that drugs were an issue for Jennifer, she might have wanted to stay on this topic. But she didn't. Besides, drugs had not been her 'problem.' Escape and avoidance of her pain had been the problem that drugs helped her mask. This is what Jennifer needed to understand.

"Working at the hospital put me into a healing arena," Rachel continued. "At some level, I must have known I needed healing that could be facilitated by the kinds of therapy my students received. As I learned about the special needs of teenagers with emotional problems, I also began to confront my own therapeutic issues indirectly.

"Also, for the first time in my adult life, my closest work colleague was a woman instead of a man. That was significant. There was no sexual dynamic to our relationship. I felt 'safer' with Lily than I had felt with previous male colleagues."

Jennifer was not ready to give up on the drug use topic. "I had to ask about the drugs. You always told us how dangerous it was."

"You have every right to question me about this," Rachel conceded. "Addiction affects different people differently. Some cycle very quickly into a state where their health is adversely affected or they can no longer support themselves or sustain relationships. For others, the harmful effects of drug and alcohol use take longer." Rachel was determined to move on from this topic.

"So," began Rachel, "I was teaching again and continuing to volunteer as a Senior High Counselor at church when I learned that Jack Fuller was leaving his position as Youth Minister to work at another church. His position was part-time during the school year and full-time during the summer. Here I was, this person with a theological education, who loved working with these kids – kids who were a refreshing counterbalance to the teenagers I worked with at the psychiatric hospital. So, I decided to apply for the job. And I got it!

"But then Jay came along and told me that he'd put in a good word for me with some of the influential people on the Church Council. In other words, he 'helped me' get the job. Then he said my new job would delay our entrance as a couple into the public spotlight. It would not 'look good' for the Youth Minister to be dating a theology school professor."

"What a manipulator!" said Jennifer.

"I thought so too," said Rachel. "I was angry, and I was trapped. I could not quit the position or my kids when I'd just taken the job. To add insult to injury, Jay then announced that he wanted me to date others again."

"I don't get it. I just don't get it," Jennifer shook her head.

"The way Jay explained it, I was..." Rachel flipped through her journal to the entry dated October 24, 1985 and read "...'consolidating myself for our future happiness together.'" Rachel looked up and said, "Then he would come over after I'd been out with someone else – just like before. Here's what I wrote after going out with Jack Fuller..."

Jennifer interrupted, "So you did go out with him after all."

"I did. But it was because of Jay. I'd made the decision on my own that I didn't want to have a romantic relationship with him, though I did like him as a friend, as a person. But once Jay was in charge, well, I had to find bodies."

Jennifer was slowly shaking her head again.

"I wrote..." continued Rachel.

November 4, 1985

Jay came over tonight and we got high together. He knows I went out with Jack, so he wanted to know what had happened. The truth is that we rushed into sex and I mentally "checked out." My body performed the task of fellatio while I was thinking of ways to explain this event to Jay. After it was over, I didn't want to see Jack again. I felt dirty and worthless.

When Jay asked, I told him the lines I had rehearsed in my head about giving Jack a blowjob, using the glowing terms I thought he wanted to hear. But Jay didn't believe me! He said there was more I was keeping secret. I told him there wasn't any more to tell. I went over my story again, telling him exactly how it had happened and how I had deliberately saved sexual intercourse for us. He still didn't believe me. Jay *would not* believe me. It makes me feel crazy. I don't know what to do.

"A few days later, Jay seduced a fellow theology student who was going through a difficult time in her marriage," said Rachel.

"He was punishing you," declared Jennifer.

Rachel nodded. "I couldn't stand not being believed. That goes back to being a rape victim. Not being believed is crushing. So, I needed to get back in Jay's good graces. But the only way I knew to do that was to accomplish another of the schemes he devised. This one concerned the hospital social worker on my unit whose name was Tim Marsh. Jay said he wanted to *watch* me have sex with Tim. I wrote about this too…"

November 19, 1985

Jay planned to watch from the closet in my bedroom through the doorknob hole while I had sex with Tim…

Rachel remembered the preparations. Jay had come to her apartment with tools to remove the doorknob. He brought a container that he could urinate in if he needed to while he waited. Her stomach had been in knots.

…He talked about how wonderful it would be to have sex with me immediately after Tim left. He said I would be "warm and wet and opened up." After three and a half years of losing arguments with Jay, I don't even try to talk to him about his need for control.

Tim and I met and went to my apartment. I convinced him to move with me to the bedroom. He was gentle and tender, and he flattered me in every way. I know that, for him, this was a romantic experience with a beloved friend, a way of stretching the boundaries of the ways we care for each other on a daily basis. But I just wanted Tim to treat me like a piece of meat. I did not count on his response and I was overcome with guilt and shame. At the same time, my mind jumped back and forth between what I imagined Jay to be seeing, doing, and feeling in that closet and what I was seeing, doing, and feeling with Tim.

After Tim left, Jay emerged from his dark hole. He seemed shaky at first. I could see that Jay recognized how wonderful Tim had been with me. This shifted the burden to me to make Jay feel comfortable again. I needed to minimize the experience with Tim to elevate Jay; and, at the same time, I had to validate and glory in the conquest enough to give Jay the sense he was winning in a very tough race. I had to show that I was comfortable with my sexuality, but fully passionate only when I was with Jay. What a balancing act I perform!

Jennifer realized she had been holding her breath again and released the air. "I don't know how you did it. You say it like you had job responsibilities and you performed them well."

Rachel nodded. "It was like that when it was happening. But, later, when I had to be at work with Tim, I felt terrible. All I wanted was a *normal* relationship."

"What happened with Tim?" Jennifer asked.

"I ended it. He had served his purpose. I don't remember the details. I probably used 'working together' as an excuse. He handled it."

Rachel felt the tightness in her neck. She didn't want to dwell on thoughts about Tim. He, like Jack, and like so many of the others, were good guys. She'd used them. Why hadn't she been able to stop herself?

She said, "The irony is that all of these sexual experiences made me, in some ways, a better Youth Minister than I might otherwise have been. I was a good listener when the topic of sexuality came up because nothing shocked me. I was available for all the little crises: 'Should I go out with so-and-so?' 'How do I know when it's right for me to have sex with my boyfriend?' 'My parents don't understand me. Will you listen?' I knew some of the pitfalls. I also knew how important the history of each person was to the decisions he or she made."

"If any of the parents or youth had known what you were doing in your personal life…" Jennifer was remembering her days in Youth Group. What would she have thought if she'd known these details about *her* Youth Minister?

"I know what you are saying. It's crazy. No one really knows what is going on in the private life of others, do they? I'm guessing I would have been judged a predator or mentally and morally incompetent. But, you see, I wasn't. There was the private, tormented, unhealthy me. And then there was the public, appropriately loving, engaged and thoughtful Minister to Youth. Most of the time, I did a pretty good job."

Jennifer thought about Chris. She wondered what she *didn't* know. She thought about the years her brother Henry had hidden his exploits from the family. Mom was right. It was hard to know the insides of another person unless they shared it with you. Jay, from all Mom had said, was a master of deception with the public.

"Once again, I'd had enough of Jay. I'd be sucked back in, do things I didn't want to do, and then strike out. This was our cycle. This time, I thought the only way to shift the power imbalance between us was for me to *really* start dating. Frankly, I wasn't sure if I was breaking away or trying to make Jay jealous so that he would finally be willing to bring us out of the shadows," said Rachel.

"I started dating the Youth Choir Director, Tyler. He was a great guy, and Jay knew it. Tyler and I went on normal dates and gradually became closer. Jay *was* jealous. On December 7, 1985, Jay surprised me with a ring – not an engagement ring – just a beautiful ring, that was accompanied by a poem." Rachel pulled another piece of paper from an envelope in her box.

To Rachel
There she was, ambling in her beauty
Poised, all opened up

toward her ascension, as the morning
mists suspended in the bright
over fields she claimed as her own -
in love, with love, to love
       with all my heart
       Jay

"But it was too little, too late. As the relationship with Tyler had progressed, I found that I was happy and peaceful, and I wanted to remain that way."

"Finally!" exclaimed Jennifer.

"Well…" Rachel bit her bottom lip.

"Oh, no," sighed Jennifer.

"Here's what I wrote…

December 15, 1985

As Tyler and I grow closer, Jay becomes more desperate. This evening he followed us in his car. He drove by, motioning to me, and mouthing the word "Why?" I felt embarrassed, but I can't help being affected by Jay's obvious pain.

I don't know what I want. I still believe that the day Jay chooses me over other women will be the day all the awful things that came before will vanish.

I received another poem from Jay today:

My Best Beloved, My Beautiful Rachel,

As these few days have passed and midnights reach out to entangled shadows - no moon to carry my candle - I have known as never before that all roads are perfectly safe (and at any hour) when you are at my side. Then night and day are given over to pleasure as you dance nimbly in my mind.

But without you, the night about me is ruthless, and winter's wounds fester, unstaunched.

I pray that you, soft as Spring wind and soul, will feel the lure beyond our cloudy peaks; that you will meet me; that no rumors of heaven more high or courts more desirable will ever again set us asunder.

So dark these hours, grief, discord, and sadness:
Will we not rather, when our freedom's won,
get to some clear place wherein the sun
lets drift in on us a liquid glory?
I love you now - and I always will – Jay

Jennifer said, "The poems are so romantic. You'd never know from them what he was really like."

"And there's no 'evidence' of the other side of Jay. This is all I have – a few letters and poems. I don't know if he was calculated in what he wrote or if it just worked out this way. If it came to a test, it would be my word against his."

Jennifer's thoughts turned to David Reese. Just like Mom and Jay, it would be her word against his. He hadn't left any evidence, had he? She suspected the motels were paid for with cash. She had never seen anyone she knew when she was with him. There were no letters or notes exchanged.

Jennifer gulped at the gravity of her mother's words. "*I* believe you, Mom."

"Thank you, my darling… Once again, I was not strong enough to resist Jay's charms. I broke up with Tyler and went back to Jay."

"And was he different then, after you returned?"

"You would think so. Sadly, he turned on me again. I had gone to him with demands: no more lovers, a public commitment, and a shared family life. But Jay accused *me* of being the one unwilling to commit. And he said he would not allow me to see Ben anymore until we were clear about our own relationship."

"Back to the status quo," remarked Jennifer.

"Well… almost. Jay requested that I get a tattoo that would be a symbolic reminder of my allegiance to him," said Rachel.

"That's why you have an angel on your ankle!" exclaimed Jennifer.

"That's right."

"You never talked about it that I can remember," said Jennifer.

"What could I have said?" replied Rachel.

Jennifer nodded. "But why an angel?"

"First, you need to know that tattoos were not nearly as common and popular among young people with college educations as they are today. In fact, I had to drive to a different part of town to find a tattoo parlor. The people who worked there were scary to me. And a tattoo is permanent. People I loved were going to see it. I insisted that it be in a place where I could hide it most of the time with socks or long pants.

"As to 'why an angel,' Jay did the research. Angel wings are a symbol of devotion. Angels can also be intended as figures of guidance and protection. Jay saw himself in that role. He thought the angel was perfect because I could explain it as a symbol of my faith while we would know its secret meaning," said Rachel.

"Jesus, Mom. I can't help thinking of cattle or slaves branded with their master's mark… Did Jay get one too?"

Rachel shook her head. "No. He said he would if he could. But his position at the theology school prevented him."

"How convenient," said Jennifer, sarcastically.

CHAPTER TWENTY-FOUR
FEMALE FRIENDS

"Yes, I was marked, and we were back to the status quo. But in the meantime, I had my work and I made a new *woman* friend," said Rachel. "I wrote…"

January 4, 1986

I met Amanda Shepherd, a senior at Austin University, through a mutual acquaintance. Amanda and I have many similarities. Our fathers are both ministers, and we grew up involved in the church. We both love men who are very intelligent and academically successful. Their peers are awed by and jealous of them. Some people dislike them because they often appear aloof or uncaring. Amanda and I understand each other's attractions and the pain it sometimes causes us. We can share stories of past and present hurts that have been inflicted and our mutual fear that we will be forgotten or replaced for failing to live up to the expectations of our men.

Rachel looked up. "This passage really doesn't do justice to my relationship with Amanda. There was an immediate bond between us. We were passionate about each other. But it was a safe passion because we were both heterosexual women. I wanted to be with her all the time, and I think she felt the same.

"I could talk with her about my disagreements with Jay, and she fed me hope and confidence. Being able to speak my thoughts and opinions freely and receive Amanda's support and praise made me feel alive again. We saw beauty, grace, and potential in each other that we were not afraid to express."

"Did you tell her *everything*?" asked Jennifer.

"Not everything," responded Rachel. "But I could share my *feelings* about Jay with Amanda, just as she shared her feelings about her boyfriend with me. Getting my feelings out on the table allowed me to look at them and begin to get a different perspective.

"During those same first few months of 1986, I was conducting seminars with the Youth Group. Let me read to you about one in February," said Rachel.

February 12, 1986

We just finished a series of seminars for the youth and their parents on drugs and alcohol. For this last session, I asked my friend, Vince, who is a recovering alcoholic and drug user to speak about his personal experiences. He told the kids how he had started using drugs as a teenager. He told them about all the money he made, and how he spent it on apartments and cars and women in several cities. He told them about getting on a plane with thousands of dollars in his faded blue jeans and coming home from Miami with large quantities of drugs. Then he told them about the night he consumed bottles of alcohol and pills and cocaine and had most of his bones broken in a car accident. No one thought he would live. He wasn't sure he wanted to live. The money dried up. The apartments and cars and women disappeared. He was alone with himself for the first time in almost twenty years.

One of the things that Vince said really caught my attention. He said that once he started using drugs, he stopped maturing. Instead of struggling with the issues of sexuality, identity, self-esteem, etc. that teens usually struggle with, he was high all the time. When he finally sobered-up in his thirties, he was still emotionally fourteen years old. He did not know how to relate to women. He did not know how to make mature decisions. He was just a

kid... That makes me wonder if I am doing that to myself --
thwarting my maturity process -- by being high. I wonder if
I would make different decisions if I had never encountered
cocaine.

Jennifer was nodding. "So you were starting to think
differently about your drug use," she said.

"Between the hospital kids and this, I was. But I was still
convinced that cocaine wasn't interfering with my life. And I
was still using it, on occasion, to numb myself with respect to the
abuse.

"Meanwhile, Katherine, the young rape survivor, was
forcing me – just by her presence – to take a look at my rape
experiences. Amanda, because she was dating a manipulative
young man, enabled me to think about Jay in this way too. I
wasn't telling Amanda everything. Still, her relationship
provided a mirror for my own. All of this was nudging me to
take a closer look at what I had become," said Rachel.

"Jay was so controlling. I can't imagine he just *let* you
spend a lot of time with Amanda," said Jennifer.

"He was jealous all right," said Rachel. "In fact, he said I
spent so much time with Amanda because I was probably
bisexual. He also said Amanda might be the one to give us the
sexual experience he had tried to set-up with Sarah in the
summer..."

Jennifer slammed her hands on the arms of the recliner. "I
knew you were going to say Jay wanted to have sex with
Amanda!" she exclaimed.

Rachel laughed. Jay had been so predictable in some ways.
"Oh, Jen," she sighed. "Where were you when I needed some
perspective on this?!"

"I couldn't ask my best friend to do what Jay desired," she
said. "But, the only way I knew to distract him from this agenda
was to agree to find yet another stranger to have sex with so that
I could bring *that* story back to Jay.

Rachel took a deep breath. "Let's see if I can sum this up," she said. "In 1985 and 1986, there were safe places and unsafe places for me. My safe places were the hospital, the church, and with Amanda. My unsafe places were anywhere I was isolated with Jay. The safe places were places that supported my healing. I was safe with Lily because we were mutually engaged in a profession that, most of the time, promoted the mental health of patients and staff alike. The hospital encouraged recognition and sharing of feelings, just as my family had done when I was a child and felt nothing could harm me inside their embrace.

"I was also safe with the youth group. It was a place that encouraged the open testing of values. I could take my knowledge about sexuality and substance abuse and turn the bad experiences into good lessons. I was examining my own beliefs, away from Jay, while I helped to give others valuable insights about growing-up.

"The more time I spent with Amanda, the less time it gave me to spend with Jay. Jay was feeling squeezed out because that is exactly what was happening!"

Rachel and Jennifer heard Sam come galloping up the carriage house stairs. "Mom, I need a ride. I'm going to be late if we don't hurry," he said.

"Give me a few minutes?" Rachel questioned Jennifer as she rose from her seat.

"Sure, Mom," Jennifer replied.

While her mother was gone, Jennifer thought about the trade-offs she had made between spending time with her female friends and the man in her life at the time. She hadn't always sacrificed one for the other, had she? There had been mixed gender group dates to movies, restaurants, or games when she was younger. She had experienced sleepovers with girlfriends without guilt about time away from the boy she was dating. But all that had changed in recent years. The men she had loved more recently expected... expected what? Expected that she give up her girlfriends? Expected that she devote all her time to them?

She had thought this must be the natural evolution of growing up. Now she wondered if she, like her mother, had been fooled.

=====

Once Rachel returned from delivering Sam to his dance rehearsal, she settled back down with Jennifer in the carriage house.

"We were talking about my friendship with Amanda and Jay's attempt to control it by sexualizing it. I was able to prevent that. However, something happened that gave Jay the opportunity to spoil my friendship," said Rachel. She lifted the next spiral bound notebook to read. "Oh. First I need to tell you that by this time, both Sarah *and* Lucas knew I was dating Jay, even though our relationship was not generally public.

April 13, 1986

Amanda had lunch with a long-time friend of hers who knows Jay, and she mentioned that I was dating him. The friend told Amanda that Jay was dating someone else. Amanda later told my brother Lucas about the conversation. Lucas decided to confront Jay. He went to Jay's office and told him, in effect, that Jay had better not "screw around" on his sister or he would make sure Jay paid dearly for it.

"Way to go, Uncle Lucas! Wait. How old was he then?" asked Jennifer.

"Let's see. If I was 28, then Lucas must have been almost 23. He was very protective of his big sister," said Rachel. She continued reading…

Jay immediately came to me and told me about Lucas's confrontation. How could my brother and Amanda betray him, he asked. How could he trust them again? What was I going to do about it? He said he was extremely hurt.

I feel sick, but I have to believe Jay. I said I would take care of it and rectify their wrong impressions. Jay said he was sure that Amanda's friend had a secret attraction to him and that this was her motivation for the lies. I didn't ask Jay if he was guilty of the allegations. I couldn't.

I told Lucas and Amanda that they were wrong. I asked them how they could believe such an impossible story. They looked stunned, but both apologized. I feel nauseous. I am worried about my relationship with Amanda.

Rachel looked at Jennifer and said, "Amanda and Lucas were right, of course. I just couldn't admit it. I couldn't bear losing Jay. When I told Amanda she was mistaken regarding this alleged affair, my relationship with her changed forever. Never again would we share the innocent bliss we once shared.

"Those had been happy days – walking dogs in the park, sharing meals and conversation, going out at night. Amanda is the one who introduced me to *Harmony* by the way." Jennifer knew her mother had long been a big fan of *Harmony*, a local Austin band that had become a national and international success by the time she was born.

"Afterward," continued Rachel, "we analyzed our interactions. We were distrustful of each other – or that's the way it felt to me. We were both hurting."

"Poor, Mom," Jennifer said without meaning to sound condescending. She knew what it felt like to be without women friends. As she and Chris had grown closer, she had spent less time with her college friends. They had moved into an apartment off campus, away from most of the college-related activities, and Chris often preferred that they stay home or socialize with *his* friends.

"Why is this important?" Jennifer asked, sensing that this particular friend held a special place in her mother's heart. "I mean, why mention Amanda as part of this history?"

"I had become isolated from other women except at work. And you don't usually tell your deep dark secrets to work colleagues. Friends, *real* friends, tell us things we need to hear even if we don't want to hear them because they care about our well being. Amanda tried to warn me about Jay. I didn't heed her warning. But she still managed to chip away at my armor."

Jennifer thought about her best friend at Meriweather College, Diane. There had been many times with Diane called her or stopped her on campus to say: "Go out with me tonight" or "Can you meet me for lunch?" or "So-and-so is having a party. Want to go with me?" Jennifer's world was Chris. She had abandoned Diane and her other friends. She wondered what Diane might have said to her about Chris if she had given Diane he opportunity.

Jennifer refocused on her mother who was talking again.

"After a year with Scott Johnson, who was my co-Youth Minister, he graduated from theology school and moved on to become an Associate Minister at another church. I became the Senior Youth Minister and another theology student was hired to be my Co.

"Jay was still not willing to be my public boyfriend. He was still waiting on a tenure decision. Our nights of snorting cocaine and having sex continued. I was fine while the high lasted. But, afterward, I felt empty and ashamed."

Rachel cast her eyes toward the ceiling and then said, "You know, I said that my professional judgment was not impaired by using cocaine. But maybe it was... indirectly. It numbed me to Jay's power and influence, and *that* affected my other relationships. I'm remembering that I promised to take a group of girls to the beach for their spring break. I reneged when Jay said it was unprofessional of me. Katherine wrote me a letter later, after she graduated from high school and was on her way to Africa. She wrote about how special I had been to her. But she also expressed her disappointment that I had broken my promise without giving an adequate explanation. A certain line from the letter remains etched in my mind. She wrote: 'Ignoring things that are uncomfortable does not make them go away.' I had been ignoring my emotional pain for a long time. I had not been honest about what drove me to change our plans, and Katherine knew that, even if she didn't know the details."

Rachel turned to Jennifer. "I was dishonest with the people I loved. I was dishonest with myself. Jennifer, *you* know me as an honest person. I've made it a priority since that time in my life."

"Sometimes you are *too* honest," Jennifer said to break the tension. Her mother was obviously in pain.

"Maybe so. Maybe I'm still trying to make up – to compensate – for being dishonest back then, especially when it concerned the teenagers. I was supposed to be their role model and teacher for God's sake!" Rachel flipped through the journal again.

"There is a note… Here it is… that one of the Senior High boys wrote to me after a program I led. We had gone around the circle telling each other what animal he or she reminded us of and why. He writes…"

The animal you remind me of is a deer. A deer is an animal that is very pretty to me and makes me just want to pet it one time, but I can never get close enough.

"That was me, Jen. I was like a deer - always darting away." Rachel's sadness filled her and spilled into her eyes.

Without thinking, Jennifer stood up, went over to where her mother sat, and put her arms around her. All of this intense, terrible stuff, and these were the first tears her mother had shed. It was probably because she had children of her own now, thought Jennifer.

Rachel let her daughter hold her, and she hugged Jennifer back. "You are so precious to me," said Rachel, wiping her eyes.

240

What was Jennifer thinking? Rachel wondered. Maybe Kevin had been right. Maybe it wasn't good for Jennifer to know this much about the road she had traveled. Rachel gave her daughter another squeeze and then gently pushed her back to stare into her eyes. "Is this too hard for you – knowing all my flaws?" Rachel asked.

It was hard, thought Jennifer. Would it feel different if this was someone else's story? Probably. She wanted to give her mother an honest answer.

"It's hard. And part of me wishes I didn't know. But… well… I feel even closer to you now. You always said I could tell you anything. But that was just words, you know? Now I really believe it," Jennifer said sincerely.

Rachel let out a long deep breath. "That's worth something then," she said.

She hadn't anticipated this response from Jen. It was easy, as a parent, to believe that if you said something, your children understood it and took it to heart. "I'll always be there for you, no matter what" was one example. Hadn't her own mother said these words to her? But somehow she hadn't believed it. She had not trusted that her mother could handle "no matter what." If this was all she accomplished with Jennifer by telling her story, it *was* worth something.

CHAPTER TWENTY-FIVE
MUSIC AND THERAPY

Jennifer had quietly climbed back in her chair and looked ready, like a student, to hear more. Rachel stretched, unknotting her back, and picked up the journal to remind herself where she left off.

"Okay," she started. "So, now it was the summer of 1986. The new youth minister who was hired to be my partner decided to leave -- ironically, to 'find himself' -- after the first of *many* summer trips, service projects, and events with the kids. I had no choice but to do the job of two full-time employees. I was so busy with the youth that I had little time to spend with Jay. On the occasions when we did see each other, he frequently questioned me about alleged affairs I was having with certain men who crossed my path during work. It was exhausting to repeat over and over that nothing had happened. Nothing *had* happened. I began to look for reasons to avoid Jay and his badgering even when it might be possible to schedule a few more hours of private time with him.

"As I mentioned earlier, Amanda had introduced me to the local band, *Harmony*. As you know, the band is led by two women, Laura and Nicole, who play acoustic guitars and write most of their own music. That summer, I started going to more of their shows at night after work. I found myself developing a powerful 'crush' on Laura. I had always had women idols. When I was young, they were teachers or famous women -- movie stars, singers, and so forth. I'll show you my scrapbook someday.

"Laura was real and approachable. She was talented and beautiful. And I always felt *safe* in the places where *Harmony* performed – mostly in bars full of women. What you may not know," said Rachel, "is that, in the 1980s, Laura and Nicole were not 'out' as lesbians. But their fans in Austin knew, including me.

"For a long time, I had associated bars with seduction of men and tasks I had to perform by a certain hour to achieve a certain result that was frightening to me. This was different. I was free to drink, talk, laugh, and listen to music without expectations. I felt, well, *safe*. Also, the music spoke to me. Sometimes I could almost believe Laura wrote her songs with me in mind.

"Let me read to you about my feelings that summer…"

August 11, 1986

Tonight I was out by myself at a bar where Harmony was playing and my MG Midget broke-down. I asked Laura for a ride home. During the drive, I told Laura that I was sad because Amanda and I are no longer close. Laura asked me if I was gay. I was surprised by the question, but tried to be "cool" and responded that I didn't think so. Laura confided that she had assumed Amanda and I were lovers. That surprised me too. I wonder if the pain I am feeling is the pain of losing a "lover" instead of a friend. My feelings for Amanda were complicated, intense feelings. They were in many ways "passionate" feelings.

August 17, 1986

I did something crazy -- but a different kind of crazy for me. I told Laura I love her. Without missing a beat, she responded that she was flattered, but that she was already in love with her girlfriend, Tricia. I winced a little and felt embarrassed, but I am also glad that I risked rejection and grateful that Laura responded as she did. Life goes on. Our friendship has not changed. We still care about each other. Relationships with men are so different.

August 23, 1986

Laura continues to be an undemanding friend with whom I feel safe to be simply a woman in search of her identity and destiny. We share a simple trust through conversations and letters that gives me peace. I let myself *feel* on the nights I go to hear Harmony play. I know that is good for me. I feel sad about losses. I let myself realize that I am made of flesh and bone and mushy stuff that sometimes gets hurt and sometimes feels ecstasy. Laura expresses a kind of religious faithfulness through her music and a trust in family and love that enables questioning. Her openness and honesty has been a treasure to me. She has a realistic understanding of the limitations of human tolerance and, at the same time, a kind of expectancy and optimism. It's a magical combination. She makes me realize how much I want to be honest again.

Rachel looked up. Jennifer looked puzzled. She said, "Did you think you were a lesbian?"

"You know, I wasn't focused on what I was – what label. I was more aware of how free I felt," said Rachel. "I felt liberated to think about and explore that possibility. I'm sure my emotional attachment to Laura was exaggerated by my unconscious desire to escape Jay. The contrast between how *good* I felt when I was in Laura's presence and how *bad* I felt about my activities related to Jay was enormous.

"Through Laura -- or my perceptions of Laura -- I also recognized that religious or spiritual faith should not be defensive. With Jay, it was 'us against the world.' For Laura, faith seemed to incorporate the positive aspects of her family's life and values. She gave me strength to examine my decisions, motivations, and goals by providing not only a sympathetic ear but also a model of the kind of human being I wanted to be."

"So you weren't gay?" Jennifer asked again, not quite believing she was asking this question of her married-to-a-man mother.

"I wasn't sure what I was. I wasn't sure if I *needed* to be a lesbian to continue feeling the good feelings," said Rachel.

Jennifer guessed that made sense. She had been to observe a rugby club team practice at the encouragement of her lesbian friend, Jill, during her first year in college. Jill thought Jennifer would be a good addition to the team because of her strengths in soccer. Jennifer had been very aware that most, if not all, of the players were lesbians. Although she thought the game might be fun to learn and play, she couldn't get over the feeling that she didn't belong. Perhaps, her mother was just trying to find a way to fit in.

Rachel continued, "When the summer ended, the teenagers went back to high school, and my peers returned to higher education or advancing their careers. I was saddled with a part-time Youth Minister job and had to take another paper route to support myself. That was frustrating, and I was lonely.

"Jay was angry with me for 'abandoning' him during the summer months. I was angry because he didn't seem to appreciate how hard I was working at the job he said was necessary for me to prove my maturity and ability to keep commitments. I was still making demands about going public. He complained that my behavior toward him was 'sexual punishment.'

"I was sufficiently confused myself and sufficiently empowered by the women I'd been hanging around with, that I finally, *finally*, got into therapy," said Rachel. "My dad, your Papa, found a pastoral counselor for me to start meeting with in October. He was a colleague of Papa's, an older man named Williams."

"Why a man?" asked Jennifer. "Wouldn't it have been better for you to see a woman? Remember how Henry insisted you find a therapist for him who was young, a guy close to his age, a guy who liked video-games, because he thought he could relate to somebody like that better?"

"You make a good point," said Rachel. "That might have made better sense. But finding a therapist was new territory for me in those days. I let Dad handle it, and this is who he found. It wasn't a *bad* match. Any therapist worth his or her salt can be helpful if there's a connection made between patient and therapist. Remember, I was new to this. With whomever I saw, initially, I was going to tiptoe cautiously into the water, hoping to discover that the water would buoy me rather than drown me.

"You and your metaphors," Jennifer laughed. "So, what happened?"

Rachel read from her journal again...

October 7, 1986

I saw a pastoral counselor today. When he asked "why" I was seeking therapy, I told him that I had been raped two times and that those experiences were interfering with my relationship to my boyfriend. I was not being completely honest. But I am not sure I can talk to anyone, even a therapist, about Devon and Jay's "birthday present." I don't want to be condemned. What I want is complete sympathy, understanding, and comfort. Today I talked about family relationships and past relationships with men. I was as honest as I felt I could be while, at the same time, hiding information about Jay that might affect his tenure chances if it ever leaked out.

"Did Jay know you were in therapy?" asked Jennifer.

"He did. And I promised him I would not reveal too much. I justified my need for therapy by telling him I still had some 'rape issues' to work out," said Rachel. Meanwhile, Jay and I were back to the old pattern of secret meetings for the sole purpose of having sex, involving other people to satisfy Jay's longings, and using cocaine to block out any real feelings."

"So, therapy didn't help," concluded Jennifer.

"Papa once told me that he never agreed to see a couple for marriage therapy, when one person in the couple had been caught having an affair, unless the adulterer agreed to give up the affair. Until the affair ended, Papa said, the adulterer wasn't really ready to work on repairing the marriage. I didn't completely understand what he meant when he said it. But later, when I was in therapy while continuing to do things that harmed me, I did begin to understand.

"You can talk until you are blue in the face about kicking an addiction and why the addiction is bad for you. But until you actually stop using, you can't work on recovery.

"So, to answer your question, therapy helped me in certain areas, but not in others. I wasn't *being raped* anymore, so I could work on that. I could work on my relationships with family members. But I couldn't work on using versus not using cocaine, and I couldn't get much perspective on my relationship with Jay."

Rachel paused and then said, "There can be ah-ha moments in therapy. But, mostly, it's a process of healing that takes time. Initially, the most significant thing that happened to me was that I started having vivid dreams again." Rachel flipped pages in the journal. "Like these…"

October 28, 1986

Last night I dreamed that Laura told me she was attracted to me. I felt passion stir and I was brightened by her response. Then I discovered she wanted me to be a secret mistress while Tricia continued to be her public girlfriend. My heart sank and the old anger and victim feelings resurfaced… I think the dream reflects my struggle with the heartache of being a secret mistress for so long.

It feels like an identity that is destined to follow me no matter who I am involved with, even if that person is my dearest friend.

I had a second dream: I was searching and searching for Amanda at her room and around campus. I could not find her, but I needed her. I bought her a present so that I would have something more to give than my desperateness when I found her. I saw her coming out of a building as I am driving up. I tried to greet her warmly, but she was already opening her car door and stepping in. I hurriedly gave her the present. She thanked me but said she had to run. I feel like I am the gift -- tossed to the back of the car -- unable to speak urgency -- waiting, always waiting...

I believe this dream reflects the strain I feel acutely in my relationship with Amanda. I don't know how to fix it or how to approach her. In the dream, I decided to approach her with a "gift," a time-tested remedy with Jay. He responds so well to the gift of sexual experiences neatly tied in bundles. The trouble is that this approach makes me feel like the equivalent of the gift -- the sexual experience. I am an inanimate bundle that can be tossed aside.

"That's pretty insightful," suggested Jennifer.

"Yes. And that's the kind of thing therapy can facilitate. So, it wasn't all a loss," said Rachel. "I was becoming conscious of the fact that when I did as Jay directed to fulfill *Jay's* expectations and motivations, I lost. I felt empty, restless, and out of control. I was an outsider to my life. I could perform because I was tough, but I could not enjoy the performance. I knew that in the future I needed to take a more active role in creating myself through decisions I could claim as my own."

Rachel suddenly realized that she didn't know if Jennifer had ever been in therapy – if she had ever needed to speak with a counselor during the years she was in college. "Jen, you've never been in therapy, have you?" she asked.

"No. What I know about therapy is because of Henry," said Jennifer.

Jennifer shouldn't be using Henry as her "model" for who needs therapy, thought Rachel. She said, "Henry was kind of an extreme case. He had legal issues and mental health ones. But people go into therapy for lots of different reasons. They may be depressed or anxious. They may be 'stuck' in their lives and want to get 'unstuck.' They may be grieving the loss of a loved one. They may be going through a difficult transition. I guess, the one thing I would say that is common to everyone in therapy is that we all have *wounds*. But to heal a wound, you first have to open it up again, and let it heal from the inside out. A wound becomes more vulnerable before the real healing begins."

Rachel swallowed hard. "As I was opening up old wounds and becoming more vulnerable, Jay came up with a new plan that he promised would bring us closer." She looked directly at Jennifer and said, "What I'm about to read is another particularly graphic episode..."

"... but necessary to the story or you wouldn't be reading it," Jennifer completed Rachel's thought.

Rachel half-smiled. "That's my call – that this part of the story can't be avoided." She turned a page and read.

January 6, 1987

Jay has been trying to get me to arrange a ménage-a-trois for many months. As I was not able to find a woman to serve that purpose, Jay settled on the idea of a threesome with my friend, Jeff. I met Jeff in college and we had a brief romantic relationship, but we remained friends afterward. Jeff is an adventuresome person, and he agreed to give Jay's idea a try.

As usual, I arranged the event, but I was terribly nervous. We sat in Jeff's the living room, had drinks, and talked until I took a deep breath and removed my blouse. Then it began. We were in different rooms, in different positions. I was with one, then the other. I was with both. There were tongues and penises all around me, in my mouth, in my vagina, on other parts of my body. I mentally stepped outside myself and watched. I worried about who was being satisfied, who was feeling neglected. There was only one of me and all this male sexuality surrounding and invading me. I remember Jay watching Jeff enter me from behind and then taking Jeff's place and ejaculating. I remember we all finally wore ourselves out. I was sore and pulpy and wanted to be left alone, but I certainly didn't say that aloud. Jay and I said goodnight to Jeff and we returned to our car. As we started our drive home, Jay turned to me and said, "Let's do that again."

Something inside of me snapped. I was revolted and repulsed. I have never felt this extreme distaste for Jay before. I know with certainty I will not do that again -- never, never, never will I do that again! Jay is a stranger to me. He is gross and unfeeling. And he will never change. I pity him. I told him then that I would no longer use my friends this way. I told him I did not want to see him for a while. Now that I'm home and writing this, I feel nauseous.

Jennifer was speechless again. Rachel waited a few seconds for Jennifer to process what she had heard – if she could. Rachel also needed a moment to steady herself. Although she knew the story, reading it aloud took her back to that place and time. She had to return to the present and help Jennifer, as best she could, to understand what this meant to her, then and now.

"This was my 'rock bottom,'" Rachel said. "I had previously taken steps forward and stumbled a few back, but I was unable to let go of the myth of the Jay-Rachel relationship.

250

If only it could be salvaged, I imagined, all my pain would disappear.

"But that night with Jay and Jeff sickened and outraged me as never before. Yes, this should have happened on any number of previous occasions – particularly after Devon. But I couldn't see any alternative back then. I didn't really believe that using cocaine and alcohol to keep me from feeling the pain was wrong. I couldn't see that Jay had no regard for my safety and self-esteem. But, perhaps most importantly, *this* time I had sexually used someone I cared about, who predated Jay, like Sarah did. I had not forgotten Jay's attempted seduction of Sarah. And though Jeff – who I cared about - may not have felt used, *I* knew he was present solely for the use of his body. I may have lost the part of me that protected *myself* through the years, but I had not lost the part of me that protected loved ones. I was done."

"*Really* 'done,' Mom?" asked Jennifer in disbelief.

Rachel smiled and shook her head. Her daughter knew by now that "done with Jay" was not a statement she could trust.

"Well, let's just say I was a helluva lot closer to 'done.' I *was* done having sex with multiple partners and strangers. *Truly* 'done.'"

CHAPTER TWENTY-SIX
TENURE AND CONFRONTATION

"*I* went to hear *Harmony* play as often as I could, including road trips with Adagio," said Rachel.

Jennifer smiled at the mention of Adagio.

"I stopped using cocaine. The people around me didn't use drugs. It had become clearer to me that my use of cocaine was intimately connected to Jay and to all the bad stuff I wanted to forget. Since Jay wasn't around anymore, I didn't need cocaine," said Rachel.

"That means you weren't addicted to it? You could just stop?" asked Jennifer.

"I wasn't physiologically addicted. Thank God! I had been emotionally addicted because it helped me cope," replied Rachel.

"With Jay out of the picture, I probably should have been intentional about staying single and figuring out who I was. Instead, when a substitute paper carrier asked me out on a date, I said 'okay.'

"Gabe was delivering his friend's paper route and running the friend's small business for a few months." Rachel debated with herself whether or not to tell Jennifer that the friend had gone in search of Big Foot in California. She decided against it. This story was crazy enough without Big Foot!

"As Gabe and I got to know each other, I learned that he had left his family home at age sixteen, had been in technical school for a short time, and had played semi-professional football. He said he didn't demand too much from life – only 'happiness.' Gabe was young, athletic, and extremely good-looking. He could have been a professional model." Rachel smiled at the memory. She also remembered that she had wondered why he picked *her* when he could have picked any woman.

"Still, given my track record with men, I was wary. But, from our first date, I could tell that Gabe liked me for reasons other than my looks. He was content to tag along and help with my youth work. The teenagers liked him and thought he was a good match for me. I enjoyed having a boyfriend who could be with me in public. Almost without any conscious choice on my part, Gabe became part of my life. He was always with me."

"Something tells me that this is not going to end well," said Jennifer, a concerned look crossing her face.

Rachel felt warmed by her daughter's protectiveness. She said, "You are right. But I'm betting you can't guess the reasons 'why.'"

Jennifer shrugged. She had too many possibilities running through her head to venture a guess.

"The first trouble had nothing to do with Gabe directly. It came when I discovered in May that Jay had received tenure at the theology school and took Elizabeth Nash to his celebration party. I was *so* hurt," said Rachel.

"That *bastard*!" shouted Jennifer, jerking upright in the recliner.

Rachel laughed, and Jennifer blushed in embarrassment about her language.

"I'm not laughing at you, Jen. Gosh, given everything you've heard, that was the perfect response," said Rachel reassuringly.

Jennifer recovered. "That was *the thing* you'd been waiting for – *the thing* that was supposed to make all your suffering go away." She paused. "Okay. I knew it wouldn't. But *you* believed it would."

"I really did... still... after all this time. I called Jay, determined to let him know just how angry I was. But all that came out of my mouth was the pain. I recorded the conversation on paper verbatim. This is what I wrote..."

"Jay?"
"Yes."
"This is Rachel... How are you? I heard you got tenure, but I didn't hear it from *you*. I'm really hurt, Jay. What

happened? What happened to the promise? I thought --
you promised -- it was going to be our second chance. How
could you, Jay? How could you do that to me after all
these years? -- After all we've been through?"

"I don't know what you mean. I haven't known for
very long."

"But there was a party, wasn't there? I heard you took
Elizabeth... Are you dating Elizabeth now?"

"Yes."

"Are you in love with her?"

"I love her very much."

"Are you going to marry her?"

"That would be premature to say."

"Does she... I mean, it doesn't matter if I know. I
mean, I just want to get a clear picture... does she spend
time with Ben?"

"We spend time with Ben. And we spend time alone."

"Oh, Jay! Oh, it hurts, Jay. It's what was supposed to
happen for us... And is it a relief to have tenure at least?"

"It came too late. I work... but it came too late."

"You just have to know that I feel used and abused."

"I'm sorry to hear that."

"Well,..."

"Thank you for calling." CLICK

Jennifer's mouth was slightly ajar. This time she whispered,
"That bastard."

"The only redeeming part of the conversation was the fact
that Jay *still* wasn't satisfied with his life despite the long-
awaited tenure. But, most of all, I felt like someone had kicked
the wind out of me. Somehow I had to come to terms with the
fact that I was no longer at the center of his life -- if indeed I ever
was. The latter was a more frightening possibility," said Rachel.

"With Jay dating Elizabeth *publicly*, secure in his tenure, I
realized that I needed to get on with my *own* life. I needed a full-

time job, not a part-time Youth Minster position and a part-time paper route – jobs with no future. So, in June, I found work as a teacher in another hospital on another psychiatric unit. At this hospital, there are five adolescent psychiatric units, one child unit, and one young adult. I was part of a staff of twelve teachers who had regular staff meetings and weekly supervision with our school director. Almost every interaction I had at the hospital, whether with peers or students, was conducted on a therapeutic model. Co-workers seem to really care about my feelings. We were expected to discuss our feelings and any personal problems that might be interfering with our work.

"Pretty soon, I was pegged as insecure and overzealous as a caretaker. I was pushed to explore the ways my victimization experiences carried over into my present life and work. I wrote…" Rachel again flipped through her journal to the relevant passage.

July 12, 1987

I feel like I'm on a roller coaster -- sometimes up, sometimes down, trying to catch my breath, always frightened, never really in control, and never knowing what's around the next bend. I feel caught in some kind of emotional freeze as well. I can't quite cry or laugh or be angry. Everything feels stilted and not quite real or quite me. I want desperately to fit in here - but I don't know how.

"More opening up the wounds, right?" queried Jennifer.

"Uh-huh. It was both the perfect setting for me to be in and the worst. My perception was that my supervisor and the other teachers were skilled at making decisions about what to share and how much. I wasn't. When I opened up, I felt like I had no control over what might come pouring out," said Rachel.

"Meanwhile, there was my relationship with Gabe. In the beginning, we were perfect playmates. I could relax and get away from it all with Gabe. He was very strong and athletic, so we exercised together. We watched movies and made enormous meals and just sat around swapping stories. There was no heaviness, no profound decisions to make, just happiness."

"That's what Gabe said he wanted," commented Jennifer.

"He did," said Rachel. "But by October, Gabe was beginning to confide in me about *his* dark side. I didn't notice it at first, but his confessions seemed to increase the more alcohol he drank. Listen to this..."

October 7, 1987

My curiosity got the better of me. I wanted to know where Gabe had come from. What was his family like? What were his beliefs and values? He told me he had grown up in a large family that was very religious. At first he described light-hearted moments and the special character of each brother and sister. But after a while, dark secrets began to emerge. He told me that his father physically and sexually abused family members. Gabe, as the oldest son, was required to accompany his father to bars where his father picked up women. Gabe was required to watch them have sex. His father sexually abused at least one of the boys and more than one of the girls. Gabe tried to protect them but could not. He remembers his father kicking his pregnant mother in the stomach. He remembers his father taking a sister's cat into her bedroom and making her watch him cut the live cat open with a coat hanger.

Jennifer gasped.

He also remembers taking some of his siblings to the pastor of their church and trying to tell that pastor what happened in their home. The pastor didn't believe them and called their parents to come get them.

Gabe left his family home because he wanted a new life. But, he says, it seems that he can never stay in one place for long. Gabe says women have used him. When he was broke, he would go to bars and women would buy him food and drink. Then they would take him home for sex. Gabe told me about having trouble getting aroused and about feeling dirty and guilty afterwards. I understand.

I listen to Gabe and I hurt for him. The world is so screwed-up and, unfortunately, so are many churches. I asked Gabe to get help from a therapist. Instead, he says he wants to *marry* me and have babies. It is crazy. Gabe is sweet and tender with me most of the time, but I wonder if he will ever be "well." *I* want to be well.

Rachel didn't give Jennifer a chance to respond. "I couldn't believe what I was hearing from Gabe. I panicked. Gabe was another version of *me*. He was a victim of sexual and emotional abuse. I wanted to help him as much as I wanted to run in the other direction. On the outside, he was so beautiful. But on the inside – Damn!"

"You wanted to help him even though you were not healthy yet yourself," Jennifer said with assurance. Jennifer knew this about her mother. She knew her mother never shied away when she saw someone in pain.

"You know my personality," said Rachel. "That actually makes telling this story easier for me." Rachel smiled appreciatively at Jennifer.

"Yes. I wanted to help Gabe. But I couldn't get him to go to a therapist. For one thing, he didn't have the money for one. He also wasn't convinced he needed professional help. I decided to tell *my* therapist Gabe's stories," said Rachel.

"What happened?"

"Williams went ballistic. This is what I wrote…"

October 13, 1987

Last week I shared some of the stories about Gabe's childhood and adolescence with my therapist. He lost his cool for the first time in all the months I have been seeing him. He stated - in no uncertain terms - that I should get out of the relationship immediately. I was shocked into silence. I wasn't sure I wanted to come back this week. I did go back, and the first thing my therapist did was to apologize. He told me that what he had done was wrong. He had been taking the role of my father. That makes sense to me. They are both older men with grown children. He said he was trying to control me the way my father had controlled me through outbursts of emotion, knowing I trusted his judgment, knowing I felt powerless to rebut his opinion or deal with his emotions.

This is a turning point for us. We are acknowledging that the father-daughter relationship is part of the way my work with him is done. He says that what I can benefit from the most during these months of therapy is the opportunity to practice saying to my "father" what I feel and what I have done. I am learning that although a father can be wrong, I do not have to run away. I can confront him with the truth. I can learn to stand my ground and believe in myself even if he does not respond with acceptance -- my greatest fear.

"Wow. That's big. I'm guessing your 'father' might also be Jay?" suggested Jennifer. "What you were saying about connecting to a therapist – I get that now. The therapist doesn't have to be *like* you. But there has to be a way of relating that moves you forward."

"Exactly," replied Rachel, proud of her daughter's insightfulness.

Jennifer had never thought she needed therapy. But now, she wondered. Had David been her "father"? She had done whatever he asked of her. She had never confronted him or questioned his authority.

"I was so empowered by therapy at that point," said Rachel, "that I was ready to do battle with Jay again. I wanted answers." Rachel thumbed through her journal, finding the letters she had written. "I wrote to him twice in mid-October. I listed the risks I'd taken." Rachel read from her list: "adultery, finding multiple lovers, staging performances, contacting and buying from drug dealers, lying to family and friends. I listed what I'd received in return: herpes, love letters returned to me for 'safe-keeping,' the loss of Amanda and Jeff as friends, fears and suspicions about men, an inability to love anyone else. I demanded a response. I didn't get one. So, I wrote to Jay again. This time I pleaded with him for answers to my questions: Was he ever in love with me? Was he ever serious about marrying me? Was Elizabeth *always* in the picture? Did he really believe our sexual stunts would ever end? Did he worry that I'd get caught buying or possessing drugs? Did he have other affairs? Did he really think I was gay? And so on."

"You really laid it out there for him," said Jennifer. "Did he answer the second time?"

"He must have known I would persist unless he did. I received this response…"

October 25, 1987

The time we spent together was important and compelling. All the questions you have asked were discussed at length in the context of the time. I have no desire to attempt to re-think now, with such distance in experience and mind-set as is evident, or to re-hash what is over. It is inappropriate.

I, too, am trying to put my feet on the ground, and - just as I would not dream of intruding upon you - expect that you will afford me the same minimal courtesy.

"I would have been pissed!" exclaimed Jennifer.

Rachel couldn't help feeling touched that her daughter was angry for her. "I was furious," she said. "Jay had moved into a house with Elizabeth and Ben. They are his public family.

"But think about this," Rachel said to Jennifer. "If Jay had done battle with me, all of the details of the past six years might have come out. Would that have been a *good* thing for me? I didn't mention this before, but I had gingerly approached my advisor at the theology school years before when I was at a low point with Jay. I wanted someone to intervene and get me out of these bizarre sexual scenarios. I don't remember exactly what was said – and this was something I didn't write down – but he dismissed my concern about Jay and his control over me. Everything was 'fine.' It was sort of like the pastor at Gabe's church. If you aren't believed, you go back into hiding.

"Anyway, if the truth had come out, jobs, relationships – all of it might have been thrown into disarray or destroyed. I don't know, but in some ways I'm glad it didn't come out then. I was so fragile. I might not have faired well… The fact is, the past stayed hidden. And that created other problems for me that I would deal with later on."

Jennifer was trying to wrap her mind around her mother's conclusion that circumstances and timing determine when one tells the truth. "So, you are saying that the truth should only come out at certain *times*? What about your admonition to 'always tell the truth'?"

"'Always tell the truth' works great if you tell the truth at the time of an event," said Rachel. "That's why I'm forever encouraging my children to fess up to errors, mistakes, or accidents when they happen. Later on, it gets trickier. People rely on your deceptions. Whole worlds may come crumbling down with the revelation that a lie was told if it's revealed years later." Rachel knew she might be exaggerating to make her point, but she didn't think she was far from a fair statement.

"Think about this. I'll use a real example. Jay eventually married Elizabeth and they had kids. Is it fair to those kids to know the truth about their father? What would that do to them? Should that matter? I'm not sure I have an answer to my own question. But I do think it helps if the recipients of the truth are healthy enough to hear it," said Rachel.

"I see what you mean. I'm going to have to think about this some more," said Jennifer, looking genuinely perplexed, Rachel thought.

"I hope you do. If you figure it out, let me know," she smiled.

Jennifer yawned and Rachel took this as her signal to stop for the day. "Next week, then?" she asked. And Jennifer nodded.

=====

Over the next few days, Jennifer was aware that she felt lighter – happier – than she had in the past few months. She reckoned that she had grown accustomed to her mother's painful stories. 'Comfortable' was too strong a word. But she had settled in. She no longer awakened in the night, frightened by her dreams.

Jennifer was venturing out more. She spent more time with Cheryl or Louise. She had been to the movie theater alone – something new for her. She thought she sounded more authoritative when customers asked her questions. She had become aware that she walked with her head held high more often now, unafraid to look around and take in her surroundings, including the men who stared or gawked at her. She was changing in a good way, she thought.

It didn't add up. How could her mother's misery make *her* feel better? All she knew was that she felt 'hopeful' instead of 'defeated.'

SUNDAY
NOVEMBER 9, 2014

CHAPTER TWENTY-SEVEN
HOSPITAL LESSONS

"*L*ast week, we left off talking about Gabe's dark side and my response to Jay's tenure," began Rachel. "Now I need to tell you what I was working on professionally. I had been at the second psychiatric hospital for only two months when I landed on the idea that I wanted to be an attorney. Actually," said Rachel, "the idea percolated throughout all my years working with teenagers – but particularly in the hospitals. I knew I had the ability to help students who had been unsuccessful in school to achieve success by tailoring an academic program to their specific needs. But I had also learned that I could not control many of the contextual changes they needed in their lives to continue to be successful *outside* the hospital. For example, one of the students I helped get his GED was observed selling drugs on the street not long after he left us. His home life was miserable and it propelled him back to crime. I thought that, as a lawyer, I would have the power to advocate for structural changes in home life, in schooling, and in larger social issues."

"Pretty optimistic," stated Jennifer, somewhat sarcastically. She'd heard other stories from her mother over the years about roadblocks to justice for certain clients, particularly those in poverty. Mom gave the impression that legal remedies where not always available to solve some of the most difficult problems.

"Yes. But I *was* optimistic in 1987. What did I know?" Rachel smiled. "The grass always looks greener on the other side of the fence, as they say. Besides, I was frustrated at work for some other reasons, and I thought being an attorney would free me of those."

"What reasons?" asked Jennifer.

"I often disagreed with the hospital's general approach to treatment. There was a prescription for 'normal' that was routinely imposed on patients regardless of their individual differences. For example, a seventeen-year-old girl was hospitalized on my locked unit for her homosexual activities," said Rachel.

"Seriously?" Jennifer questioned.

"Seriously," confirmed Rachel. "This was the 1980s. Thank goodness we've progressed *some* in our thinking about sexual orientation and gender identity since then. For a time, homosexuality was considered a mental illness."

Jennifer shook her head in disbelief. She'd known that homosexuality had been misunderstood as illness. But she didn't realize this misunderstanding had been as recent as her mother's young adult life.

"In the case of my patient," said Rachel, "her diagnosis was 'depression.' It seemed apparent to me, however, that her depression was the direct result of being rejected by her family because of her sexual orientation. Her treatment plan called on the staff to try to 'convert' her to heterosexuality. I simply could not comply."

"That amazes me," said Jennifer.

"Your generation – in general – knows better," said Rachel. "You know that this kind of rigidity to others' expectations is unhealthy and destructive to individual lives.

"'Professional power' had also become an increasingly important issue for me," continued Rachel. "In hospitals, only doctors were referred to by their titles while the rest of the staff were called by their first names. The vast majority of doctors were men. Many of the staff members had advanced degrees, but we were indirectly, and sometimes directly, made to feel inferior. Insights about the patients from activity therapists, nurses, and teachers were given limited weight despite the fact that we spent many more hours with the patients than their doctors did.

"Also, while I was working at the hospital, insurance became an issue. The rules changed regarding what diagnoses insurance companies would cover and for how long. Generally speaking, insurance coverage was *less* than before. So, for example – and I don't remember the exact number of days – a person with the diagnosis of depression might be entitled to five paid days in the hospital while a person diagnosed with bipolar disorder might be entitled to ten days. Suddenly, the staff was being asked to 'chart' or take notes on each patient in a way that moved them quickly through treatment and out the door. It was clearly about getting paid and not about what was in the best interests of the patient… in my humble opinion." Rachel wasn't sure everyone who worked with her would agree with this assessment.

"The bottom line is - I wanted more autonomy and control. I thought that becoming an attorney would give me a better chance at achieving that power," said Rachel.

"You should have been focused on power all along," said Jennifer.

"You're right. After years of being suffocated under a heavy blanket of shame, my feminist inclinations were beginning to be reasserted."

Rachel opened a journal and looked at Jennifer. "Another reason I thought I might make a good lawyer was because of my caring nature and sensitivity other's feelings. I write about this in my journal…"

October 2, 1987

I think about Charlie, a sixteen-year-old boy I worked with who was diagnosed with schizophrenia. Under medication and through therapy he became increasingly healthier over a course of months. As his release date approached, however, his visions and random thoughts returned. It is the practice of the hospital not to tell young patients what their diagnoses are. The theory is that each teen should approach group therapy predisposed to think of him/herself as more like than dislike his or her peers. Diagnoses, it is assumed, will interfere with this assumption.

My schizophrenic patient learned through some error on the part of a staff member that he had been labeled "psychotic." He came to school and looked up the definition of that word in our dictionary. He was very troubled and unable to work in school that day. Toward the end of class hours, I approached him. As his peers were leaving the room, he told me how scared he was. He was afraid he would never be better. Knowing that Charlie is a skilled guitar player, I told him that I had heard James Taylor, the famous musician, was psychotic too. I heard that he wrote "Fire and Rain" about another patient he met in a mental hospital. I asked Charlie to think about what Taylor had achieved despite his diagnosis. He left the room without responding.

Later that day, during group therapy, Charlie said he had gone to his room and listened to James Taylor's "You've Got a Friend." He said he had been really frightened by what he'd learned about his diagnosis, "But I talked to Rachel, and I think I'm going to be okay"... It is a small thing, but at that moment I felt like I could make a difference. My compassion for people, for victims of forces they cannot control, will help me be useful to others in the legal profession, I think.

Jennifer noticed that her mom seemed lost in thought. "What's wrong, Mom?" she asked.

"I was just thinking how I never really proved if that last statement is true. After you were born, and even though I worked part-time until Henry came along, I was more focused on being a good mother than on finding out if I was capable of as an attorney," said Rachel.

"There's still time," said Jennifer brightly, seeing that her mother needed cheering up.

Rachel took comfort in Jennifer's encouragement. "Of course there is," she said, not sure if she meant it.

266

Rachel cleared her head and returned to the story.

"I took the LSAT or law school admission test in October and waited for the results. I also received a letter from the parole board informing me that they were considering releasing Isaiah Barry from prison in December of that year. The letter said I could write to the board and express any concerns I might have. I wrote that Barry had threatened me and that I was frightened he might come after me. I asked if he had been rehabilitated. Could I be assured of safety? And I waited to find out the results of that too."

"I thought you said Barry was sentenced to twenty years," Jennifer said.

"He was. I wish I understood this better, but I don't. What I know is that sentences rarely refer to the actual time one spends in prison. Depending on behavior, some prisoners only spend a fraction of their sentence inside. The rest of their time is on parole, outside the prison walls. It would have been roughly five and a half years that Barry had been in prison," said Rachel.

"That must have been scary for you. But I guess you had the handsome, football player Gabe to protect you," Jennifer grinned. "You never said what happened to Gabe. Did he get better? Did he get help?"

Rachel turned serious. "Gabe was not getting better. Here, let me read from my journal to you…"

November 3, 1987

I am really worried about Gabe's drinking. I am surrounded by people with substance abuse problems every day at work, and I can't help but notice that Gabe has all the same symptoms. He drinks to escape. He drinks to excess. His drinking drives him to remember more about his family life, and this makes him drink more. I recommended that he go to Alcoholics Anonymous, but he didn't go. I then asked him to go to AL anon -- because he admits his father is an alcoholic -- knowing he might recognize his own problem if he goes. I can't get him to go without going myself. But I am willing to do that.

Rachel continued, "The friend with the business and paper route had returned and resumed his jobs. Gabe was out of work. He looked for work, but found nothing consistent. I wrote..."

November 27, 1987

When Gabe's latest temporary employment ended, I told him he could move in with me -- but only for one month, unless he paid his share of the bills. He tried to hold a job, but couldn't. He borrowed money from me and promised to pay me back. I went to a hospital-sponsored meeting to learn about confronting Gabe with his alcoholism. I set deadlines for his getting a job, paying back money, and seeking treatment. I told him that if he did not meet my deadlines, I would kick him out.

Three days ago, the last deadline came and went, so I asked Gabe to leave. It felt terrible, but I did it. He disappeared last night in a friend's car with several hundred dollars in unpaid debts to me. Have I been too cruel?

"No!" answered Jennifer. "You didn't need another man to take care of in your life."

"That's my girl. That's the answer I want you to give yourself *if ever* ... "

"Oh, Mom," sighed Jennifer.

"At the time, I felt like I was being selfish," said Rachel. "I thought I had chosen my health over his. I did not yet understand that taking care of myself was not *selfish*. Taking care of myself meant that I was in a *better* position to take care of others too. It's the logic behind the airline safety demonstration that instructs the adult to put on an air mask before putting one on a child."

Jennifer felt the indictment of her mother's words. As a religion major, there had been no obvious professional goal at the end of her education. She had been attracted to the degree because of the multi-cultural, multi-ethnic world she lived in. She was fascinated by differences, and she knew that religion was often the basis of a person's values and beliefs. Everyone had faith in *something*. For some people, what was of ultimate value derived from their Christianity, Judaism, Islam, Hinduism or some other formalized religion. For others, it was a belief system that elevated power or money or beauty and so forth. Conflicts arose between people and groups in politics, in law, in schools, in communities, between countries – basically *everywhere*, Jennifer had determined, because of these differences in belief.

At one point or another, she had considered a variety of careers for which this knowledge base – this religion major – would be useful. She might join the Peace Corps or the Foreign Service. She might go into teaching or journalism or law or international business. The possibilities had seemed endless.

But by the end of her junior year in college, Jennifer realized, she was no longer focused on what *she* might do. She had turned her destiny over to Chris. He would be applying to medical school and moving to an undetermined location. She would be following him, so she couldn't make plans of her own. She would find something to do wherever they landed, she had thought. What a fool she had been!

The sound of her mother's voice brought Jennifer back to the present.

"So, Gabe was gone by the end of November and, that month, I also learned that I had done really well on the LSAT. Basically, my high scores opened the door for me to go to law school almost anywhere I chose. *And* I received another letter from the parole board informing me that Barry's review for release had been moved back to December 1988. My life had definitely taken a turn for the better," said Rachel.

"Meanwhile, I was in a therapeutic environment at work. Plus, my own therapy was paying off. Even though I didn't reveal all my secrets to Williams, he opened me up to work on my private stuff privately," said Rachel.

"I found a journal entry I wrote near the end of 1987 that I'd like for you to hear…"

December 7, 1987

The man who became my savior during the ordeal of that first year after I was raped brought his own agenda of sexual needs to my recovery process, an agenda that adversely affected me and, indeed, slowed my recovery. Jay was the most brilliant and sensitive man I'd ever met. I adored him and would have done anything to sustain his affection for me.

The following emerged as the ground rules for our relationship over several years. This occurred gradually; and so I met each of his new requirements as isolated events rather than seeing them as a pattern. I knew he had been used by women, and so I rationalized that whatever was necessary to convince him that I was not an abusive woman was part of the price I had to pay to win his trust and love. Jay's rules for Rachel can be summarized:

Rule 1: The more you love sex and admit you love sex, the more I'll love you and the more likely I'll be to make a lifelong commitment to you. And –

Rule 2: The more you love sex, the less likely I'll trust you to be faithful to me. So –

Rule 3: The more often you have sex with others and tell me or include me or let me watch, etc., the more likely I'll trust you.

I was caught. The only way to prove fidelity and earn fidelity was by infidelity. Believe me, I did not go passively along in these endeavors. We fought over them; but then I'd give in. This did two things: It reinforced my sense of powerlessness and reinforced the thesis that people who like sex can't be satisfied with one partner.

"You nailed it, Mom!" Jennifer said excitedly. "You simplified the whole thing into something that really makes sense..." she smiled, "in an insane kind of way."

"I'm pretty impressed with my insightfulness then too." Rachel then shook her head and pursed her lips. "I guess it's one thing to figure out a pattern or see the logic or to draw conclusions from a bunch of data. It is something quite different to *use* the knowledge effectively. It's like I said before about Jay. What he 'knew' in Montana didn't translate into a change in our relationship. That requires a day-to-day commitment. You know, like a recovering alcoholic stops drinking one day at a time."

Jennifer straightened. "It's also about creating a new habit, right? I remember you used to tell me how hard it was to get back in shape after you let yourself go for very long. You lost muscle tone and had to rebuild it. Plus, it was painful to get those muscles built and working again."

Rachel was nodding. "Yes. I had an understanding of how Jay and I related. I knew it wasn't healthy and couldn't be sustained. But I didn't have anything else to replace it with yet. No healthy habits."

Rachel swallowed hard and said, "Believe it or not, after telling me we were done, Jay called me again in late December."

"Oh, no!" moaned Jennifer.

271

"It wasn't as bad as you might imagine," said Rachel. She wondered if she had left *anything* to the imagination after all she had shared with Jennifer. "Here's what I wrote..."

December 27, 1987

Yesterday, I received a phone call from a humble-sounding Jay Winchester who wanted to see me again. We spent another torrid night of passion together. But instead of feeling exposed or remorseful afterward, I feel like I am on solid ground. Life is complicated. Though I know Jay is wrong for me in many ways, I also know he has not been wrong about everything. When I met Jay years ago, he tapped into some core truth, some yearning in me for a richer life, a life that challenged cultural expectations -- religious or otherwise. This hunger we shared is why our relationship began as consensually as it did. As a stronger individual I can still learn a few healthy things from Jay about the importance of sexuality. Sure, he distorted that message, but it is a message that in a different, respectful form I believe in. It makes sense to me that part of the reason recovery from sexual assault is so difficult is because talking about anything that affects our sexuality is difficult.

Jennifer looked perturbed, Rachel thought. Jennifer said, "You are saying it was 'just sex' and you could handle it. Come on, Mom! We've had this talk. There is no such thing as 'just sex.'"

"Oh, Lord," Rachel thought. Jen was turning her own pronouncements of "truth" against her. She had to laugh. "You're right. Of course, you're right. It would never be 'just sex' with Jay. We had a deep and abiding connection – an unhealthy one – but a connection that went beyond sex. But, hey, can you give me credit for gaining some perspective and for no longer being under his complete control?

"Frankly," Rachel continued. "I was feeling a little smug that Jay had come crawling back to me. Elizabeth out. Rachel in."

"Truth, Mom. Did you get sucked back in?" asked Jennifer.

"Not completely. I had too much else going on – but not romantically. Jay and I met from time to time to have sex. But he didn't have the same power over me," stated Rachel. "I had something else on my mind."

Chapter Twenty-Eight
Sexual Orientation

"This is how I described myself at the beginning of 1988…" said Rachel.

January 1, 1988

I am more hopeful than I have been for many years as 1988 begins. I am excited about visiting different law schools and considering the possibility of moving away from Austin. I have, on more than one occasion recently, been successful at limiting the contact I have with Jay to an amount and kind I can handle. I also feel ready to learn more about the part of me that is so enamored with women. Ever since Jay and Laura at separate times and in very different ways suggested I might be romantically and sexually attracted to Amanda, the issue of homosexuality has been on my mind. Would I be happier with a partner and lover who is female? Is that my destiny? I am not at all sure I am a lesbian, but the idea of "coming out" of hiding appeals to me. "Coming out," for me, means being honest about what is and about who I am in the aftermath of rape.

"And this too," said Rachel.

January 20, 1988

My principle concern this month has been to prioritize a list of possible law schools. Toward that end, I traveled with my mother to the East Coast to visit some schools while she attended a business-related conference. At the conference, I met a colleague of Mom's who recently announced publicly that she is a lesbian. I talked some with

Ellen and felt comfortable with her. I wrote to her about questioning my own sexual orientation. She wrote back:

...Right now I am sensing there is a lot of energy among lesbians and woman-identified, heterosexual women. Bookstores, music, new age hopes/theology, positive ambiance, peace concerns seem to focus here. But as with any other group, there is a wide spectrum of experience which might bring commitment to a lesbian lifestyle. Some of us grew up 'knowing' (from age 12 or 13 when we first 'fell in love' with a woman). Others come to a lesbian lifestyle after long years in a heterosexual marriage. Still others are young (like yourself) and still seeking a core identity and life commitment. So the types of women cover a wide range and style.

I guess my own bias is that no one end up in the lesbian lifestyle unless there is no other choice. This is because it is simply too difficult and painful in terms of social norms, families, having children, etc. I would not have chosen it; it chose me, and I spent some years trying to change myself and become heterosexual. I enjoy men enormously, work with them daily, and yet finally, intimate needs cannot be met by a man. And so the choice is clear. But from what you have written about yourself, it is not clear. It does sound like you need some space away from your family. But no matter where you end up geographically in terms of law school, I think it is very important that you not hide major decisions from your parents. This takes so much energy and is severely draining. So I hope you can figure out how to let them in a bit more on your questions and explorations, while at the same time giving yourself space to BE.

As I reread your letter again now, it does strike me how at-home you feel with women -- but I am not sure that makes you gay. One of the most helpful experiences in my life was to have a relatively successful, intimate relationship with a man who was relatively healthy and loving as well. Through him I discovered I simply did not fit emotionally in the heterosexual world. But, as I said before, my early experiences as an adolescent helped to clarify this too.

...We all need to go towards what is life giving, no matter what the price. The only really comforting or encouraging word I can offer is that things usually come clear with time. But I sure hope it does not take you the 25 years it took me.

Rachel looked up from her reading. "Remember that Ellen is from an older generation. I suspect your generation would not have a bias against a 'lesbian lifestyle' as she writes."

"That's for sure," said Jennifer. "Many of the women I went to college with were 'experimenting' with lesbianism like it was a new drug or take-it-or-leave-it proposition."

Jennifer paused. "So what did Ellen's letter mean to you?"

"I appreciated her sensitivity to me and her candidness about her own life. Three things that she wrote about, in particular, stuck with me. I should be *honest* with myself and with the family I love. I should *find out* about my sexual orientation sooner rather than later. I should get *distance* from my current circumstances. She also said: 'Go toward what is life-giving.' I needed to figure out what that meant for me," said Rachel.

"The distance part is why you went to law school in California, isn't it?" suggested Jennifer.

"That was part of it. But before we talk about law school, I wanted to address the sexual orientation aspect."

Jennifer raised her eyebrows. "Sounds intriguing," she said.

"In the spring of 1988, I was playing soccer," began Rachel.

"*You?* I thought you told me you were a terrible soccer player," said Jennifer.

"I was pretty bad compared to my teammates." Rachel grimaced. "But I spent all those months hanging out at bars to hear *Harmony* play. Along the way, I met some women, mostly lesbians, who invited me to play on a mostly-lesbian women's soccer team. You know I love team sports and being outside. Well, I decided to give it a try. My social group became this group of women who were attracted to other women. It *got* to me. Here's what I wrote..."

March 1, 1988

My teammate, Jessie, is one of the prettiest and, at the same time, most athletic women I have ever seen. Her body is perfect. She is blond and has piercing green eyes that seem to search a person's soul. She is the best player on our team. I feel light-headed around her. As discreetly as I can, I have been asking others about her. What is she like? Is she dating anyone? Friends say she is shy, but nice, and very thought-full about life. She isn't dating anyone. One person suggested I ask her out. I have no idea how to do that! Not only am I inexperienced in the area of dating women, Jessie seems as unavailable to me as the quarterback at my high school was. She barely knows me. And I know I can't impress her with my novice-like soccer playing ability. Nevertheless, I am interested...

"Mom! You had another crush on a girl! And was Jessie more available than Laura had been?" Jennifer seemed more delighted than disturbed by the idea, thought Rachel.

"Did you ever do anything about the 'crush'?" Jennifer smiled.

"As a matter of fact, I did," Rachel responded a little sheepishly. Jennifer raised her eyebrows again.

"In April, I found out where Jessie worked and I dropped by to discuss something trivial just to get some time alone with her. I felt about twelve years old, but Jessie was great. She seemed to understand why I was there and she didn't shut me down.

"We went out for a drink one night and the conversation went well. A few days later... well, here's what I wrote..." Rachel opened the journal and found her place.

April 16, 1988

Jessie and I went out to dinner and spent another several hours talking. I could barely eat anything because my stomach was so full of her presence. When we got back to her car and before she got out of mine, I asked her if I could kiss her. To my surprise, she said "yes." It was a kiss like nothing I have ever experienced before. It was so gentle and soft. I started to be more aggressive, but she gently stopped me. I wonder if that aggressiveness is a product of my heterosexual training. It was a perfect kiss.

"Wow. I'm surprised," said Jennifer. "I never would have guessed."

"It's funny," Jennifer continued, "as you were reading, I was hoping something would happen. Is there more?" she asked expectantly, not quite believing this was her *mother* she was cheering for.

"Yes and no," replied Rachel. I need to go back and fill in the 'professional' piece of the story first." Rachel flipped the journal back a few pages and then looked up.

"I had applied to several law schools including Austin University Law School. In February, I got a call from AULS notifying me that I was a finalist for a prestigious scholarship that included full tuition and a $2500 a year stipend for three years. That was a lot of money in those days. It was a great honor. But after the initial rush of excitement, I started to feel depressed about being 'trapped' at AU for three more years.

"I went through the interview process successfully and received the written scholarship offer. I had very little money saved for school. So, two weeks later, with mixed emotions, I accepted the scholarship to AULS and turned down every other law school that had accepted me. *But,* I had not yet heard from Challenge University School of Law. That was in March.

"Then in early April, I received notice that Challenge University had accepted me into its joint degree program and was offering me a partial scholarship. This was a three and a half year program, at the end of which I would receive a J.D. or Juris Doctor, a law degree, and a M.A. or Master of Arts in history. If I chose to accept, I would begin my studies that summer with forty other members of the first-year class who were pursuing various joint degrees.

"I was excited about the possibility, but there was a lot to consider. The AU scholarship was the main reason to refuse Challenge's offer. And I was somewhat fearful about leaving my family and friends in Austin.

"But there were so many other reasons to move at that point in my life: Challenge was considered the better law school. Challenge graduates seemed to have better options for employment. The additional degree might give me an edge if I decided to pursue doctoral work or teaching at the college level. I also wanted to do the thing that would make me a better, healthier and happier person -- whatever that meant!

"I remembered something your Papa said to me about his decision to move to Chicago for his Ph.D. work, after having lived in and around Austin all his life. He said, 'You can't *choose* home if you've never *left* home.' Does that make sense?" Rachel asked.

"*I* went away to school," Jennifer was nodding. "I saw and experienced new things – being in the mountains, Southern culture, snow! I would not have experienced those things or met the people I met if I had stayed in Austin. It gave me a different perspective. And I learned new things about myself."

"So, you understand," said Rachel. "I thought that understanding who I was – my identity, post-rape – would always be a problem for me unless I got some distance from this place of my origin and, virtually, all of my experiences thus far. I might eventually choose to make Austin my home. But I wanted the *choice*. And I wanted to know myself and how I operated without the familiar supports I had in Austin… But I was grateful that Adagio was going with me."

Jennifer smiled at the mention of Adagio again. She said, "So you went to California."

"I was leaning toward that decision when another opportunity or experience came my way in April that would clinch the deal."

CHAPTER TWENTY-NINE
LEAVING HOME

*L*isten to this…" said Rachel.

April 8, 1988

My dance therapist friend, Sally, persuaded me to attend a weekend workshop at the hospital based on Arnold Mindell's *The Dream-Body in Relationships*. Mindell's premise, as I understand it, is that people communicate simultaneously with two very separate languages without realizing it. Their first language, the intended one, consists of the issues and themes they focus on. It is so powerful that it obliterates their awareness of the unintended, dream-like communication process. This second process, called "dream-body language," consists of grunts, shrugs, sounds, eyebrow movements, sitting positions, and other forms of unintended language. It is also expressed in dreams. One's goal should be to uncover this second language.

Mindell's ideas are particularly intriguing to me at this point in my life because he talks about a detrimental split, and I have lived for so long with the sense of being split into different parts: public and private, mind and body, sexual and romantic, etc. I know I want to merge my public and private lives, to put the soul back in sex, and to bring sex back into the whole of my life.

When I got home from the workshop, I continued to read the book. There is an example given of a couple who reminds me of Jay and Rachel. The analysis suggests they represent two parts of the same dream: one part wants passion and the other part represses it. As a body with two parts, one is sexual partly because the other is shy. The analysis concludes that as long as the couple is together they will share this dream... Reading this worries me. It suggests that sex might always be the paradigm for my relationship to Jay; and I know by now that our "dream" is an unhealthy one, at least for me.

April 9, 1988

After I had read two-thirds of the book, I drifted off to sleep and had this dream: I was in a vacation house in the mountains with Dad. We were waiting for Mom. There was an upstairs and a downstairs to the house. I had been eating a package of peanut butter cookies downstairs and left them half eaten to do something else. When I came back downstairs later to clean up, I saw a tail sticking out of the cookie package. Then I saw a group of chipmunks and knew they had come in to eat the cookies I left out. I didn't know what to do because I was scared. Suddenly I saw some baby kittens who had come out to get the chipmunks. The kittens weren't much bigger then the chipmunks. One kitten pawed at a hungry chipmunk and it turned and bit a hole in the kitten's side. The kitten got angry and started fighting back. They were putting holes in each other. I wanted to stop them and help the kittens, but I was paralyzed. I was afraid I'd hurt them more if I intervened. I just stood there and screamed for Mother over and over again until I woke up and thought, 'All the animals are dead.'

I think the house is me. The upstairs, where Dad is, is the conscious, ruling, public part. The downstairs is the unconscious or hidden and conflicted part. The cookies are my sexuality. The chipmunks are Jay. They come after the sweet stuff. They are sinister in that they eat up the cookies; but they are also cute. I can't -- or I am scared to

-- shoo them away. The chipmunks bring out the kittens -- my innocent, adoring, and playful nature. The kittens are attracted to the chipmunks. But the chipmunks turn on the kittens and hurt them because they interfere with devouring the cookies. I don't want any of the animals hurt, so I stand paralyzed with fear as they destroy each other. I scream out for my mother as I become a child who needs a rescuer. It never occurs to me to call on the rule-maker or conscious part because there doesn't seem to be a connection to this unconscious conflict. Because I can't help the situation as a helpless child, the warring parties destroy each other.

I am now more in touch with how split and out of control I have felt for a long time. The course I have taken over the past six years has cut me off from my father, but it has also cut me off from the part of me that my father represents -- conscious or ego control. If I cannot regain that control, I have only my child-like dependence on others to protect me from self-destructing. It is painful to be feeling this way. Nevertheless, I still feel closer to resolution than ever before.

"You have such *amazing* dreams, Mom," Jennifer marveled.

Rachel laughed. "I was just in the habit of being *aware* of my dreams and of writing them down. I was working in a therapeutic environment and I was in therapy myself. Psychology finds significance in dreams. That was my mindset.

"Today," Rachel smiled, "I don't have time to think about or write down a dream unless it's especially alarming and wakes me up in the middle of the night. Then I tell your dad. Dreams can be an interesting window into what's troubling or concerning you if you pay attention to them.

"My dreams were telling me I needed to leave Austin. That was the final factor in making my decision to go to Challenge University School of Law."

Jennifer realized her dreams over the past few weeks had been telling her what she needed to focus on too. Right after her mother told her about Jay and the first rape, she had dreamed about snakes devouring Katie and her inability to stop them. David had been tearing her apart too. She didn't – or couldn't – stop him either.

After the initial glow of their relationship wore off, she had been tormented by the secrecy. She wanted so much to share her joy with her friends, but David had said "no." When she was around him at school, she had to pretend they were not involved. She monitored her speech and behavior. It was exhausting.

As time passed, the sneaking off to the woods behind the school for a quickie or lying to her parents about where she was going had sapped all of her energy. She stopped wanting to work out. She found it difficult to eat. She only felt alive when she was with him. Oh, she *was* her mother's daughter, thought Jennifer.

"And now to get back to your earlier question about what happened with Jessie," said Rachel. "I had to tell her that I was moving out of state to go to law school. That reality prevented us from getting any closer. I guess I will always wonder what might have happened between us if I had chosen to stay in Austin."

"Oh, and perhaps this goes without saying," smiled Rachel, "Jay made a request to have sex with both of us."

"Of course he did," smiled Jennifer.

"I said 'no.' Jessie was much too precious for that," said Rachel. Jennifer noticed a faraway look in her mother's eyes, no doubt remembering the promise of something that might have been.

"We've been sitting a long time. How about a walk with Katie to the creek?"

"Sounds good," replied Jennifer. Katie, who had been napping on the rug, perked up at the mention of her name.

Jennifer observed her mother reach for a spiral-bound notebook from the box labeled "First Year Law School." She knew that meant the story would continue on their walk.

Jennifer retrieved two water bottles from the kitchen and met her mother in the garage where she was leashing a wriggling Katie. Once they were on the sidewalk, Rachel began talking again.

"Let's see. Where were we?" asked Rachel.

"You were about to leave for law school," said Jennifer.

"Oh, yes. Almost. I need to tell you about more one more person I got to know before I left Austin," said Rachel. "His name was Doug Moore. He was the father of one of the members of my former church youth group. He called and asked if he could come over to my apartment to visit. It was a little strange. But I had a reputation with his son and his son's friends for being a good listener. Doug came over, appeared nervous at first, but then settled down to spend the next few hours telling me the story of his wife's affair with another man over a long period of time – an affair he had only recently discovered."

"Why would he talk to *you*?" Jennifer asked.

"He was very polite. Yet, I sensed Doug was attracted to me."

Jennifer rolled her eyes.

"I know," said Rachel. "But I was leaving for law school, moving to California in a few days," said Rachel. "So, I was compassionate with Doug, and that was as far as it went."

"But?" asked Jennifer, knowing there had to be more.

"Well. Once I got started with classes, I was pretty overwhelmed. I was afraid I wouldn't do well and afraid I'd made a mistake deciding to go to law school in the first place. Doug was a lawyer – an expert in the field I was entering…"

"Oh, NO!" interrupted Jennifer. "Don't tell me you got involved with another older, married, '*expert*.'" She emphasized *expert* with sarcasm.

"Not right away," Rachel grimaced. "Remember. Old habits are hard to break – *especially* when you are feeling weak and vulnerable. When you're scared and unsure of yourself, it's easy to revert to familiar behaviors.

"But, listen. My relationship with Doug – it wasn't like Jay. I first reached out to Doug by letter, about a week after summer school started. In my letter, I told him I appreciated the honesty and courage it took for him to confide in me. Being in an honest mood myself, I also told him that I had once been a mistress and that he shouldn't count on me to be entirely objective regarding his wife's behavior. Further, I said that I would never be a mistress to a married man again," said Rachel.

"That sounds like a good start," Jennifer said, unconvincingly.

"Doug wrote back, admitting that he was attracted to me. He hoped that, because of the geographical distance between us, a relationship might develop for the 'right reasons.'

"Nanna's words of advice to protect myself were echoing in my head. Little alarm bells were going off inside me too. Doug had confessed that he was traumatized by marital crisis, and he affirmed me as special, attractive, and intelligent…"

"Just like Jay," Jennifer interjected.

"Yes. But Doug was 1300 miles away," said Rachel. "He was a connection to Austin and news from home. And, as a lawyer, he could understand conversations about my academic program and give me guidance."

"Were you falling for him?" asked Jennifer.

"No. Not really. But he was a comfort. He made me feel better about my capabilities as I was struggling to get my bearings," responded Rachel.

"He was a crutch," suggested Jennifer.

"Yes. Or a lifeline. At least in the beginning. Let me tell you what it was like for me to start law school at the age of thirty.

CHAPTER THIRTY
LAW SCHOOL

"*A*dagio and I moved to San Francisco, California in early June 1988. I was taking classes with forty other joint degree students who came for the summer semester to take two of the required first-year law courses so that we would have time in our schedules to take various graduate school courses for our other degrees beginning in the fall. Most of my classmates came directly from college or with one year off between college and law school. I was among a handful of older adults who had done other graduate work or held professional positions for a few years.

"I felt as though I was in another world. Our reading consisted of case books filled with appellate court legal opinions. I could stare at a single page for ten, twenty, or thirty minutes and not understand the language or meaning. Classes were conducted largely according to the Socratic method. Do you know what that means?" Rachel asked Jennifer.

"I had an introductory course in Philosophy and we studied Socrates. But I'm not sure I remember the specifics," said Jennifer.

"I don't think I can give you a formal definition, but I'll tell you how it worked in my law school classes. The teacher would choose one student to recite the facts of the case and the court's opinion and reasoning. Then the teacher would continue to ask questions of the same student to expose assumptions and contradictions or alternatives in pursuit of discovering the 'truth.' Because I wasn't even sure what I was reading, I was terrified of being called on," said Rachel.

"So, this Doug – from a distance – helped you feel like you could survive?" Jennifer asked.

"Yes. *And* because Doug was pulling for me, I found it easier to rebuff Jay. Jay would call and say he wanted me to 'open up,' to confess to all the sex I had since coming to law school."

"Jay?! I thought he was out of the picture," said Jennifer. "Hadn't he moved on to a public relationship with Elizabeth?"

"He had. It's ironic, really. I'd done all this work to let go of my attachment to Jay – even moving to another state – and now *he* was the one refusing to give up his claim on me," responded Rachel.

"I tried to explain to him that I had no social life. My time was consumed with simply staying on top of the reading. Jay wouldn't believe me. His understanding of how I operated was so centered on *sex* that I couldn't get through to him. He said he wanted to come and visit me. I said 'no.' I couldn't deal with him. So, Doug was both a buffer between Jay and me and someone who understood what I was *really* going through in law school," said Rachel.

"There's one other thing I want to mention about those early law school days," continued Rachel. "One of my classmates, a young woman named Kelly, sat in front of me in classes. She was bold and self-assured. She encouraged me to speak out too, and we became friends. I guess I gave off the gay-friendly vibe because Kelly confided in me that she had dated women before coming to law school. At this juncture, she was confused about her sexual orientation. That story is hers to tell. *My* experience with her was that she started dating one of the men in our class, but she also touched me with affection occasionally and invited me to spend the night with her several times. My response was always to ask her if she was *sure* that was what she wanted to do. Each time she rescinded her offer.

"I tell you this because observing Kelly struggle with the issue of sexual orientation in her way helped me clarify my own thoughts and feelings on the subject. I had tried to imagine having sex with Kelly, but, as much as I cared for her, I was not 'turned on.' I thought for a while that I might just need training. But, I still found myself attracted to men in a sexual sense. On the other hand, I was no longer afraid to admit that I was also attracted to strong, beautiful, intelligent, or talented women in other ways.

"I realized that I would never let a man keep me away from other women again. Without other women, I am less of a person than I can be. A part of me dies. That's something I want you to know and think about for yourself. Okay?"

Jennifer was reminded again of how isolated from her girlfriends she had become in the years she and Chris had been a couple.

"Let me read you something I wrote about my attraction to women," continued Rachel. They were walking beside the creek now, and Katie was off leash, racing up and down the path and into the woods in pursuit of small animals or birds. Rachel stopped walking and opened the notebook she had tucked under her arm, and Jennifer stopped to listen.

August 3, 1988

I had a dream that involved Katherine -- the teen who had been raped by a stranger. In my dream, I was coaching Katherine's basketball team. Then the scene shifted to me alone with Katherine. We were discussing our feelings about rape. We started crying. We were holding each other. We kissed and touched each other's faces. In the dream, I tried to visualize what sexual intimacy with a woman would be like. During the dream, I worried about this seemingly sexual attraction to Katherine.

When I awoke, I saw the dream in a different light. The experience of rape created an intense bond between Katherine and me, a bond that I feel in varying degrees with other victims of sexual assault. And although I understand why rape is classified as an act of violence perpetrated against vulnerable and, often, random women, I also know there is something deeply personal and deeply sexual about rape. It affects our feelings about men and about being penetrated. The intensity of the emotions experienced in the aftermath of rape affects our "passions." But the passionate nature of the dream wasn't about wanting sex.

Jennifer said, "Let me see if I understand. Your being attracted to women wasn't about being a lesbian. It was about other things, like identifying with someone else who had been victimized or finding your strength and beauty through other women."

Rachel began walking again, and Jennifer followed.

"Right," nodded Rachel. "Women – relationships with women – helped me heal in the ways you suggested. Going forward, I knew I always wanted women in my life. I might someday find *the one* man I could make a commitment to for a lifetime. But that would never 'complete me' – as you sometimes hear said about marriage partners. I love women in all their variety – gay, straight, young, old, artistic, nerdy, athletic, spiritual – you name it! I had figured out that I was heterosexual, but I had also figured out the fallacy of being at war or in competition with other women. I hope that makes sense."

"I think so. I've enjoyed reconnecting with Cheryl and Louise these past weeks. It's different than friendship with a man. Not better or worse, just different. And important, like you said," Jennifer replied.

"Throughout the summer, Doug and I were pen pals... If you can believe this – I got my first computer when I went to law school. Well, it wasn't really a computer. It was a word processor for me to use to write papers. So, yes, Doug and I wrote letters back and forth, or talked on the phone – landline, no cell phone.

"As our friendship grew, he asked to come visit me on a couple of weekends, and I agreed. Those visits were very non-threatening, non-sexual. Doug described possible dates with me: dinners, movies, concerts and church. He envisioned me with him at family gatherings with his kids and their dates. He saw us walking hand-in-hand along rivers, by mountain lakes and on the beach. It was very romantic. It was exactly what I had wanted from Jay.

"When I went home to Austin at the end of the summer, Doug and I finally consummated our relationship. We were officially dating," said Rachel.

"He was too old for you, Mom. He'd already had his family, and they must have been almost grown," said Jennifer with concern.

"That's true," responded Rachel. "I knew Doug wasn't my 'forever guy.' But I was enjoying the romance. I was too busy trying to learn how to be a lawyer *in the moment* to be thinking much about long-term. I do remember thinking to myself − not sharing this with Doug − that I hated the idea of going back to Austin anytime soon."

Rachel paused and took a deep breath. "Now. Brace yourself. I want to tell you about the professor."

"Another Jay?" asked Jennifer. Her mother couldn't be *that* stupid, she thought.

"Just wait. Hear me out…" said Rachel.

"I was taking two classes that summer, one of which was Criminal Law. In early August, we finally got to a discussion about rape. The procedural part of the discussion confused me because it differed from my own experience in Texas with the legal system. After class, I mustered up the courage to ask Professor Nathan Taylor my questions. I discovered that in order to make my point, I had to talk about my own experience as a victim in a trial. Professor Taylor said he appreciated my openness and would like to discuss my views further. He seemed to think I could enlighten him about all kinds of 'oppressive' experiences known only to women. I said I would try."

Jennifer was shaking her head. "This is not sounding good."

"Professor Taylor and I corresponded by notes left in each other's boxes and through conversations in his office. He also began telling me *his* stories. He was currently separated from his wife. There were children involved…"

Jennifer interrupted, "There is *no way* you were falling for this!"

"It was all on the up-and-up until mid-August when Professor Taylor invited me to dinner. He said the decision of how 'close' we became was in my hands. I didn't want to insult him, but I told him that because he was my professor, I could not date him," said Rachel.

"Good for you. I was worried you wouldn't do that," said Jennifer.

"The semester ended. I officially became Doug's girlfriend. Even though I announced this to Professor Taylor when I returned to law school, he continued to ask me to go out on dates. He was now my instructor in another required class, so I refused to go with him *again*."

"But you caved," suggested Jennifer. Men could be so stubborn and dense sometimes, Jennifer thought. Yet, she sensed that, in this case and at this time, her mother had not been adamant enough. She was too weak. It hurt her to think what a pushover her mother must have been.

"Listen to what I wrote…" said Rachel. She and Jennifer stopped walking again.

September 20, 1988

As soon as the legal writing class was over, Nathan Taylor asked me out again -- "as a friend." I gave in. Nathan is very interesting and so bright. His experiences and perspectives fascinate me. He bathes me in flattery. I know this is reminiscent of my beginnings with Jay, and I want to guard against any problems that might arise, so I am telling Nathan a lot about Jay. I think that if Nathan really understands what I've been through, he will be less likely to repeat any of those actions.

"*Or*," Jennifer said cynically, "he would be turned on by your sexual experiences."

"That wasn't my intention," Rachel protested. She pulled back on her defensiveness. She really wanted Jennifer to understand this. She needed her to understand this. She said, "Once again, I was probably naïve. This is what I wrote a few weeks later…"

October 15, 1988

Despite my good intentions and every reminder of my commitment to Doug that I utter to Nathan, a romantic attraction has grown between us. He is impossible to resist. Nathan knows all the right things to say to me. I am afraid of being taken advantage of again, afraid of becoming embroiled in another couple's marital dispute, afraid of being a secret mistress, and afraid of being cut off from the important child or children in a man's life, as I was cut off from Ben by Jay. But Nathan reassures me that none of these fears are realistic in relation to him.

Reassurances aside, when I am alone I know I must surely be crazy. I am now sleeping with two married men who both think they love me and I have no idea what I really feel! Nathan is going abroad in a few days to teach and do research for the remainder of the semester. He wants me to visit and says he will pay for my trip. I am glad he is going. I can see the heartache ahead. Haven't I been here before? There is his tenure to worry about. There is a separation period and then divorce. Men don't seem to understand how emotionally devastating that whole experience can be when they tell themselves: 'Divorce is the best thing for all concerned.'

"You *were* crazy! You were completely *nuts*! Were you wearing a sign: 'Pick me. I'm the vulnerable one'?" Jennifer said angrily. Then she sighed. It made her sad to think of her mother this way – a hamster on a wheel, going around and around.

Rachel hated to see her daughter look at her with such pity. She had tried to explain this before to others, and it always came out wrong. She had to do better this time.

Feeling guilty for yelling at her mother, Jennifer said, "I'll bet you were lonely so far away from home." Jennifer was feeling her own loneliness. She wondered if she would pick the wrong guy if that guy found her sexy and irresistible, just to be held again. Maybe...

"I'm sure loneliness played a part in it. But every time I've tried to tell this story, I end up sounding like an over-sexed woman, someone who can't help herself because of her passion... Jennifer, I'm *not* that woman.

"Think about your dad and me. I know, the last thing you want to think about is your parents' sex life. But I can guarantee you that your dad and I are a pretty 'normal' couple.

"During that period of time, in the months after I left Austin, I was still pretty fragile in my commitment to start my life over. I had left my therapist, so no one was questioning me about my activities. Frankly, in the core of my being, I was still a victim and a 'bad girl' who acted out sexually just as Jay had fashioned me to be. In a strange environment, with no other support, when another man like Jay came along and confirmed that I was indeed a 'bad girl,' I didn't have the fortitude to fight back. I wasn't good at my chosen profession yet. But I was good at sex. I was praised for that," Rachel shook her head, remembering how weak she had been.

"And, yes, I was wearing a figurative sign. I'm easy. I'm vulnerable. Pick me. That was still my identity. But I wanted it to change. So..."

October 21, 1988

Nathan's departure coincided with a fall break at the law school. I decided to go to Austin, not to see Doug, but to see Jay. I was angry. I know this latest mess I have gotten into is Jay's fault even though he is hundreds of miles away. I vented my rage, but Jay said there was nothing to discuss. He said, "You have your set of problems and I have my own." For a few minutes I couldn't move. All I could do was cry. Jay sat nearby, completely emotionless.

When I left Jay's house, I knew I could not date Nathan Taylor any longer. Even if Nathan doesn't see the similarities between himself and Jay, I feel disturbed by our relationship in a way that is reminiscent of the some of my worst feelings about Jay.

Rachel tucked the notebook under her arm again and turned toward home. Jennifer followed her lead.

"On October 30, 1988, I wrote to Nathan that I was going to stay with Doug who was, by then, close to a final divorce. He accepted my boundary and we both moved on," Rachel said.

"Then," continued Rachel, "in December, at the end of my second semester of law school, I received notice that Isaiah Barry was being released from prison. That event was a bookend for me. I suddenly knew I needed to understand what happened to me in-between getting involved with Jay and Barry's release from prison.

"My New Year's resolution for 1989 was to reflect on and write about my experiences over the past seven years. I began by reading these journals and letters that I've shared with you. I purchased my rape trial transcript from the State Archives. And then I met some amazing women while I continued to learn more about myself, history, and law for the next few years," said Rachel.

She suddenly felt exhausted and needed a break. She wanted to breath in the fresh air, to listen to the sound of rushing water, and to hear the leaves crunching under her feet. "Do you mind if we just walk silently for a few minutes?" Rachel asked Jennifer.

"Sure," said Jennifer absentmindedly. She was deep in thought about her own married man, David Reese. She had been so stupid! She thought she loved him. She gave herself to him. She didn't even ask him about his marital status until… well, she didn't ask until she already knew.

They were in an inexpensive motel about 20 miles from Austin. He was on top of her, thrusting up and down, and she turned her head to the right. As he grabbed a pillow for better positioning, she noticed the tan line on his left hand ring finger. It startled her. He finished and rolled over on the bed beside her.

David must have sensed her concern because he asked, "What's wrong?"

She couldn't ask him directly. If he lied, what then? She said, "You're married."

He propped himself up on his elbow to study her face. With complete calm, he said, "Yes. I thought you knew that."

'I didn't know!' she wanted to scream. Instead, she blubbered, "How would I? You never said…" and melted into a puddle of tears. David held her tightly.

He whispered, "I didn't think you wanted to discuss it. My wife was my high school sweetheart. We married after college. It seemed like the thing to do. But after a few years, the magic was gone. We were too young. We focus on our careers now."

David moved closer to look into Jennifer's eyes. "I love *you*," he said. Then he pulled her in close.

Jennifer had wanted to say, 'Then why don't you get divorced?' But she wasn't really sure she wanted to hear the answer. She had felt bad about the secrecy. Now she felt something worse. This was the moment, Jennifer now realized, that she had started counting the days to graduation and her escape.

CHAPTER THIRTY-ONE
WRITING AND WORKING FOR RECOVERY

Back at the carriage house, while Katie gnawed on a rawhide bone beside them, Jennifer asked, "Where was Dad in all of this?"

"I wasn't ready for Dad yet," smiled Rachel. "I was ready to start writing my memories. I wrote about the night I met Barry. I had access to other written materials that chronicled that night in great detail. But as I turned to write about other events and the suffering that came privately during the following years, I was lost. My memories consisted only of brief episodes of humiliation and pain in contexts where I seemed to have little or no control. Some of the journal entries that I've been reading to you, Jennifer, are re-creations of events I could not remember in detail at this time. At the beginning of 1989, I was having difficultly locating events in real time and in relating them to other less traumatic events in my life. I was feeling worse when I wanted to feel better.

"Fortunately, at the same time I started this memory recovery project, I took my first women's studies course as part of my M.A. program in history, and stumbled into some significant relationships with women who were concerned about feminist issues, including sexual violence. One of these women was Claire. Claire would later become the Director of the Women's Center on campus and hire me as the first and Interim Coordinator of Sexual Assault Support Services. As you know, Claire is still my friend though she has moved to North Carolina," said Rachel.

"Oh, I know Claire. I remember one time you took us to visit her and she painted my toenails," said Jennifer.

Rachel smiled. "That is the Claire I'm talking about here."

"Another woman I met through Claire was Ruth, the Director of Residential Life. She also happened to be a licensed psychologist. I was ready to do the work of recovery, and Ruth agreed to help me with my lost memories. We reached an agreement according to which she would prompt me with questions about my past life; I would write what I could remember; and we would discuss my writing and memories in a therapeutic setting. Ruth became my friend, confidant, and therapist. Our meetings went on for several months. Ruth believed in me when I had difficulty believing in myself. We explored my past together and, in time, once lost memories began to resurface. I owe Ruth a debt of gratitude I can never repay," said Rachel.

"Before therapy, I knew that sexual violence was about taking power and control away from its victim, but I fought tooth and nail to convince myself that I was immune, that I was still in control. So, every time someone else – Jay or another man – managed to do something to me or with me that I did not want to do, I felt like a failure. I had to get to the point of acknowledging and *owning* my powerlessness before I could begin to feel better. Therapy helped me do that," said Rachel.

"This is going to sound strange… The other thing I had to do was figure out what to do with my *body*. A life without sex to avoid sexual violence results in the loss of certain kinds of relationships that can, potentially, bring so much joy and fulfillment to human lives. Marriage, companionship, commitment, and the creation of children come to mind. For me, there was a period of celibacy, a period of coming to terms with *me alone*, and embracing my sufficiency. But I wanted more. I wanted marriage with the right man. I wanted a family. The alone time helped me get beyond *needing* a man to feel complete. By the time I met your dad, I had found my way to *wanting* a sexual relationship and being able to let go and trust in that relationship despite what I had experienced in the past," said Rachel.

She shifted in her seat. "There is no doubt in my mind that sexual violence changed me and changed how I express my sexuality. I remember hearing a rape survivor tell me that her rapist had worn a leather jacket and his breath smelled of beer.

She said she could no longer tolerate the smell of leather or beer. Certain acts, smells, sights, or words are triggers. In my experience, getting to the point where I could have a 'normal' sexual relationship meant acknowledging, stopping, and addressing each trigger as it occurred. This requires a loving, caring partner who is willing to participate in the process. I am now desensitized to some of the original triggers, but there are other sexual activities I will probably never do again. Is it a loss? Maybe. But I have come to believe that what is most important is that I feel *whole*, as does my partner."

"I hope this makes sense," said Rachel to Jennifer. Jennifer nodded, thinking that she would never meet someone in a cheap motel for a sexual rendezvous again.

"After that first year of law and graduate school," said Rachel, "I came back to Austin to work for the summer in the District Attorney's office that had prosecuted my rapist. I steered clear of Jay and appreciated the time I had with family and friends. With my head clear again to focus on *my* goals, I discovered that, although Doug was a good man, we wanted different things in our futures, so we parted ways.

"I returned to law school and graduate school a truly independent woman. I delved into my studies, enjoyed my new friends, and helped lead a public interest law group. I worked on projects related to date rape prevention. I interviewed for summer jobs and agreed to work in law firms in California and Arizona the following summer. My future was open ended. I could do anything or go anywhere. The one thing I knew for sure was that I didn't need a man in order to be okay.

Jennifer felt inspired. These were reassuring words.

"In the early part of 1990, I went to a 'reunion' party of the forty of us who had started law school together in the summer of 1988. One of my classmates brought his new roommate, Kevin. You've heard this story," said Rachel.

"Tell it again anyway," Jennifer said brightly.

"I noticed Kevin, but didn't think much about him at the time," said Rachel. "A few days later, the classmate approached me and asked, 'Are you married or anything?' It was a funny question, but I was an older law student who didn't party with the younger crowd, and he didn't know my relationship status. Kevin wanted to ask me out, he said. I replied, 'Okay.'

"I rejected your dad twice before I agreed to go on a date with him. He still has a hard time believing I was *really* studying on a Friday night. But I was! I was in a trial practice class and the mock trial was on a Sunday. I finally agreed to go out with Kevin *after* the trial. It was my 32nd birthday.

"Your dad was *so* young – almost seven years younger than me. But he wasn't married or engaged to be married or a parent. He wasn't a professor or lawyer or any kind of expert. He thought I was beautiful, smart, and charming – despite my serious, scholarly persona. I was no longer wearing 'the sign' that labeled me good-for-nothing-but-sex."

Rachel snickered. "This is going to sound funny to you. But one of the things that drew me to your dad was that we *played* together: tennis, swimming, running, basketball, and even golf. The older, scholarly or stuffy types I had been dating didn't play. Kevin was a breath of fresh air.

"Your dad was also a feminist like me, and he supported my activism in relation to women's issues on campus. He loved Adagio and the music of *Harmony* from the get-go. And your dad listened to my story... over time... piece by piece... and loved me anyway. He wanted children, as did I, and he was willing to start a family sooner rather than later as he planned to marry this 'older woman' the spring I graduated from Challenge University," said Rachel.

"Oh, that reminds me..." Rachel said as she dug through her box once again. "In the summer of 1990, the summer your dad proposed, I had this dream..."

Last night I had a dream that I saw Jay Winchester and, instead of running away as I would have done a few months ago, I called out to him exuberantly. He looked a little surprised to see me. I introduced my new boyfriend,

Kevin, and then asked Jay how he was and a series of other questions about his life. Kevin seemed to wander off during this exchange. I dreamed that Jay told me he had two more children, in addition to Ben. He said that his wife, Elizabeth Nash, was a wealthy businesswoman and attorney. Jay was still writing and teaching. I was aware that I wasn't jealous of any of his good fortune. Jay then changed the subject to how unfulfilled he still felt. As he began to talk about how I "understood him," he started to nuzzle and touch me. I began to panic. I closed my eyes. Then I relaxed. As I relaxed, I recognized the touch as Kevin's touch, not Jay's. I opened my eyes and Kevin was with me. Jay stood somewhere off in the distance.

When I woke from this dream, it was morning. It felt like my whole body was smiling and warmed. I knew that whatever power Jay had had over me all these years was waning. And I knew that this was, at least in part, because I had the courage to begin to tell my story.

I have a long way yet to go before my intellectual understanding connects with some of the pain still locked away. But now, I am optimistic about the future. Somehow, I will take what I have learned and turn it toward a good end. I have already turned a corner of some sort that enables me to be grateful for the blessings of opportunity.

"Wow, Mom. That is so cool," Jennifer said as she smiled.

"I didn't get to this point simply through therapy. As I worked on my personal stuff in early 1989, I was also moving out into the community that cared about the issues of sexual violence by volunteering at the Rape Crisis Center of San Francisco. By April 1989, I had written a handbook for victims of rape and sexual 'offense' – as it was referred to by state statute – called 'RAPE and the Criminal Justice System.' It covered the Victim's Bill of Rights, financial assistance, legal courses of action, reporting crimes and police response, and going to court. I included the statutes, definitions of legal terms, and other resources for victims," explained Rachel.

"I think it was also in the spring of 1989... or maybe it was the fall... but I read an article in the school newspaper about a young woman on campus who had been raped. The article implied that this victim held some responsibility for the assault because she was running at night and wearing earphones. The article might as well have said: 'Rachel was raped because she worked at night and chose to help a stranger who said he needed assistance.' I was outraged! I immediately composed a Letter to the Editor in which I stated my position that *men* have a responsibility to stop rape. Boy, did that letter generate some response! It seemed everyone had an opinion and the whole campus was talking.

"I guess you could say my activism regarding education about and prevention of sexual assault on campus began then. Both during law school and after I graduated, I was involved in educating the community about sexual violence and generating resources and support for its victims.

"In November of 1989, the university formed a Rape and Sexual Assault Task Force to develop a coherent response to the discovery that an average of one Challenge University female student per week was reporting having been raped or sexually assaulted," said Rachel.

"One a week!?" Jennifer exclaimed.

"Yep. Frightening, isn't it? I was hired in the spring of 1991 as Coordinator of Sexual Assault Support Services for the Women's Center on campus at the recommendation of the Task Force.

"But before I was hired, in the spring of 1990, I wrote a play called 'Date Rape on Trial' that was produced in the student auditorium. The play was taped. In those days, everything was recorded on videotape. It was to be used for educational programming in dorms and with student groups about the legal consequences of rape. I may still have a copy somewhere. Your daddy was one of the actors in the play," said Rachel.

"Cool. I'd love to see it," said Jennifer, glad to know that her father had supported her mother's work.

"Let me see if I can give you some specifics about what I did that year at the Women's Center." Rachel reached into the bottom of the cardboard box and pulled out several handbooks, flyers, and other documents.

"Ah. Here it is." Holding up a multi-page document, Rachel said, "This is a report of my activities as Coordinator for the 1991-92 school year. Okay, so I helped develop a 'response protocol for sexual assault of Challenge students.' I worked with members of public safety, student health, and student life, among others. I wrote brochures on our sexual assault support services, helping acquaintance rape survivors, the University Judicial Board and sexual assault, a resources and referral hand-out, and materials related to Rape Awareness Week. I'll get to that in a minute. I wrote a manual called 'Victim to Survivor' for survivors of sexual assault. I wrote another manual for graduate and professional students called 'Crime Prevention and Safety Guide.'

"I consulted with or trained student groups including CARE or Challenge Acquaintance Rape Education, MAC or Men Acting for Change, and MADR or Men Against Date Rape who collected signatures from men, pledging against date rape. I went to a variety of conferences on sexual violence, representing our university. I was even interviewed on 'The Today Show.'"

"Impressive," said Jennifer.

"I think there is a copy of that interview around here somewhere too. I'll see if I can find it. You may be more impressed that I'm wearing make-up than you are with the content of my message," smiled Rachel. Jennifer laughed.

"And there were other things I did," said Rachel. "I engaged in crisis intervention with individuals, and began Safe Haven, our own campus shelter for victims of sexual assault, with Caroline, my assistant. You remember Caroline too, don't you? We went to visit her when you were looking at colleges in

North Carolina. She is a minister and continues to be involved in feminist issues of all kinds."

"Oh, yeah. I had no idea how these women were connected to you, and I never thought to ask," said Jennifer.

"Why would you? I don't think I paid any attention to what my parents' friends did until I was older than you are now. But it is interesting, don't you think, because friends are clues to a person's past or interests," said Rachel. Jennifer nodded. She wondered what her selection of friends said about her.

"Of course," continued Rachel, "Caroline and I trained the volunteers and wrote the manual for Safe Haven too. We did anonymous data collection to assess rape victims' needs. There's more. But you get the idea of how much there is to do in relation to sexual violence and victimization."

"Wow, Mom. I'm so impressed," said Jennifer. "You had this *life* I knew nothing about."

"I found it difficult, over the years, to talk to you guys about that work because I wasn't ready to talk about *why* I was so interested in the issue of sexual violence," said Rachel.

"That makes sense. I mean, you can't really understand what rape is until you are old enough to understand consensual sex," said Jennifer.

"Right," agreed Rachel. "I also want to tell you about the Rape Awareness Week because that is probably the piece of my job I remember most clearly all these years later. The first thing we did was to place boxes of red ribbons all over campus, easily accessible. We advertised that members of the community – students, faculty, and staff - were to 'tie a ribbon' on the chain that surrounds the center of campus if you were a survivor of sexual assault *or knew someone who was*. Jennifer, there were literally hundreds and hundreds of ribbons tied that week. It was an incredible sight.

"We also held a 'Take Back the Night' march…"

"I went to one of those at school," said Jennifer, sitting up straighter. "It was amazing. All those candles, speeches, and chants."

"That was my experience too. We also invited a rape survivor – a woman who had a highly publicized rape experience - to give a keynote speech. We had sexual violence information tables. We hosted a panel on legal alternatives. There was a panel of men speaking about sexual violence and their work to prevent it. We had a Speak-Out in the middle of campus. This allowed anyone to 'speak-out' about her or his experience with sexual violence. At the end of the week, we had a Service of Healing."

"I just keep thinking how you did all of this decades ago, but we still have the same problems today," said Jennifer. Rachel nodded. She could have given her pep talk to Jennifer about taking up the cause. But she knew Jennifer didn't need to hear it after all their Sundays together.

"I mentioned the red ribbons," said Rachel. "Well, we also had a place on campus that was open 24 hours a day where you could write, on big sheets of paper, *why* you tied a ribbon. The paper expanses said at the top: 'I tied a ribbon…' I was so busy that I never got to the room until the end of the week when we took the pages down. At least a couple hundred people had written about their experiences or the experiences of someone they cared about. But, Jennifer, the thing that got to me, the thing I wasn't expecting, was that *so many* had written about experiences with child sexual abuse and even incest. I was blown away. I expected date rape. I didn't expect so many bright, successful, and academically capable people to be survivors of childhood and adolescent abuse. They named fathers and father figures, coaches, religious leaders, and teachers as perpetrators. I was astounded."

Jennifer tried to hide her reaction at the mention of 'teachers.'

"I had done my thesis for my J.D. degree on child sexual abuse," said Rachel. "But I never imagined that I was surrounded by so many people who had been hurt at a young age."

Jennifer was listening in awe, trying to take in everything Mom was saying. Her mother was more animated and excited than she had seen her on any of the previous Sundays.

"Let me tell you about another experience I had when I was wearing my Coordinator of SASS hat. A young man, an undergraduate, who was clearly in distress, approached me. He told me that he and several others were on a 24-hour-a-day suicide prevention watch for a friend of theirs who had previously tried to take her life. She had been hospitalized. But now that she was back in the dorm, he and his friends were worried that she was not out of danger. This is the story he told me.

"The young woman – I will call her 'Anne' – had grown up in a home with an older brother who had drug addiction problems. When Anne was in her mid-teens, the brother had raped her. He threatened her so she wouldn't tell. These sexual assaults continued. Their parents became aware of the boy's drug problem – but not the sexual assaults. They told him that if he used drugs again, they would kick him out of the house. Anne's brother raped her again right before she left for college and, to save herself from any more abuse, she told her parents that he was using drugs. The parents made good on their threat and kicked the boy out. Anne went off to school at Challenge University. A couple of months later, right before mid-terms, the brother killed himself..."

"Oh, my God!" said Jennifer.

"Yes. But because the parents wanted Anne, their gifted student, to do well on her mid-terms, they *didn't tell her*," said Rachel.

"What?" said Jennifer, not sure that she had heard right.

"They buried the young man. And only *after* mid-terms did they tell Anne."

"That's horrible!" exclaimed Jennifer.

"I couldn't agree more. Anne was devastated. She felt responsible. If she hadn't told on him, he wouldn't have been kicked-out, and perhaps he would still be alive. A month later,

Anne tried to take her own life. Fortunately, she was unsuccessful.

"She was treated at the university hospital. Her parents came, of course. But she never told them about the rapes. So, now, riddled with guilt and unable to share her story, her friends worried for her safety," Rachel said.

Jennifer felt ill. She wasn't sure if the nausea was a consequence of the story or the knowledge that she was holding back information from her own mother.

"You okay?" Rachel asked. "It's such a sad story. Maybe I shouldn't have told you." Rachel wondered if she'd hit too close to home. Anne was a woman close to Jennifer's age.

"I'm okay. It makes me wonder about other people I've known, you know? Did I miss the signs? Was I too busy worrying about the wrong things – what to wear, how my hair looked, if I'd prepared well enough for a test. Stuff like that," said Jennifer, her nausea beginning to subside.

"We don't know what's going on in other people's lives most of the time – unless they let us in. I'm sure you've been a good friend. Now, you know a little more. And with that knowledge, you may be a better friend to someone who needs compassion and listening." Rachel hoped she had been reassuring enough. There were no easy answers.

"I'm reminded of something else that I learned when I was working at the Women's Center that may help you understand how... what's the right word? 'intractable'? 'embedded'? 'entrenched'?... these behaviors can be. I mentioned Men Acting for Change or MAC earlier. MAC was a group of men concerned with issues of masculinity, sexuality, and gender equality. They provided education through forums and presentations, and they advocated about political and social issues. They also met as a support group to look at themselves and at their socialization as boys and men in an effort to end sexism," said Rachel.

"I was allowed to sit in on support group meetings occasionally. At one particular meeting, the topic was pornography. Again, you need to remember that we were dinosaurs in comparison to the type of Internet access you have now. Most pornography that men used then was still in the form of magazines. The men talked about how their first exposure to sex came through the magazines and the women in the magazines. In other words, as teenage boys, they masturbated to the pictures of women. One particular man in the group that night talked about making love to his girlfriend, and what he said had a profound impact on me. He said that he could not climax with his girlfriend unless he closed his eyes and imagined her as a picture in the magazine." Rachel looked expectantly at Jennifer for her reaction.

It took a few seconds, but then Jennifer said, "Oh! You are saying that he had to objectify his girlfriend in order to reach orgasm."

"Exactly! Pornography trains young men to think of women as objects, not people. Women as people are complicated and messy. They have feelings and desires all their own. But pictures of women are simple. They are there to serve the sexual needs of men." Rachel paused. She was coming on strong. But it felt good, in a way, to be this passionate again about a role that had changed her life.

Jennifer was reliving a multitude of moments in her life when a boy or young man she was involved with had been demanding in a way that made her uncomfortable. Could this be part of the explanation?

"It's complicated, Jennifer," said Rachel. "Sexual relationships, the way we socialize our kids, the variations along the gender identification spectrum… it's all complicated. I don't think we are going to solve all these issues today." Rachel reached out her hand to pat her daughter's knee.

"It's late. Your dad is already concerned about how much time I'm spending with you on *this* subject. But I need one more Sunday morning to wrap this up."

"You can have it," Jennifer smiled. This had been a strange and awful and *awesome* way to spend her Sunday mornings. She wasn't sure she wanted them to end.

SUNDAY
NOVEMBER 26, 2014

CHAPTER THIRTY-TWO
RETHINKING THEOLOGY

Jennifer had accepted Mom's stipulation that they not discuss the content of their Sunday mornings outside of their time together *for now*. Dad had expressed concern that it would cut into 'family time.' So Jennifer almost exploded when she sat down with her mother on their seventh Sunday together.

"You lost most of your twenties and your early thirties to all of this, didn't you?" asked Jennifer.

"It preoccupied me, for sure." A wave of regret washed over Rachel as she said it. "That made me angry for a while. But I can't do anything to change the past. And everything I went through contributed to making me the person I am now. I turned out all right, didn't I?" Rachel looked hopefully at Jennifer.

"Absolutely," Jennifer smiled back. Her thoughts turned to herself and the life that was slipping away while she worked a dead end job. She didn't want to lose her twenties. But hadn't she turned her destiny over to Chris? She'd had dreams. Why did she let him make all the important decisions? She had to figure it out so that it never happened again. Mom had been in therapy. Maybe she needed to talk to a therapist too. Maybe there was even a connection between what happened with David and how she related to Chris. She wasn't sure...

Jennifer said, "Mom? As you can imagine, I've been doing a lot of thinking about *all* these things you've shared with me. I guess you know I've been lonely. I'm guessing you decided to keep these Sunday appointments with me partly because of that." Jennifer looked to her mother for confirmation, and Rachel gave a slight nod.

"As you know, it's been hard for me to come home. I thought – well, I guess you know I thought I would be going with Chris to Colorado. That didn't exactly turn out the way I planned." Jennifer forced a grin.

"One of the things I've realized as you've told your story is that I stopped pursuing my goals when I latched onto Chris."

Rachel knew this about Jennifer, but she also knew that Jennifer had to figure this out for herself. It had been the same with her and Jay. She was silently shouting 'hallelujah' that Jennifer had made this discovery so soon.

"So, here's the thing," continued Jennifer. "I know there's not an obvious career path for a person with a religion degree – except for becoming a minister – and that's not for me. I've considered a lot of other possibilities. I think having a basic knowledge about religious and cultural differences between people all over the world can be a real asset..."

"I do too," interjected Rachel, wanting her daughter to know she was supportive.

"Well, as you've talked about the mental health issues of kids you worked with in hospitals, and as I've thought about so many of the current issues – immigration and sex trafficking and violence that has its origins in religious intolerance... well, I've decided I want to be a social worker and work on some of these issues. I know I'm not articulating this very well..."

"You are doing a great job," said Rachel, trying to look appropriately excited without overdoing it. What she really wanted to do was jump up and crush Jennifer in a hug.

"I'd have to get a Master of Social Work degree. I'd have to go back to school," Jennifer said, trying to assess if her mother would support such a large, new endeavor.

"I think it's a great dream, Jennifer. You'd be a wonderful social worker," said Rachel.

Jennifer breathed a sigh of relief. If Mom approved, she was probably on the right track. She would take charge of her life again. She was sure of that now.

"I'm very excited about this new plan, Jen," said Rachel.

"I was stuck and you got me unstuck... I love you, Mom."

"And I love you too," smiled Rachel, "I always will."

"There's another question I've been meaning to ask you," Jennifer continued, but then hesitated. "After all of this, are you still a Christian?"

"That's a good question," responded Rachel. "By the time I got to law school, I had almost lost my faith. When I met Jay, I was enthralled by his ideas about God. But after six years of being subjected to Jay's God who was never satisfied with me... well, I had to learn different ways of envisioning God. Through my associations with certain women in law school and the Women's Center at Challenge University, I became reacquainted with a Creator God, a Mother God, and a God of Forgiveness who loved me as I am. This God didn't pass judgment on my past. She claimed all of me and urged me to use the 'good' *and* the 'bad' to make my life and the lives of others better.

Rachel paused, then said, "There's a mystery to life that can't be explained with logic. I believe in transformation and change through Love. I believe that Love – with a capital L – is something that is both part of us and comes to us even when we don't earn it or even deserve it. Most of the time, I experience Love – which is, for me, another word for God - through relationships. But sometimes it's in nature or in being part of a community, like church. My own life was transformed through the love of all the people I've told you about in the later parts of my story.

"Does that mean you *are* a Christian?" Jennifer asked again.

"I have faith in a Higher Power that I call God. But am I a Christian? I've thought about that a lot over the years – not just because of what happened to me, but because I have friends of different faiths. My two best friends growing up..."

"Were Susan and Margaret," Jennifer completed her mother's sentence. Susan and Margaret were godparents for the Adamo children and had been a constant presence in their lives.

"Yes. Susan is Jewish, as you know. Margaret is a devoted United Methodist whose father was a minister. I remember wondering as a kid, 'If Susan isn't a Christian, does that mean she doesn't go to heaven with Margaret and me?' And that just didn't seem fair because Susan was and is a good person."

Jennifer had wondered the same thing about her friends of different things, she thought.

Rachel continued, "It seems to me that if you call yourself a Christian, you have one of two different ways of viewing God's saving work through Jesus Christ. Some people believe that a person must *accept* Christ as Savior or they go to hell – whatever that is," Rachel smiled. "Other people believe that Jesus' life, death, and resurrection is a gift to *all* people. In that case, no one is left out. I am inclined to believe the latter.

Rachel paused again before saying, "The problem with calling myself a Christian is that I'm not sure I believe in the resurrection. I do believe there was a man named Jesus. I believe he was a good man, a Jewish rebel who challenged many of the beliefs and rules of his day, rules and beliefs that did more harm than good. I believe he wanted to change the world, and that he tried to teach others about the nature of God – a God who is loving and forgiving and who can transform us."

"So, you are saying you are *not* a Christian. But…" Jennifer began to protest.

Rachel interrupted, "You are going to ask me why I made you go to church, sing in the choir, attend Sunday school, go to youth group, and all the rest, aren't you?"

Jennifer nodded.

"It's because, despite my history with a pretty screwed-up representative of the church, I still believe that most of the time, the church – which is its people – is safe and loving. What better place to send my children than to spend time with people who are trying to live like Jesus? And I do believe in trying to live like Jesus even if I'm not sure about the resurrection."

"But the resurrection is the *key* to Christianity, Mom," said Jennifer, a worried look on her face.

"You may not remember this, but several months ago, our minister, Alice, preached about a passage from the Book of Matthew that is referred to as the Great Commission. Jesus meets with the remaining eleven disciples after the resurrection and gives them authority to make disciples of all people. Do you have a Bible in here somewhere?" asked Rachel, looking around the room.

"I think so," said Jennifer, getting up. She went to the bookcase near her bed and found her Bible with her textbooks and novels. She handed it to her mom.

Rachel opened the Bible to the New Testament and thumbed through the pages. "Here it is. Matthew 28, verse 17. It says, 'When they saw him, they worshipped him; but some doubted.'"

Rachel looked up. "Alice preached about doubt. Doubt, she said, is not *un*belief. Doubt is being caught between two worlds. We know how imperfect we are and how messed up our world is, so it's hard to believe in another 'world' where we are saved and chosen by God. But this passage is telling us that even some of the original disciples doubted.

"Let me say it this way. I try to live 'as if' the resurrection was true. The resurrection represents life after death, right? It represents good following the worst possible scenario. Think about my life. I've experienced some pretty horrible things. I've made some bad choices. But then your dad, you, and your brothers came along. I've been given new life – a resurrection of sorts.

"For me, Christianity is about looking to Jesus as my guide. Jesus models hope and possibility for change. Jesus condemns practices that treat human beings unfairly or unequally. Jesus values the natural world, God's creation. Jesus forgives and shines a light on God's grace.

"Sometimes life hands you a 'dead kitten' or a day in the ER. But I've experienced the grace of God through my father's embrace and my mother's abiding care. My hope is that living 'as if' somehow enables God's grace to flow through me in similar ways.

"Maybe all my doubt means I shouldn't be a member of a church. After all, I've repeated a lot of words in church that I'm not sure I believe. But I trust God knows my heart. I trust that God knows I'm trying when I help those in need or when I work to correct injustices."

Rachel paused. "Is that enough of an answer for now?"

"I guess so, but it's kind of disturbing," said Jennifer.

Rachel laughed. "And it shocks you that I would say something *disturbing*?"

Jennifer chuckled too.

"The bottom line is that you are the only one who can figure out what you believe. And your beliefs may be different than mine. But I do think it's harder to make much progress on answers to the knotty questions of life in isolation, without a faith community, even if you move from one faith community to another in search of the answers you are seeking. As my mother said to me, I'm giving you the best thing I've found as a foundation. What you choose to do with it is up to you," Rachel said.

Chapter Thirty-Three
Looking Forward

"More burning questions?" Rachel smiled.

"Not right this minute. Tell me more of the story," said Jennifer, making a mental note to think about her own faith later, when she could give the subject her full attention.

Rachel said, "You know what happened next. Your daddy received his M.B.A. in the spring of 1992, and you were born that summer. We moved to Austin where Daddy found his first job with a real estate development company and I worked part-time at Austin Legal Aid. We chose Austin because of family. Living in Austin has allowed you and your brothers to see your cousins, aunts and uncles, and grandparents on my side of the family more often."

Jennifer did know that part of her mother's story, she thought. Suddenly, her breath caught and a great weight landed on her chest. She said, "Does Jay still teach at AU?"

Rachel nodded.

Jennifer exploded, "He got to live his life as a tenured professor and you had to suffer?! How is that *fair*?"

"As your Papa always said to me: 'Life's not fair.'" Rachel regretted her flippancy as soon as she spoke the words that she knew to be true but not helpful.

Jennifer stood up and paced, waving her arms in emphasis. "That's too easy, Mom. He needs to pay!" Jennifer stated authoritatively. When her mother didn't respond right away, she added, "What if he's doing it to someone else?"

Rachel winced. That was the question that had tormented her. What if she didn't prevent this from happening to other women? It was one thing to break away from Jay's hold and achieve her own recovery. It was quite another to ignore or refrain from announcing a potential danger to others. But she'd done *something*, hadn't she? By putting her story in his file in 1992.

316

"There something I left out. I didn't tell you that, in 1991, while I was working in the Women's Center, Anita Hill testified at the confirmation hearings of U.S. Supreme Court nominee Clarence Thomas. She stated that Thomas had sexually harassed her while he was her supervisor at the Department of Education and EEOC. Specifically, Hill testified that Thomas spoke to her of women having sex with animals and about films showing group sex. At one point, according to Hill, Thomas asked, 'Who has put pubic hair on my Coke?' That did it for me. Despite criticism of Anita Hill coming from various quarters, I *knew* she was telling the truth. No one makes up that kind of detail. I thought: 'If Anita Hill is brave enough to go public with her story, so can I.'

"Having worked with Ruth for many months, I had a fairly complete rendering of what I had experienced with Jay. So, in the spring of 1992, I took a copy of my story to the Dean's assistant at the theology school at AU. I told her what I had, and she put my document into Jay's file. She told me it would be there if any future accusations were made," said Rachel.

"I can't promise you that Jay didn't hurt someone else, but I did take some action. At that point in my life, I was married and pregnant with you. I had a new life and I didn't want to dredge up the past. I didn't want to do that to your dad," said Rachel.

Before Jennifer could argue with her, Rachel continued. "As to 'fairness,' Jay did pay, Jen. He has suffered from mental anguish and mental illness all these years – at least to the best of my knowledge. This isn't a competition where he wins or I win. I used to think of it that way. But then I realized I was using legal analysis to pass judgments. Don't get me wrong! That has its place. After all, I became a lawyer to fight against injustice and inequality. But something like this? Well, I could never make it 'fair.' I could never undo the damage – which is really what I wished for.

"You know," said Rachel reflectively, "I got to a point where I let go of seeking revenge and looking for 'justice' by forgiving *myself*."

"What do you mean by 'forgiving yourself'?" Jennifer seemed puzzled.

"I didn't know I needed to. But after all the work Ruth and I did together, she asked me to write a letter to myself. I thought that was a silly request, and I resisted her at first. But, eventually, I sat down to attempt the assignment and, much to my surprise, the words came pouring out." Rachel reached into the cardboard box and pulled out a document, preserved in sheet protectors. "This is the last thing I wanted to read to you," she said.

Dear Rachel,

I have finished reading the story of seven years of your life -- really more years than that. I read about the men who penetrated not only your vagina, but your soul. Shouldn't they be held accountable for what they did?

I want you to heal. You have come so far. It's awful reading about what happened to you. You were so vulnerable then, but you couldn't show it. You were tricked and manipulated and used. You saw it, but at the same time couldn't see it. For so long you held on to the hope that Jay would marry you and make all of the hurt go away by his claiming you publicly. I know there were times when you doubted that vision, though you couldn't let go of it entirely. Your instinct that going "public" was the answer was a healthy one. Silence was killing you.

Reading about your private life is like reading about someone else that isn't you. You were so kind and forgiving and loving. Why couldn't those bastards see it? You didn't deserve what you got. I know you often thought the "punishment" was deserved. But I'm here to tell you that you were deceived. The culture that silenced many of your responses to being sexually abused and exploited is sick. And Jay was sick. You understood Jay's pain and you were patient with him -- patient to the point of denying your own needs. Being raped obliterated most of your sense of what was right and fair for you. People always told you that you were impatient like your father; but you were not impatient at all with Jay. You were more like your mother. I wish you could have seen how much like your mother you were. I think that if you had recognized your mother in you, you might have protected yourself more. On the other hand, you had to stand on your own. You had to make independent decisions and branch out into worlds unexplored by your family. Mother represented naiveté and dependency to you. After all the work you've done to heal yourself, you are now able to appreciate the gifts and shortcomings of both your parents more.

Listen. You have to understand that I forgive you for every awful thing that happened. I know there are events that still plague you -- instances when you used people you loved for what appeared to be selfish ends. Please remember that you were not intentionally hurtful. You were more dependent on the graces of men than you wanted to believe. They held the power. And if you think about it, you know *you* never forced sex on anyone. They each got something they wanted from you.

Honesty is probably the most important gift you can give yourself today. All the dishonesty you lived with for years took you away from the Rachel you love, feel proud of, and respect. Sexual violence takes a lot out of a person. And, baby, you were raped three times in three years and subjected to other kinds of sexual abuse for even longer. I know you did the best you could. It's a wonder you can trust anyone at all. But you hung in there and kept trying to love and trust. You did a damn good job given the circumstances. You really did. And now that you are being honest, there are many people close to you who will support you. They already have.

When you were told at a young age that you were smart and pretty and strong, you weren't lied to. All that positive stuff got twisted around; but you are back now. I know there will be times when you feel out of control. Everybody feels that way sometimes. But, believe it or not, you are in a better position than you ever were before to recognize when control has been taken from you, to recognize when you need to fight back and how to fight back. And please remember that when you fail to prevent being sexually harassed or violated in the future, when you feel helpless and afraid, you are fighting a battle you cannot win alone. Sexual violence is a social problem as well as a personal one. It will take a long, long time to change the conditions that make it so easy for some of us to be abused.

You have learned an awful lot. Continue to hold on to your tenderness. It has caused you pain at times, but you know it brings so much more joy. I'm proud of you, Rachel.

Jennifer sat quietly for a few minutes. Her mother's head stayed bowed toward her lap. Jennifer needed to let the full impact of her mother's words sink in – her history, her discoveries, her road back to health – before she spoke. Her mother had recovered. Or, maybe, she would always be *in* recovery, Jennifer thought. Her past would always be her past. But she had moved on. She had graduated from law school, married, worked, started a family and raised her and her two brothers. She knew it hadn't always been easy – what with Henry's struggles, Sam's differences, and her own ups and downs...

"Mom?" she finally said. "That was beautiful. It really touched me. This whole story... This time with you on Sundays... It's really meant a lot to me." Jennifer struggled with what to say next, how to ask what she wanted to ask. Rachel waited expectantly.

"If you could say. No… If you had to tell someone what sexual victimization is, how would you describe it?" asked Jennifer.

Jennifer's question triggered a 'concern response' in Rachel, but she decided to ignore it and address the question directly.

"As you might imagine, I've thought a good deal about that. What I believe is that to avoid sexual victimization, a relationship has to be both *consensual* and *healthy*. A consensual relationship is between equals – equal in the sense of power and control. No sexual relationship between a child and an adult can be consensual. Likewise, sexual relationships between employers and their employees or teachers and their students cannot be consensual. You can probably think of other relationships where there are different amounts of power and control. In those cases, there is always a risk of sexual victimization.

"By healthy, I include physical, spiritual, and emotional health. Is the sex harmful to the body? Is it psychologically damaging? Is it destructive of the values and beliefs one holds most dear?"

"And you would include drugs as unhealthy?" asked Jennifer, remembering that towards the end of her relationship with David Reese, she had used marijuana to help her forget her discomfort with the situation.

"If you are asking whether using drugs automatically qualifies as unhealthy, I guess I'd have to say 'no.' A glass of wine at dinner for someone who doesn't have an addiction problem and isn't dependent on the wine to agree to sex – I don't think that is necessarily a problem. There are so many variables. Is the intoxication sufficient to remove the person's ability to consent? Is the drug necessary for health – as in a prescription? Or, does it have potential harmful side-effects – causing rapid heartbeat, high blood pressure, damage to organs, etc.?"

Rachel hesitated and then continued, "I'd even go so far as to say it's 'unhealthy' to have unprotected heterosexual sex if you are unwilling or unable to consider the possibility of pregnancy. If a pregnancy does occur under those circumstances, the woman is left without any good options. Parenting, abortion, and adoption all require some form of sacrifice.

"Of course, an unplanned pregnancy can be a blessing." Rachel was remembering her unplanned pregnancy with Sam. She and Kevin had wanted to wait another year because Henry had been such a demanding baby and rambunctious toddler. But Sam came along anyway. And he had, miraculously, had the opposite of the expected affect on Henry. He had calmed Henry for a few months. It was as if Henry knew, at some level, that his parents didn't have time to deal with so many tantrums.

Jennifer's voice brought Rachel back to the present. "That sounds so old-fashioned, Mom. *No sex until you are ready to make babies,"* Jennifer said in a lower, authoritative voice.

"I know it does, honey. Maybe I *am* getting old. But the older I get, the more I realize how complicated sexual decision-making can be. I don't want to spoil your fun. Sex *should* be fun. It's not just about 'making babies.' My point is that it comes with risks. The better able you are to identify and make conscious choices about those risks, the better off you are likely to be."

They had veered away from her original question about sexual victimization, Jennifer thought. She wanted to get back to it.

"So, Mom, if a person can be sexually victimized when there isn't consent between equals and when it's not a healthy situation..." Jennifer swallowed. "I think *I* have a story to tell you too. And I may need to *do* something about it," she said, remembering her legal research. Jennifer looked up to see how her mother would respond.

Rachel's eyes were wet, but she softly smiled. She looked directly at Jennifer and said, "I'm here. Tell me."

Rachel knew that, no matter what her daughter had to say, she would *believe her* just as Jennifer had listened and believed her own story. And she would be by Jennifer's side, supporting her all the way through whatever needed to be done, and for all the time after – no matter how long it took. She knew, as well as anyone did, that it sometimes took a very long time.

A Brief Resource Guide

Faith Trust Institute
www.faithtrustinstitute.org/resources/learn-the-basics/sv-faqs

Feminist Majority Foundation
www.feminist.org/911/resources.html

National Alliance to End Sexual Violence
www.endsexualviolence.org

National Center for Victims of Crime
www.victimsofcrime.org

National Center on Domestic and Sexual Violence
www.ncdsv.org

National Sexual Assault Hotline
1.800.656.HOPE (4673)
Free. Confidential. 24/7

National Sexual Violence Resource Center
www.nsvrc.org

Not Alone
www.notalone.gov

Pandora's Project
www.pandys.org/recommendedreading.html

Questia
www.questia.com/library/law/areas-of-law/sexual-assault-and-the-law

Rape Abuse & Incest National Network
www.rainn.org

Sexual Assault Training & Investigations
www.mysati.com

Workplaces Respond to Domestic & Sexual Violence
www.workplacesrespond.org

About the Author

Rebecca Patton Falco has degrees in psychology, history, theology, and law from Duke and Emory Universities. Her articles have been published in *Adoption Today* magazine and the 2002 *Adoptive Families Together Anthology.* Rebecca's first book, *Everything In Its Own Time, a Mother's Memoir about Adopting Five Children and the Ones that got Away*, has received awards and honors from Next Generation Indie Book Awards, International Book Awards, and USA Best Books, 2011

Rebecca is a former high school social studies teacher, youth minister, litigation associate, coordinator of sexual assault support services, and branch director of an open adoption agency. An Atlanta resident, Rebecca is an author, attorney, athlete, adoption advocate and activist for causes involving women, children and issues of equality. She's married to John Falco and adoptive mother of Emily, K.J., Skye, Journey and Becton.

www.ingramcontent.com/pod-product-compliance
Lightning Source LLC
Chambersburg PA
CBHW060002100426
42740CB00010B/1372